T0267199

Vegetarianism, Ecology, and Business Ethics

VEGETARIANISM, ECOLOGY, AND BUSINESS ETHICS

Three Essays of Judaic Insights into Contemporary Concerns

DANIEL SPERBER

Foreword by Martin Palmer

URIM PUBLICATIONS
Jerusalem • New York

Vegetarianism, Ecology, and Business Ethics:
Three Essays of Judaic Insights into Contemporary Concerns

by Daniel Sperber
Foreword by Martin Palmer

Typeset by Juliet Tresgallo

Printed in Israel
First Edition
ISBN 978-965-524-367-3

Urim Publications
P.O. Box 52287, Jerusalem 9152102, Israel

www.UrimPublications.com

Library of Congress Cataloging-in-Publication Data in progress

Contents

Foreword by Martin Palmer   7

Introductory Note   11

Essay One
Vegetarianism: Moral and Halachic Aspects   15

Essay Two
Ecology: New Areas of Religious Responsibility   99

Essay Three
Business Ethics and Ethical Investment   199

Conclusion   235

FOREWORD

by **Martin Palmer** CEO of FaithInvest and Senior Advisor to WWF International on Beliefs and Values

I have had the honor of knowing Daniel Sperber for many years. His has been one of the most outstanding voices in the emerging world of Jewish environmental reflection and passion, and his writings and contributions lie at the heart of much that contemporary Judaism now sees as its distinctive gift to the world of faiths and ecology. He recalls in his Introduction being with me at the tenth anniversary of the Alliance of Religions and Conservation in 2005, invited by Rabbi Arthur Hertzberg, one of my dearest friends sadly no longer with us. Arthur had written the first Jewish Statement on the Environment at the invitation of His Royal Highness The Prince Philip, Duke of Edinburgh, when he invited faith leaders to come to Assisi, Italy, in 1986 to explore how the faiths could partner with the major conservation organizations. I had the honor of organizing that historic event with Prince Philip.

When Daniel arrived at the Archbishop of Canterbury's London Palace (yes, Anglican Archbishops have palaces!), he made a huge impression not least on Prince Philip. In Daniel's quiet, firm, scholarly way with his passion for sharing, discussing, and thinking, he stood out from the hustle and bustle of so many religious and secular representatives. This book shows why.

Daniel was also deeply involved in what has now become a very significant movement, namely, enabling the major faiths to be the powerhouses of investing in a sustainable and ecological world. In particular, and as always, he is ahead of the game – his wisdom in facing the challenges of contemporary business and its lack of values has set an example for many to follow. Daniel was grappling with this many years ago, which is why we involved him in setting up one of the very first multifaith ethical investment groups, the International Interfaith Investment Group 3iG. He is right to highlight that until the world of business and investment begins to move, we will lack the engine for real change, and his breadth of experience and knowledge in this world speaks powerfully to the possibilities and the necessity for such change.

There are few people who can span so many fields of human endeavor as Daniel can, from theology and philosophy to business via biblical studies, science, and, of course, his passionate call for vegetarianism. Daniel doesn't just study; he doesn't just reflect; he doesn't just suggest. He lives what he believes in ways that are challenging, thought-provoking, and deeply seated in his faith.

I am not Jewish, and although a theologian and environmentalist, whenever I talk with Daniel or read what he has written, I am humbled by the sheer range of his knowledge and profoundly challenged by the logic of his values and lifestyle derived from this knowledge.

He is also, in the great tradition of Jewish teachers, a master storyteller. The book is enriched by his personal stories, the stories he has heard and learnt, and the sense that he is inviting us on a journey of faith, wisdom, and yes, even fun! I must confess that much of the Talmudic wisdom and textual analysis sails over the head of this Anglican, but what even I can see is that Daniel is mining a depth of spiritual and practical wisdom that has guided Judaism for millennia and is exhorting all of us – Jewish or not – to be alert to the insights, inspiration, and urgency of what he has found.

For me, his tale of the two Nepals – one many years ago and the one he saw again recently – highlights why we must urgently attend to the faithful care of our planet, what the Pope has called in his landmark ecological Encyclical (Laudato Sí) "Our Common Home." The passion with which he records the degradation of that astonishingly beautiful world cannot but move us as readers to reflect upon places we know where we too have seen the damage done in such a short period of time. He challenges us – as he was challenged – to respond and to look at our own lifestyles, our own beliefs and values, and ask hard questions.

As we emerge, God willing, from the crisis of Covid-19 and see perhaps more clearly what was so fundamentally wrong with our economic and environmental way of living, we need guides. Real guides.

Not campaigners with their short attention spans, but guides who know the pathway ahead because they know how we got here in the first place. Daniel is such a guide, and I hope and pray that all of us who read this will be drawn to emulate the pathway that Daniel doesn't just point out, but has and is traveling himself.

Introductory Note

Each of these three essays has its own individual history of development. The first one, on vegetarianism, actually began as an interview. R. Yonatan Neril, CEO of the Interfaith Center for Sustainable Development, interviewed me on December 11, 2012. Since then I have modified the text and greatly expanded it, while retaining the original question-and-answer structure.

The second topic, on the subject of ecology, has a long history beginning with a short article in *The Edah Journal*, January 1, 2002, pp. 1–5, followed by another short one in Bar Ilan University's *BIU Today* publication of June 2008, pp. 8–9, entitled "The Jewish Mandate to Preserve and Conserve." I then revisited the subject in the journal *Milin Havivin: Beloved Words*, vol. 5, 2010–2011, in an article entitled "*Bal Tash'hit*: Waste Not Want Not," pp. 85–92. During those years, I was a member of the Alliance of Religions and Conservation (ARC), a British-based international organization founded by His Royal Highness, Prince Philip in 1995 as a sort of offshoot of WWF (World Wildlife Fund), which he also founded. Martin Palmer served as the Secretary General of ARC, and I represented the Jewish view.

For an understanding of the nature and aims of ARC, I shall cite Martin Palmer's welcoming statement on the Tenth Anniversary Celebration of ARC at Lambeth Palace on May 4, 2005, which I attended as the Jewish representative:

> When the Chinese Premier Zhu En Lai was asked his opinion in the early 1970s of the French Revolution of 1789; he replied it was too early to tell quite how significant it had been.

It is on a different scale of course but after just ten years we find ourselves saying something similar for ARC. Much of what we do is rooted in the understanding of timescales by which the great faiths operate. The faiths – which could be said to be the very first multinationals, and are certainly, the most successful and long lasting of all human institutions – think in terms of generations not in three- or five-year campaigns or plans. Developing major programs with the faiths takes time. Immediate targets can of course be achieved, such as creating a management plan for religiously owned forests or investment policies for centrally held religious funds. However, the real significance of ARC's work with the faiths will be seen in the coming decades and even centuries through the degree to which care of nature has become axiomatic for all believers.

ARC is simply an instrument. We exist to create links, initiate and assist innovative projects on the ground, broker new partnerships and convene groups who otherwise might never find it possible to come together. This ranges from bringing major religions together with groups such as the World Bank or national governments, through convening different African Muslim groups who have never sat together before, to helping faiths find the experts in land management that they need to conserve their land holdings.

ARC's strength is the strength and commitments of the faiths. And increasingly our strength is also the growing interest and engagement of major secular bodies with the faiths as serious partners in caring for what the specialists call bio-diversity and what most of the faiths call, perhaps more beautifully, Creation.

Palmer further gave a practical example of how ARC functions:

THE ENERGY OF THE FAITHS
The Story of the Religious Climate Change

ARC was asked in 2000 to help bring religious leaders to bear upon government leaders to ensure that the Kyoto Protocol would be passed. We initially refused, but set about instead organising an international programme which saw religious leaders from 30 countries and over 1,500 organisations make commitments to cut their own use of energy, and thus their production of CO_2. Only after the faiths had made such commitments themselves were we able to ask them to speak to their governments urging support of the Kyoto-Protocol. Twenty-one countries were eventually involved and we played a small part in helping the Protocol be accepted. As a direct result of this, ARC has produced a practical handbook for the faiths on how to cut energy use. It has been translated into several languages and forms the basis for our pioneering work with faiths on climate change in Zambia, Mexico and Mongolia undertaken in collaboration with the United Nations Environment Programme (UNEP), and our wider work with groups such as The Climate Group.

Later he established 3iG: The International Interfaith Investment Group, of which I was one of the founding members. Its Mission Statement was as follows:

• To contribute to a just and sustainable society through responsible investment. 3iG intends to do so in a spirit of genuine inter-faith dialogue and co-operation.

• Creating a platform for exchange of information and for dialogue on all issues which contribute to its mission. The platform should be open to Members, Associate Members and Partners.

• Engaging in an active dialogue with corporations about ethical concerns, human rights and the environment.

• Using the combined economic power of their assets, including shares, land, water resources, and intellectual properties to press for changes in the corporations where they have relevant share holdings.

• Providing information on socially and environmentally responsible investment opportunities.

So I have had an extensive involvement in this field under the guidance of a great mentor, Martin Palmer,[1] and that of the wonderful Chairman of ARC, Brian Pilkington. I would add here that I was introduced to ARC by the late Prof. Arthur Hertzberg, one of the original members, who, when he became too sick to attend one of the meetings, asked me to take his place and read his address. Subsequently, at his request, I became his successor as a member of ARC.

In this second essay I have attempted to summarize some of the Jewish ethical and halachic aspects of this very broad and crucial subject, which is, of course, of global significance.

The third essay is on a subject I treated briefly in an article entitled "Ethical Investment: A Jewish Perspective," which appeared in a volume entitled *For the Sake of Humanity: Essays in Honour of Clemens N. Nathan*, eds. Alan Stephens and Raphael Walden, Leiden 2006, pp. 3003–3007, and has been considerably expanded here.

Every one of these subjects is, of course, of global significance, and has therefore vast bibliography. Here, however, I wish to present at least some of the Jewish halachic perspectives on each of them.[2]

Finally, I believe the subjects discussed in these essays are supremely relevant, most especially in view of the recent Covid-19 pandemic. Surely, it is a most meaningful moral lesson in mankind's humility before the forces of God's nature.

---

1. I should also call attention to the invaluable book he published together with Victoria Finlay, *Faith in Conservation: New Approaches to Religions and the Environment*, The World Bank, Washington, DC, 2003, which in Part 2 also contains 11 statements by prominent authorities representing the different religions on this subject (Bahaism, Buddhism, Christianity, Daoism, Hinduism, Islam, Jainism, Judaism, Shintoism, Sikhism, and Zoroastrianism).

2. For a global overview, see most recently David Wallace-Wells, *The Uninhabitable Earth: A Story of the Future*, Penguin Books, 2019, with a rich bibliography in the Notes.

ESSAY ONE
Vegetarianism: Moral and Halachic Aspects

When first I was asked by R. Yonatan Neril[1] why I am a vegetarian, I replied that I decided to be a vegetarian[2] approximately 70 years ago. What happened was that my mother, *aleha ha-shalom*, was very sick with tuberculosis and for almost two years had to be hospitalized in Switzerland in a sanitorium in Davos. We children, three of us – I was youngest – were allocated different jobs. One of my jobs was on Thursday afternoon to go to a neighbor's house to pick up a bag which had a symbol on it of kosher meat, to bring it home, open it up and *kasher* (make kosher) what was in it. It was usually a chicken. I had to chop off the legs; I had to pluck off those feathers that remained; I had to cut open its belly and then take out all the innards. And this I did faithfully for almost two years, but I found it truly repulsive and I hated doing it. Cooking it was done by my sister. So from that time onwards, I already was repelled by the idea of taking an animal, ripping it apart,

---

1. He is mentioned in the "Introductory Note" and initiated an interview with me on this subject.

2. I would call attention to Roberta Kalechofsky's book, *Vegetarian Judaism: A Guide for Everyone,* Marblehead, MA, 1998, which has, inter alia, chapters on *Tsa'ar Ba'alei Hayyim,* pp. 110–148, and *Bal Tash'hit,* pp. 149–165 (see next topic), and contains much interesting material. It also has a rich bibliography on the subject, pp. 217–224. And, more recently, David Sears, in his excellent *The Vision of Eden: Animal Welfare and Vegetarianism in Jewish Law and Mysticism,* Spring Valley, NY, 2003, to which I shall frequently refer. I should also like to call attention to a delightful little book published almost half a century ago, called *Tree of Life: An Anthology of Articles Appearing in the Jewish Vegetarian,* edited by Philip L. Pick, South Brunswick and New York, 1977, which does not deal with halachic concepts of vegetarianism but the "humanity" of non-carnivorism.

and then actually eating it. No meat! No fish!

When my mother came home finally, and *Baruch ha-Shem*, she was already better, I said, "That's it, I am not doing this anymore, and from now on, I am not going to eat any more meat or fish, and if necessary, I'm going to cook for myself." And from that time onwards, I have tasted neither fish nor meat, and eventually my parents also became vegetarians.[3]

---

3. Maybe in part this was because I found it difficult to eat at the same table with people who were eating meat or fish, since I found this repellent. See *Aruch ha-Shulhan Orah Hayyim* 170:12:

> It is simple and straightforward that one does not do at the table that which others find repulsive, like strongly spitting out of one's mouth or [picking at] one's nose; nor should one pick at one's teeth with an open mouth when others find it difficult to watch [such activities]. And so too, passing wind from one's mouth, which, as is well known, is offensive to others. And indeed anything that is repulsive to another should not be done in his presence, also not at time of eating, as is written in *B. Hagigah* 5a, on the verse in *Ecclesiastes* 12:14, "For God shall bring every work into judgement concerning every hidden thing...." Shmuel said, "This is one who spits before his neighbour and repulses him," and in *B. Eruvin* [99a] it is stated that: If one spits or salivates before one's mentor, one is deserving of death.

See also *Derech Eretz Zuta* 5:19 and my English edition and commentary to chapters 5–8, Jerusalem, 1990, pp. 13–17, and my Hebrew edition, Jerusalem, 1994, p. 119.

On the Jewish attitude to "repulsive food," see E. Jacobowitz, *Ha-Refuah ha-Yehudit*, Jerusalem, 1966, pp. 65–66, who wrote that:

> The Jewish religion is the only one that gave a legal status to the feeling of repulsion towards contaminated food and objected directly to eating revolting materials, and it was only the influence of science that can explain the fact that the *Shulhan Aruch* and other halachic works permitted the medical use of human bones, menstrual blood, animal feces in pharmaceutical prescriptions....

But see Avraham Ofir Shemesh's comment in his article "*Ha-Shimush be-Terufot* in *ha-Hai le-Or Sifrut ha-Halachah me-ha-Me'ah ha-Shesh Esreh ve-Elach*," *Korot* 15, 2001, p. 119, idem, *Sugiot Refuiot be-Teshuvotav shel Rabbi David Even Avi Zimrah*, 14, 2002, pp. 144–146, and fish.

I am not suggesting that meat eating is the same as eating human bones or feces, only that I felt a feeling of repulsion to such foods. See further the observations of Zohar Amar in his article "*Ha-Admonit u-Terufat ha-Nichpeh be-Tekufot Kedumot*,"

But here I would like to add the following halachic considerations:

One of the five rules required for a valid *shehitah* – slaughtering[4] – is that the knife must be visible at the moment it severs the animal's gullet. If not, the *shehitah* is invalid (*haladah*, see *Entziklopediah Talmudit* 15, 192–205). However, there is a difference of opinion as to whether, when the *haladah* is caused by the sheep's wool, for instance, which may hide the knife, the *shehitah* is valid or not (*Shulhan Aruch, Yoreh Deah* 24:8). And the ruling is on the side of stringency. For this reason, later authorities required that the feathers around the chicken's gullet be plucked[5] so as to make certain that the knife is always completely visible

---

Mahkarei Yerushalayim be-Folklor Yehudi, 2001, pp. 161–162.

4. I recently came across a book which deserves mention. It is Y. M. Levinger's *Ha-Shehitah u-tza'ar B'aalei Hayyim: Skirah Makifah le-Or ha-Reka ha-Madai ka-Yom* (Schechita and Cruelty to Animals: A Critical Review), Jerusalem, 2004. Though largely technical, it deals with humanitarian aspects briefly (pp. 11–16) and has a copious bibliography (pp. 161–174).

5. Of course, at that time I was quite unaware of the halachic complexities associated with feather-plucking (*melikah*). Thus, after the *shehitah* the rest of the attached feathers have to be plucked and in such a way that the chicken's flesh which is attached to them does not get ripped out, as that would influence the amount of flesh and the price of the chicken. It was once a practice to soak the slaughtered chicken in boiling water which would open the pores so that the feathers would come out more easily. This also has been the subject of a different controversy, namely whether a chicken that was boiled, but some feathers remained attached to it, may have those feathers plucked on Shabbat, or whether that would be regarded as *gozez* (shearing), an *issur de-Oraita* on Shabbat. If the boiling loosened the feathers, such would be permitted; but if they were still attached to a certain extent, it might be forbidden. (See, in detail, R. Ovadiah Yosef, *Yabia Omer*, vol. 5, Jerusalem, 1986, *Orah Hayyim* sect. 34, pp. 118–121; R. Moshe Feinstein, *Igrot Mosheh, Orah Hayyim* 4, sect. 74, *Borer* 9, p. 140, etc., permitting it.) But all this refers to the state of the chicken after it has been fully koshered and is ready to be eaten. However, in the initial stages, before salting, etc., the soaking in boiling water was to ease the plucking of the large feathers covering the chicken. But, it was agreed, this would also boil the blood adjacent to those places. Consequently, the Maharil did not permit soaking in boiling water (*Hilchot Issur ve-Heter* sect. 10, ed. S. S. Spitzer, Jerusalem, 1989, p. 558, especially note 2 in var. lect.) but only in cold water. But again, the water must not be too cold, since that might prevent the blood from flowing freely and from coming out during the salting (see *Beit Yosef* to *Yoreh Deah* 69 and init., and *Taz* [*Turei Zahav*] to *Yoreh Deah* 36:5). Happily all these halachic details were quite unknown to me at that time, and only many years later when I learned *Yoreh Deah* did I become aware of them and the multiplicity of aspects and the complexities of this subject.

at the time of slaughtering, in order to avoid the possibility of *haladah*. However, the plucking of the feathers may at times cause internal damage to the chicken's gullet when tearing the feathers from the skin around its neck, and the chicken would then be *tereifah* (*Yoreh Deah* 23:6, *Shach* ibid. 20, etc.). The plucking is carried out, of course, while the chicken is still alive and undoubtedly constitutes *tza'ar ba'alei hayyim*, causing pain to the fowl. So in order to avoid *safek tereifah* by *haladah*, the rabbis recommended something that surely was halachically forbidden, namely inflicting pain on a living creature![6]

Nowadays, most of the chickens slaughtered are very young, as opposed to during earlier times when they lived a longer life before slaughter. Consequently, their feathers are much shorter, partially reducing the nature of *haladah*. However, their skin is more sensitive, increasing the likelihood of wounding the chicken through plucking and causing blood to flow from the wound, which in turn would make the chicken *treifah*.

Here, then, we have a combination of problems both technical-halachic as regards the validity of the *shehitah*, and ethical-halachic as to inflicting pain on a live animal.[7] Not eating chickens avoids both of these problematic situations.

We might add that their short life is due to the fact that they are artificially hatched from eggs in electrically heated incubators, and they rarely live a full year. Indeed, for this reason, the Maharsham in his responsa (3:378) was of the opinion that they are all *tereifah*, while the author of Responsa *Yad Hanoch* 34 regards them as *nevailah*. Either way,

---

6. See on this subject, R. Ovadiah Yosef, *Yabia Omer*, vol. 4, Jerusalem, 1964, *Orah Hayyim* sect. 44:4, pp. 203–203, on the *Pri Megadim*'s question in *Yoreh Deah* 24:8, on how this is permitted since it obviously causes pain to the fowl. And see ibid. for related issues. See also ibid., vol. 9, *Yoreh Deah* 32:2, that according to the *Or Zarua* (sect. 386 ad fin.) in the name of R. Eliezer of Metz, this is forbidden (even on a weekday) if one can slaughter without plucking the feathers, though the practice is to remove the feathers in accordance with the view of R. Shapira in the *Or Zarua* ibid. and numerous additional authorities, including my grandfather, R. David Sperber, in his *Afarkasta de-Anya*, sect. 127 (vol. 1, pp. 304–306).

7. See in greater detail *Meorot ha-Daf ha-Yomi* 24–30 *Kislev*, 2079 HE, to *Hulin* 5–11, No. 1019, pp. 2–3.

according to these and other authorities, they are non-kosher. However, some authorities, such as R. Meir Arik (*Imrei Yosher* 1:145) permit their consumption. But the systematic breeding of short-lived creatures, bred to be consumed, is surely morally problematic.[8]

---

8. The system of battery-hen breeding was already known in antiquity. See *The History and Description of Africa* by Leo Africanus, ed. Robert Brown, New York, 1896, vol. 3, pp. 883–884, 917–918, note 63. I recently came upon a book by someone called Will Graves, entitled *Raising Poultry Successfully*, Charlotte, VT, 1985. Chapter 3 (pp. 23–62) deals with "Raising Broiler-Fryers for Meat." On p. 56 he tells us that when the *chicks are 8 weeks old*(!) they should be weighed on a hanging scale, and if they average 4 pounds "you are right on target." He then describes how to slaughter the chicks – of course not the kosher way, as he is not a Jew (pp. 57–58, with illustrative drawings):

Necessary Equipment

You will need an axe or a very sharp knife, or both. You will need a length of cord or twine with which to tie the feet of the chickens. Or you can buy a killing cone. The bird is placed upside down in this holding device, with its head sticking out the smaller end. The cone restrains the bird from struggling and exposes its head and neck.

You will also need a bucket or plastic bag to catch the blood. A large metal container, such as a 10-gallon garbage can, is necessary to hold hot water for scalding the bird before plucking its feathers. A sturdy floating thermometer is helpful.

Killing the Bird

If you are going to kill the bird the old-fashioned way, with an axe, hold the chicken by both legs, upside down, over a block wood, lower it until its head and neck rest lightly on the block, and cut off its head. Then hold the bird over the bucket or plastic bag *until the struggling stops* and the blood ceases to flow. It is best to let the bird bleed out thoroughly, as this makes for a better carcass.

If you are going to kill the bird with a knife, be sure it's a sharp one. A 6-inch boning knife works particularly well. Tie the chicken's feet with the twine and suspend it from the ceiling of the room or a rafter. Adjust the height so it is comfortable for you. Hold the head firmly with one hand, and sever the jugular vein that runs down the bird's neck. You can do this by inserting the knife into the neck close to the neckbone and turning the knife out. Or you can sever it by cutting from the outside. Cut the vein as close to the head as possible.

If possible, keep holding the bird's head over the bucket, *until it has stopped struggling* and is bled out. If you let go, it will splatter you and everything else in

the surrounding area with blood.
[My emphasis – D. S.]

Such descriptions in themselves should encourage vegetarianism.

And here I'd like to quote R. David Rosen, who in his article "The Commandments Were Only Given for the Purpose of Refining People," apud *Kashrut and Jewish Food Ethics*, ed. Shmuly Yanklowitz, Boston, 2019, p. 214, writes as follows:

> In the case of egg-producing chickens, newborn chicks are placed on a conveyor belt where a worker picks each one up to see if it is male or female. Newborn males are placed in trash bags and suffocated, crushed or ground up alive, and often become recycled for the hens and other livestock. Newborn females are placed back on the conveyor belt. The next worker then picks up the female chick, holds her up to a machine's hot iron which cuts off her beak, and then places her back on the belt. Approximately one in five dies of stress and disease. Others are ground up and turned into animal feed on site. Layer hens are exposed to light constantly so that they will lay more eggs. At the end of their laying cycle, they are killed or subjected to "forced molting," a process that entails withholding food and water for up to eighteen days and keeping them in darkness so that their bodies are shocked into another laying cycle; many of these birds die of fatigue. Layer hens are slaughtered when they are one to two years old; hens normally live fifteen to twenty years.

And in note 37 ibid., he refers us to Peter R. Checke, *Contemporary Issues in Animal Agriculture*, Danville, IL, 1999. He also writes there:

> Male calves are raised for both beef and veal. Veal calves live in particularly small confines and are often chained. They are fed milk substitute deficient in iron and fiber. In other words, they are deliberately kept anemic and their muscles are atrophied so that their flesh will be pale and tender. They never see the sun or have contact with the natural vegetation. Ten percent of veal cows die in confinement. Furthermore, farmers get more money for chickens with enlarged thighs and breasts. As a result, they breed the animals to be so heavy that their bones cannot support their weight. Consequently, the chickens have difficulty standing, and their legs often break. Like other factory-farmed animals, broiler chickens are raised in such overcrowded enclosures that they become aggressive. To stop them from fighting with one another, their beaks and toes are cut off *without* anesthetic, a painful practice that involves slicing through bone, cartilage, and soft tissue. Some cannot eat after being "de-beaked" and starve to death.

See also note 36:

And if we look at the situation from a more global aspect, Swami Chidanand Saraswati wrote in his book *Vegetarianism: For Our Bodies, Our Minds, Our Souls and Our Planet*, already in 2007, chapter 1, pp. 14–16, that:

> More than 14,000 chickens are killed every minute in the U.S.A. alone, for our consumption, totaling eight billion chickens every year. The life of a chicken is terribly violent – they are crammed together in large warehouses, frequently as many as 40,000 chickens in one building ... so closely that they frequently cannot even move ...
>
> The chickens raised to be eaten are fed an extraordinary ... amount of food ... [so that they] are so obese by six weeks of age that they can't even walk, and 90% of them have disease leucosis, otherwise known as chicken cancer ... [the reason being] ... that their manure is routinely recycled back into their feed and their water is frequently the liquid waste from manure pits ...
>
> [And as to veal] ... people prefer "white" meat to "dark" meat, so the meat industries do everything they can to ensure their meat is "white" ... The best and cheapest way is through ensuring that the calves are left anemic. Anemic tissue is significantly paler than normal tissue. Therefore, this sought-after "white" meat is actually the meat of anemic calves chained at the neck to stalls which serve as their life-long jail....

He summarizes this section (p. 19) by telling us that:

While there has been progress in veal calf confinement techniques, the quality of life improvement has still been poor. See Lawrence M. Hinman, *Contemporary Moral Issues: Diversity and Consensus* (New York: Routledge, 2016 [fourth edition]), p. 407; Linda Elkin McDaniel (Lisa Kemmerer, ed.), "Here I Stand by Faith" in *Speaking Up for the Animals: An Anthology of Women's Voices* (New York: Routledge, 2012), p. 88.

See also Y. Neril and L. Dee, *Eco Bible*, vol. 1: *An Ecological Commentary on Genesis and Exodus* (Jerusalem) 2020, pp. 38 (on veal), 146 (on chickens and cows). Rabbi Shmuly Yanklowitz, in an article entitled "How Kosher Is Your Milk?", *Jewish Journal*, June 7, 2012, suggests that milk and eggs produced in this fashion are not kosher (ibid., p. 215, note 592).

Each year sixteen billion animals (not including fish) are killed in the U.S.A. alone mercilessly for our food consumption. This is more than the total number of people on the planet.

And after dealing with the so-called "free-range" or "cage-free" organic meat and eggs (pp. 21–22), he ends this chapter by telling us that:

The lives of so-called "free-range," "cage-free" and organically raised animals are no better than conventionally-raised animals. In some cases, like when they develop illnesses from their squalid living conditions, these animals are worse off. It is a total illusion that these animals are raised in good conditions and live happy lives before their slaughter. The myth surrounding these farming practices is simply that – myth – and in no way justifies the eating of meat or eggs coming from these animals.

I was then asked why this decision included fish. To which my reply was: I also had to gut the fish and chop off the head, and the head had eyes in it, and the eyes would stare at me. And in England at that time, when you went to a fishmonger, some of the fish were still floating around in a sort of basin. They weren't all dead. They would pull them out of the water and bang them on the head with a mallet, and they would jerk about for a short while. It was quite horrific. And for a young person, aged between seven and eight, these things made a tremendous impression. So I presume that it was then that I decided to be a vegetarian. It was very much an emotional thing.

And as to the ability of fish to feel pain, fish are equal to dogs, cats, and all other animals. Dr. Donald Broom, scientific advisor to the British government, explains,

The scientific literature is quite dear. Anatomically, physiologically and biologically, the pain system in fish is virtually the same as in birds and animals ....[9]

---

9. The *Shulhan Aruch, Yoreh Deah* 13:1, states that "fish and locusts do not

require slaughtering." And the *Rema* (R. Mosheh Isserles) in his note ad loc. adds in the name of early authorities (*Rishonim*):

> But one is not permitted to eat them alive, because [of the negative commandment, *bal teshaktzu* (referring to *Leviticus* 11:43, "You shall not make yourselves – literally: your souls – detestable [with any swarming thing that swarms…"]). (And cf. *ibid.* 20:25.)

That fish do not require slaughtering – *shehitah* – is derived from the verse in *Numbers* 11:22: "If the flocks and herds be slaughtered – yi-shehet – for them, will they suffice them? Or if all the fish of the sea be gathered together – *yeasef* – for them will they suffice them?" And the Talmud in *B. Hulin* 27b teaches that "since it says *asifah* in the place of *shehitah*, one may conclude that [for fish] *asifah* – meaning here expiration – is sufficient (i.e., no *shehitah* is required). Cf. *Genesis Rabba* 7:1, ed. Theodor-Albeck, pp. 50–51, and parallels.

As to the status of locust, see Lieberman, *Tosefta ki-Fshutah* to *Terumot*, New York, 1955, p. 452, that the Rambam, *Hilchot Shehitah* 1:3, learned that they do not require *shehitah* from the verse in *Isaiah* 33:4, where the root *asaf* is related to (the caterpillar and) the locusts, though this derivation is problematic and was questioned by early authorities (e.g., Rashba to *Hulin* 27b, his responsa, vol. 1, sect. 364, etc.; Lieberman, ibid., note 107).

However, the consensus of rabbinic opinion is that locust do not require *shehitah*; see *Pirkei de-R. Eliezer*, chapter 9, etc. Likewise fish, whether they died in the water or after being taken out of the water, are permitted; see Rambam, ibid. (and Lieberman's extensive discussion, ibid., pp. 452–453, on Karaite, Samaritan and Gaonic views on this issue).

Now the *Tosefta* in *Terumot* 9:6, ed. Lieberman, New York, 1955, p. 156, states that "fish and locust may be eaten both when alive and when dead – *bein hayyim bein meitim*! There were some (*Tosafot Hulin* 64b) who had a reading "the blood of fish and locust…" which would make this ruling somewhat more palatable. Furthermore, Lieberman (*Tosefta ki-Fshutah* ibid. p. 451) noted that this ruling is said of those who are not squeamish, strong-headed – *ba'alei nefesh yafeh* – ibid., pp. 450–451. But he rejects this reading as being inaccurate, preferring the one in the standard *Tosefta* text, which states that they could be consumed while still alive – like crabs and lobsters, among Chinese and others!

But though this may be regarded as the early halachic opinion of Tannaitic times, the Talmud in *B. Shabbat* 90b to the Mishnah, ibid., which talks of live locusts, relates to us that:

> R. Kahana was standing in front of Rav (mid III cent. C.E.) and passed a [kind of] locust (*shushiva*) before his mouth. [Rav] said to him: Take it away – *shahlei*, so that people should not say, "He ate it, and transgressed [the

"Scientists estimate that fish endure up to fifteen minutes of excruciating pain before they lose consciousness (PETA), when trapped in nets, tearing at their gills, or dragged bloody hooked on to metal hooks. Every fish that is still alive is therefore conscious

---

prohibition of *bal teshaktzu* – being detestable]."

Some readings (listed in *Dikdukei Sofrim* ad loc. p. 196, note 20) state that he was passing it *to his son's* mouth, and though this may seem to be a learned addition, it does make good sense in the context of the *sugya*. This would suggest that later authorities found the "strong-hearted" ability to eat live creatures detestably – forbidden. Furthermore, that passage is talking about children who apparently, at that time, would play about with live locusts (or grasshoppers). However, the opinion of the Tosafot (*Shabbat*, ibid., s.v. *de-lo*), is that it is forbidden to eat it *whole* while alive, but *limb by limb while alive is permitted*, and this does not transgress the prohibition of *ever min ha-hai* – tearing off a limb from a live creature. (See *Deuteronomy* 12:23, *Sifrei* ad loc., *B. Hulin* 102b, Rambam, *Hilchot Maachlot Asurot* 5.3, etc.) See also Rashba Responsa, vol. 1, sect. 364. However, though perhaps from a technical-halachic point of view this might be a plausible interpretation of the passage in *B. Shabbat*, ibid., I find it morally unacceptable and contrary to the basic notion of *bal teshaktzu*. See further *Tosafot Hulin* 60b, s.v. *Be-Mai*, and for a full discussion *Entziklopediah Talmudit*, vol. 2, Jerusalem, 1967, s.v. *Ever min ha-Hai*, vol. 1, Jerusalem, 1947, pp. 48–51, especially p. 48b; ibid., vol. 7, Jerusalem 1956, *Dagim*, col. 201 et seq., especially col. 202–203, notes12, 25; ibid., vol. 3, Jerusalem, 1951, s.v. *Bal Teshaktzu*, pp. 338–339.

See further *B. Hulin* 33a and *Tosafot*, s.v. *Ehad Nochri*; Elijah Judah Schochet, *Animal Life in Jewish Tradition: Attitudes and Relationship*, New York, 1984, pp. 174–175. And on p. 158 he summarizes that:

… The rabbis conceived of this act [*of ever min ha-hai*] as being so barbarous and incredibly cruel that all humanity, Jew and non-Jew, are obligated to abhor its practice.

See, however, ibid., pp. 203, 207 on Maimonides' understanding thereof.

To summarize, in view of the scientific findings of Dr. Broom, it seems clear to me that *ever min ha-hai* of *any* creature, be it a fish, a locust, and not only a domestic animal, should be strictly forbidden, at least under the prohibition – category of *tza'ar ba'alei hayyim*. And, of course, eating a live fish would normally entail *ever min ha-hai*, unless one swallowed a small one wholesale.

A further comment on fish: the nets in which they are caught often – perhaps always – include many species of a non-kosher variety. And in many cases they are all ground up into what is afterwards marketed as "fish paste" and similar products. Here too we encounter numerous problems of kashrut which are by no means easily resolved.

and aware (and quite able to experience pain) while its gills are slit, thereby suffocating the fish, and its organs are removed... In fact, the pain a fish feels when she is hooked is like dentistry without Novocaine [anesthesia]" – Dr. Tom Hopkins, Prof. of Marine Science, University of Alabama, U.S.A. (ibid. 29–30).

A further element to be considered is the sewage generated by fish farms. In Norway alone the salmon and trout farms produce roughly the same amount of sewage as New York City, and in Canada the sewage from the fish farms is equivalent to [that of] a city of 500,000 people. This sewage which is dumped into the ocean raw and untreated can be toxic for the already strained ocean ecosystems. So the fishing industry also has severe ecological ramifications. (See below section 2.)

"But surely," I was asked, "there are many people who believe that eating meat is not just halachically permitted but even a requirement. So how do you reconcile the idea of *simha be-basar ve-yayin* [joy with meat and wine] with your practice?"

My reply was that I think that *basar ve-yayin*, which is in memory of what used to happen in the Temple,[10] was never a halachah[11] but

---

10. See also *Beur Halachah* to *Orah Hayyim* 242, s.v. *Zecher la-Man* ad fin.

11. Here I somewhat simplified matters, as was necessary with the framework of the original interview. So now I will amplify the issue, in order to support my assertion. Already R. Hayyim Eleazar Schapiro, the Muncaczer Rav, in his *Nimukei Orah Hayyim*, Tyrna 1930, sect. 271/1, pp. 122–124, noted that in the classical Talmudic sources there is no indication of *the obligation* to have meat and wine on Shabbat. Thus, in *B. Shabbat* 118b among the different foods that bring pleasure (*oneg*) to the Shabbat, meat and wine are not even mentioned. Likewise the Rambam, in *Hilchot Shabbat* 30:7, does not mention them in the context of *oneg Shabbat*. He then brings multiple sources to prove that now that we have no Temple there is no obligation to have meat and wine on Shabbat, nor even on Yom Tov. (See *Shaagat Aryeh* sect. 68–65, cited by *Shaarei Teshuvah* to *Orah Hayyim* 529:2; *Darchei Teshuva* to *Yoreh Deah* 89:19, 15b, etc.). Furthermore, the Rambam (*Hilchot Hagigah* 1:1) ruled that one cannot offer a *hagigah* offering – the source of the "joy-obligation" – with a fowl, and consequently *Divrei Yatziv* (*Orah Hayyim* 224:3) ruled that eating a chicken would not satisfy the requirement of *simhat Yom-Tov*. And this is also the view of *Moadei ha-Shem* (by R. Yehudah Nagar, Livorno 1808), 132d, but there are also some dissenting opinions (such as *Sifrei de-Bei Rav*, by R. David Pardo, Solonica 1799, 334 et seq.). It is true that the *Magen Avraham* to *Orah Hayyim* 528:3, when discussing Yom Tov (basing himself on

only something which was recommended *le-simhat Shabbat*, or *le-oneg Shabbat* (and there's a *mahloket* whether there's a *din* of *simhat Shabbat*

---

the Rambam, *Semak*, *Bah*, and *Yam Shel Shlomoh*), assert that it is a *mitzvah* to do so on Yom Tov – and how much more so on Shabbat – but the *Darchei Teshuvah*, ibid., explains that this is not an *obligatory* mitzvah, but only initially advised (*le-chithilah*). The Muncaczer goes on to prove that:

> If meat is not to your liking, then even in the time of the Temple, the only obligation for *simhah* (joy) on Shabbat would be through wine.

Nor is there any such recommendation in the *Tur*. See continuation of the Muncaczer's argumentation. As to the obligation of *simhah*, joy, on *Yom Tov*, festivals, see *Shaagat Aryeh*, sections 65–68, who sees this as obligatory on biblical authority.

However, R. Yaakov Hayyim Sofer, in his *Knesset Hayyim*, Jerusalem, 1993, sect. *Otzrot Yerushalayim*, 1980, pp. 95–96, questions the Muncaczer's conclusions, citing, in his characteristically comprehensive fashion, a plethora of sources, both Talmudic and post-Talmudic, that indicate an established practice of eating meat on Shabbat (e.g., B. *Shabbat* 119a, B. *Hulin* 111a, B. *Kiddushin* 41a, *Pesikta Rabbati* chapter 23, ed. Ish Shalom fol. 119b [where, however, the formulation is: to what extent is the honor of Shabbat, *kevodah shel Shabbat*?; the answer being, according to Rav: meat; but this does not specify an obligation], etc.).

Furthermore, the *Shulhan Aruch* 250:2 states that "A person should eat much (*yarbeh*) meat and [drink much] wine… *according to his abilities*," i.e., both economically (see ibid., 242) and in accordance with his sensitivity.

As to why the *Tur* omitted to mention this issue, R. Sofer argues that this is in accordance with his view in *Orah Hayyim* 552; that after the destruction of the Temple there is no obligation of joy whatsoever etc., and this as we saw above the view of the *Magen Avraham*. And as to the assertion that the Rambam did not list such an obligation (in *halachah* 7 ibid.), R. Sofer counters that actually he did so in *halachah* 10 ibid., where he explicitly writes that:

> The eating of meat and drinking of wine on Shabbat is a source of joy (*oneg*), and that is so long as one can afford it.

However, that implies that the poor man who cannot afford it is not obligated to do so, and, moreover, it might impugn or decrease his pleasure if he did go beyond his means to do so. See the continuation of R. Sofer's argumentation from multiple sources.

But a careful perusal of all those sources leads one to the conclusion that, though this may have been a common practice both in antiquity and medieval times and was regarded as a positive manner of enhancing the joys of Shabbat, it was not *obligatory*, but merely recommended. And in a situation where it does not enhance the joy of Shabbat but impugns it, there certainly cannot be such an obligation.

or of *oneg Shabbat*),[12] and *Simhat Yom Tov*.[13] But those people who don't

12. As an incidental footnote I would refer to R. Betzalel Stern, *Be-Tzel ha-Hochmah* 1, Jerusalem, 1959, sect. 68:4, who sought to prove that one does not inspect signs of leprosy during *Hol ha-Moed* (Rambam, *Hilchot Yom Tov* 7:16, basing himself on *Moed Katan* 7a, according to R. Meir). And Rashi (ad loc.) explains that this is so that if one be found to be impure, one would be distressed on *Hol ha-Moed*, and the Torah commanded that one should be joyful on the festivals (*Deuteronomy* 16:13), not sad. And it is for this same reason that the *Mishnah* in *Negaim* 3:2 states that:

> If a leprosy-sign appears in a bridegroom, they must suffer him to remain free [before inspection] during the seven days of the marriage feast…; so, too, [if it appears in any man] during a festival, they must suffer him to remain free all the days of the festival.

And if it were the case that the *mitzvah* of *simhah* applied also to Shabbat, why do the sources not state that one does not inspect signs of leprosy on Shabbat? For it is only with regard to a bridegroom that the verse states "and shall cheer up his wife" (*Deuteronomy* 24:5), and with regard to festivals (as in *Deuteronomy* 16:13).

However, this is by no means clear. For the Rambam, in *Hilchot Tumat Tzaraat* 9:7 writes explicitly:

> On every day one inspects [signs of] leprosy except *on Shabbat* and the festivals.

From this it is clear that also on Shabbat one does not inspect them, presumably because this would cause distress which is forbidden on Shabbat, i.e., there is an obligation of *simhat Shabbat*.

13. This issue was discussed at length by R. J. D. Bleich, in his *Contemporary Halachic Problems*, vol. 3, New York, 1989, in his long and detailed chapter (10) entitled "Vegetarianism and Judaism," pp. 246–250, section (11), "Meat on Yom-Tov," where he concludes, after a very detailed analysis of the relevant sources, that even if there is no normative obligation to partake of meat on *Yom Tov*, abstaining from meat on *Yom Tov* because of the consideration of vegetarianism would not have been looked upon with favor by our sages. That article later was also published in *Judaism and Environment Ethics*, ed. Martin D. Jaffe, New York: Oxford, 2001, who cites R. Yosef Albo's anti-vegetarianism position (pp. 373–374) as follows:

> R. Joseph Albo maintains that renunciation of the consumption of meat for reasons of concern for animal welfare is not only morally erroneous but even repugnant. Albo asserts that this was the intellectual error committed by Cain and that it was this error that was the root cause of Cain's act of fratricide. Scripture reports that Cain brought a sacrifice from the animals of his flock. Albo opines that Cain did not offer an animal sacrifice because he regarded men and animals

find it a source of joy, but rather a source of repulsion, obviously are not halachically obligated to eat meat. And let us recall that when the Temple was destroyed, originally the rabbis wanted to declare that since we should have no *nesachim*, no libations, we should not drink wine, and since we have no sacrifices, we should not eat meat. Then other rabbis said that this is not a feasible situation, and therefore all we do is leave a small unpainted patch on the wall to show that we still bewail the loss of the Temple. But nowadays, since there are no sacrifices, there is no halachic requirement to eat animals or fish.

This question was also clearly posed by Elijah Judah Schochet in his *Animal Life in Jewish Tradition: Attitudes and Relationships*, New York, 1984, pp. 48–50. Here we shall cite sections of his very pertinent discussion:

> Sacrifices are clearly required by biblical law. But is the eating of meat similarly required? Clearly it is not. Furthermore, the cultic requirements for slaughter actually serve to severely limit the amount of meat which can be consumed.
>
> Many theories have been proposed to explain the rationale of the dietary laws, ranging in nature from hygienic to moralistic, from totemistic to nationalistic. But Scripture states simply that these laws

---

as equals, and, accordingly, felt that he had no right to take the life of an animal, even as an act of divine worship.

I would beg to differ from the learned rabbi, arguing that if those sages were to live in our own times and would be fully aware of all the details of meat manufacture that pertain in our society, they might well have a different opinion.

On the viewing of men and animals as equal, see David Mevorach Seidenberg, *Kabbalah and Ecology: God's Image in the More-Than-Human World*, Cambridge, 2015, p. 151. See below near my note 40.

And see the interesting discussion in Aaron Gross' essay, "Humane Subjects and Eating Animals: Comparing Implied Anthropologies in Jewish and Jain Practice," apud *Dharma and Halacha: Comparative Studies in Hindu-Jewish Philosophy and Religion*, eds. I. Theodor and Y. Kornberg Greenberg, Lexington Books, 2018, pp. 93–108. And in this context it may also refer to Purushottama Bilimoria's article in the same volume, entitled "Animal Justice and Moral Mendacity," pp. 109–127, which also touches upon ecological aspects (ibid., p. 117).

are to be obeyed in order that Israel should be "a holy people unto the Lord," and "distinguished from other nations by the avoidance of unclean and abominable things that defile them" (*Exodus* 22:30; *Leviticus* 11:20–24, 43; *Deuteronomy* 14:3–21).

However, one ought not to discount moralistic factors. As has been noted, Scripture does not hold the hunter in high esteem, and although ancient art depicts the rulers of Egypt and Mesopotamia as personally involved in the royal sport of lion-hunting, no king of Israel is ever described participating in this or in any hunt (Henri Frankfort, *Kingship and the God*, Chicago, 1948, pp. 9–10, figs. 11–12).

Furthermore, when the early pages in *Genesis* detail the divine plan in which all creatures are to live in harmony, man is told that he may eat from "every plant yielding seed which is upon the face of the earth, and every tree with seed in its fruit (*Genesis* 1:29)." Now meat is obviously excluded from this prescribed diet! It is only after the flood that Noah and his descendants are permitted to partake of the flesh of animals – "Every moving thing that liveth shall be food for you; as the green herb have I given you all" (ibid., 9:3) – with the restriction that blood must not be consumed.

Is this accommodation due to the fact that Noah and his sons, by virtue of having saved the animals from certain death in the deluge,[14] are now partners, as it were, with God in the creation of

---

14. On Noah's various virtues during his period in the ark, see *Midrash Tanhuma*, Noah 9; ibid., 2; *B. Sanhedrin* 108b, *Y. Yoma* 4:41; see Sears, ibid., p. 35):

> "Bring my soul out of prison, that I may give thanks to Your Name…" (Psalms 142:8). This refers to Noah, who was imprisoned in the ark. Rabbi Levi said: For twelve months, Noah and his sons did not sleep, for they were compelled to feed the animals, beasts, and birds. Rabbi Akiva said: Even branches for elephants and glass shards for ostriches (*B. Shabbat* 128a mentions that ostriches are known to eat glass shards, and this has a bearing on the laws of *muktzeh*, i.e. objects that may not be moved on shabbat, [Sears, ibid., note 18]).

> They were carried aboard by hand in order to feed them. Some animals eat at two o'clock at night, while others eat at three. Thus, you may deduce that they never slept. Rabbi Yochanan said in the name of Rabbi Elazar, the son of Rabbi Yosé the Galilean: One time, Noah was late in feeding the lion. Therefore, the lion

29

these species? (See M. D. Cassuto, *Mi-Noah ad Avraham*, Jerusalem, 1953, p. 86.) Is meat now permitted to man as a concession to his apparent inability to maintain the spiritual standards (such as vegetarianism) imposed upon him in the Garden of Eden? Or was flesh-eating permitted to the survivors of the flood simply because there was nothing else extant upon earth that could be eaten? We do not know. But in any event, man is now permitted to eat meat, albeit with certain restrictions.

But *must* he eat meat? On occasion, yes, but only as part of certain specific rituals, such as the partaking of the pascal and *Hagigah* offerings, and priestly sacrificial functions. But in a broader sense, is there a divine decree *demanding* of man that he butcher and consume the flesh of fauna? Should meat be part of his standard, normal diet? Not at all.

Quite the contrary. The crucial passage in *Deuteronomy* reads: "When the Lord thy God shall enlarge thy border, as He hath promised thee, and thou shalt say: 'I will eat flesh,' because thy soul desireth to eat flesh; thou mayest eat flesh, after all the desire of thy soul," (*Deuteronomy* 12:20). Now rabbinic tradition perceives in this text a clear indication that it is *man's desire* to eat flesh, not God's decree that he is to do so, and attributes an unflattering connotation to this lust for flesh.

"So," I was then asked, "if we now shift our discussion to the issue of *tza'ar ba'alei hayyim*, what is problematic about meat production?"

To which my reply was quite unhesitatingly that from the point of view of the halachah of *tza'ar ba'alei hayyim* (suffering of living creatures), over which there is a difference of opinion as to whether it is *de-Oreita* or *de-Rabanan*,[15] the problems of eating meat or fish or

---

mauled him, and he came away limping.

15. See Shears, pp. 63–66; ibid., Schochet, pp. 151 et seq.; Avraham Steinberg, *Entziklopedia Hilhatit Refuit*, vol. 5, Jerusalem, 1996, pp. 454–459. See most recently R. David Bigman's article, *"Teshuvah be-Inyanei Tza'ar Ba'alei Hayyim,"* apud *Kashrut and Jewish Food Ethics*, ed. Shmuly Yanklowitz, Boston, 2019, pp. 171–181; R. Dov Lihzer, "Animal Suffering and the Rhetoric of Values and Halakhah," ibid., pp. 182–208; and R. David Rosen, "The Commandments Were Only Given for the Purpose of

any animal products are immense[16] at a number of different levels.

Refining People," ibid., pp. 209–217; and the many discussions of R. Ovadiah Yosef in *Yabia Omer*, vol. 9, *Orah Hayyim* 30:5, 8; ibid., vol. 10, *Yoreh Deah* 32, where he cites (p. 333) the view of the *Nimukei Yosef* to *Baba Metzia* 32b, and *Hiddushei Anshei Shem* on the *Mordechai*, ibid., sect 40, that there is a distinction between causing great pain, which is an *issur de-Oraita* (biblically forbidden) and a lighter pain which is, according to most authorities, i.e., even the more stringent one, *de-Rabbanan*, only a rabbinic prohibition.

16. Of course, biblical law permitted the consumption of meat, fish, and fowl. *Genesis* 9:1–4 makes it clear that the children of Noah could do so after the flood:

> And God blessed Noah and his sons and said unto them: 'Be fruitful and multiply, and replenish the earth. And the fear of you and the dread of you shall be upon every beast of the earth, and upon every fowl of the air, and upon all wherewith the ground teemeth, and upon all the fishes of the sea: into your hand are they delivered. Every moving thing that liveth shall be food for you; as the green herb have I given you all. Only flesh with the life thereof, which is the blood thereof, shall ye not eat....

And later, after receiving the Torah, the Children of Israel were given laws limiting the kinds of animals, fowls, etc., that could be eaten (see *Leviticus* 11:1–17, *Deuteronomy* 14:3–21).

Here I would like to call attention to a fascinating historical tract, which, however, requires some preliminary background information for a fuller understanding of its nature.

Around the second half of the tenth century C.E. there was a secretive ascetic Islamic sect named *Ikhwan al-Safā*, banned in Basra, called the "Pure and Faithful." They left for posterity an anonymous collection of treatises arranged in an encyclopedic fashion dealing with the objects of their society, including both scientific and philosophical discussions, fifty-two in number, the *Rāsā'il*. The twenty-fifth epistle entitled (in the English translation by Lenn E. Goodman and Richard McGregor) *The Case of Animals versus Man before the King of the Jinn* (Boston, 1978, and Oxford University Press, 2010), is a charming text in which the animal kingdom complains before the Kings of the Jinns how they have been enslaved, tortured, and slaughtered by humankind. (There is a considerable literature on this subject; see Carmela Baffioni's article in *The Stanford Encyclopedia of Philosophy*, s.v. Ikhwân al-Safâ, 2016.)

Now, in the early fourteenth cent. (1316), a Jewish Provençali scholar named Kalonimos ben Kalonimos made a Hebrew translation of this Arabic text at the request of his colleagues. He did so, according to his introductory note, in the space of a week! He called it *Iggeret Ba'alei Hayyim*, the *Epistle of the Animals*. It was quite popular, and went into ten printed editions, nine Yiddish ones, and a Spanish one. See Y. Toporovski's edition, with A. M. Habermann's notes, Jerusalem, 1949.

In the past, people that lived on farms, peasants, or rural folk, looked after their animals very carefully, fed them well, grazed them well, and saw to their good health and welfare. Biblical law required that they be treated kindly; so, for example, one's animals have to rest on Shabbat (*Exodus* 20:9, 23:12, *Deuteronomy* 5:13), and one may not castrate an animal (*Leviticus* 22:24), and, so too, one is not permitted to plough with an ox yoked together with a donkey, since the ox is much stronger and the donkey much weaker, and the donkey will suffer the chafing on the yoke (*Deuteronomy* 22:10, etc.). Similarly, one must not muzzle an ox at the threshing floor, as this is unkind to it (*Deuteronomy* 25:4). And if you see a donkey bowed down under his burden, you must relieve him of that burden (*Exodus* 23:5). Thus, they looked after their animals well, as indeed the Torah required of them.[17]

And when it became necessary for them to eat, then they slaughtered them and then ate them.[18] This, however, is not the situation in

_____

In it the animals complain that, though they were created before mankind, and lived in harmony with one another, mankind has enslaved them, trapping them with nets, cruelly exploiting them, then slaughtering them, skinning their bodies, shaving their fur, roasting them on spits or boiling them in cauldrons, and torturing them in all sorts of different manners (see p. 19, etc.). The King of the Jinns hears their complaints with great sympathy and requests explanatory replies from seventy-two representatives of mankind, including Muslims, Hindus, Jews, etc., who rebuff these accusations with their own arguments. And finally, the chief spokesman of mankind, in his final summation, claims ascendency over the animal kingdom, a claim accepted by the King of the Jinns, whose ruling, in favor of mankind, is that the animal kingdom remain subservient to humans, and place their faith in God who will serve as their protector (p. 159).

Kalonimos ben Kalonimos has Judaized the epistle in his translation, substituting biblical verses in place of Qoranic ones, and giving a prominent and respected status to the Jewish representatives. And though the final ruling is in mankind's favor, the whole text reflects a sincere sympathy for the animal kingdom. And it is surely interesting that Kalonimos should have chosen to translate this text, and that at the apparent interest of his Jewish colleagues. This, then, is an early plea for animal rights.

17. Furthermore, many biblical verses stress that God himself is merciful to all his creatures. See, e,g., *Psalms* 145:9, 147:9, 36:7; *Jonah* 4:11, etc.

18. That is not to say that there is no *tza'ar* in slaughtering, but only that for essential human purposes it was permitted. See e.g., R. Yehiel Yaakov Weinberg, *Seridei Aish*, vol. 3, Jerusalem: 1966, sect. 7, p. 20b. And it was for this same reason that in that responsum he agreed with R. Mordechai Yaakov Breisch, who permitted tests on

the present time, and indeed in the last several generations meat consumption has become a question of mass production. So firstly, the conditions in which the animals are kept are in all too many cases quite horrendous. We know, for example, that cows and sheep are transported by ships across the oceans in totally unacceptable conditions. They wallow in their own feces, they're jammed tight one against another, so that often their internal and/or their external organs are damaged. Many of them die of poisoning from the fumes emitted by the feces, and their corpses are thrown overboard.[19] Some of them are

---

animals for medical purposes; see his *Helkat Yaakov*, vol. 1. Jerusalem, 1951, sections 30–31, pp. 71–76. See in detail in Avraham Sofer Avraham, *Nishmat Adam*, vol. 2, 1964, pp. 9–10; and even more extensively in Steinberg, *Entziklopedia Hilhatit Refuit*, ibid., pp. 431–481; and in his *Ha-Refuah ba-Halachah*, vol. 6, Jerusalem, 2017, pp. 208–232. This is in accordance with the view that when it is essentially for human benefit, it is permitted (R. Yisrael Isserlein, *Terumat ha-Deshen, Psakim u-Ketavim*, sect. 105 – a basic discussion of plucking feathers). Hence, for example, the Rema in *Even ha-Ezer* 5:14, permitted the plucking of feathers for the use of writing with a quill. See also *Piskei Tosafot* to *Avodah Zarah* chapter 1, sect. 11, that cruelty to animals, where there is no monetary profit, is forbidden. But where there is monetary gain, in some circumstances it may be permitted. See also below chapter 2 ad fin.

We may further note what the Rema wrote in his comments to *Shulhan Aruch Yoreh Deah* 28:2:

> He who slaughters for the first time makes the blessing *She-Hehiyyanu* over the covering of the blood [*kisui ha-dam*], but not over the slaughtering itself, *so he is harming a living creature*, [*minhagim yesharim* in the name of R. Yedidya mi-Shapira].

The Hizkuni, by R. Hizkiah ben Manoah Hai, thirteenth century France, to *Exodus*: 31:8, notes that the term "pure" – *Tahor* – is only used in connection with the table of the shewbread (*Leviticus* 24:6), and the golden candelabrum, but no other vessels used in the tabernacle are called "pure." And this is because no blood was sprinkled upon them, unlike the altar, etc., upon which blood *was* sprinkled. So even the Ark of the Covenant has blood sprinkled upon the *kaporet,* which was a part of the Ark. See *Leviticus* 16:14 and c.f. *Tanhuma Va-yakhel* sect. 10 that R. Eliezer be-R. Yosi claimed that he had seen the *kaporet* in Rome (to where it was taken after the destruction of the Second Temple), and he saw the blood stains upon it. So apparently, even the holiest of Temple vessels could not be called "pure," even though they were, of course, ritually pure, because they had blood upon them.

19. See the internet films "Animals Australia for a Kinder World," and "60 Minutes

obviously not kosher because of that damage to internal organs which is not necessarily seen by the slaughterers. Add to that, for example, that in some cases these animals are starved prior to their slaughter, to ease certain aspects of their treatment, i.e., squeezing and examining adhesions (*miuch sirchah*), something absolutely forbidden (see, e.g., *Bava Batra* 8b, that hunger can be worse than death).

So the treatment that they receive before they're slaughtered, even if slaughtering is done in the most humane manner – and humane is a funny word to use for animals – those conditions that they undergo beforehand are, to my mind, absolutely unacceptable.[20] Indeed, the

Australia." In 2018, 60 rabbis signed a petition to end live transports. See *Jerusalem Post Magazine*, November 1, 2019 (which was the World Vegan Day), for the article by Uri Ballag, entitled "Thou shalt not remain indifferent" (a reference to *Deuteronomy* 22:3), pp. 8–11, where my own part in this initiative is described (p. 11).

20. Sears, ibid., pp. 72–79, discusses some of the aspects of how animals (cows, sheep, etc.) are treated prior to slaughter. Since "shackling and hoisting" such animals in order to get them lying down for *shehitah*, not only is not "humane," the animal might be injured in the process and therefore rendered unfit. As a consequence, in the U.S. the American Society for the Prevention of Cruelty to Animals (ASPCA) developed new methods which minimized the issues mentioned above, and were endorsed by R. Moshe Feinstein in his *Igrot Moshe*, vol. 5, 1973, sect. 13, and so too R. Yaakov Yitzchak Weiss, in his *Minhat Yitzchak*, vol. 10, 1969, sect. 59, etc. However, "while the majority of American and British rabbis have accepted the upright restraint pens – this new procedure – *the Israel rabbinate has been reluctant to abandon the traditional casting methods*" (p. 75, note 43). [My emphasis – D. S.].

A further aspect of "factory farming" that he points out (p. 79) is that it:

… engages in the chemical and hormonal regulation of the animals' life cycles, both for reasons of production and health. As a result of overcrowding, the threat of disease and infection must be battled with an arsenal of animal drugs, which a U.S. Congressional committee acknowledged several decades ago, "may have potentially adverse effects on animals or humans." This, too, is a subject that warrants serious halachic consideration.

And in note 54 ibid. he expands on this subject thus:

Union Calendar no. 24: Human Food Safety and the Regulation of Animal Drugs, 27th Report of the Committee on Government Operations, U.S. Printing Office, 1985. More recently, the journal *Science* (1998) 279: 996–997 declared the meat industry to be "the driving force behind the development of antibiotic

whole life is one of inhumanity being raised in narrow stalls preventing them from freely moving about, and being fed in an unnormal manner, solely in order to fatten them. And how rightly writes R. Moshe Feinstein on the halachic implications of such a regime in his *Igrot Mosheh*, *Even ha-Ezer*, part 4, no. 92, p. 164:

> Regarding the new method of fattening calves in special, narrow stalls where they don't even have enough room to take a few steps, and they are not fed any normal animal feed nor are they allowed to suckle at all but instead are fed with fatty liquids from which they derive no pleasure at all and they are also frequently ill because of this and require all kinds of medication: Those who perform this (the fattening) are surely guilty of the prohibition of causing pain to animals. For even though it (pain) is permitted when there is a purpose, for example to slaughter them for food or to use them for plowing or transport, etc. but not for senseless pain, which is forbidden even if someone makes monetary gain from it… In any case, it is forbidden to cause pain to an animal, to feed it food which it doesn't enjoy, which causes pain, or which causes it to be ill.

It's much the same with chickens. The way they are stuffed into the cages[21] causes their legs often to protrude outside the wire netting and

---

resistance in certain species of bacteria that cause human disease." The Centers for Disease Control similarly blamed the meat industry for the emergence of new, antibiotic resistant bacteria; see K. Glynn, "Emergence of multidrug-resistant *salmonella enterica* serotype… infections in the U.S., "*New England Journal of Medicine* (1998), 338: 1333–1338. The first significant response to this problem at the federal level would be HR3804, which proposes to phase out the use of eight specific antibiotics in the immediate future, including penicillin and tetracycline that are used in human medicine or which are so closely related to human-use drugs that they trigger cross-resistance.

And for problems, both halachic and ethical, connected with veal production, see ibid., pp. 79–80.

21.   Purely by chance I recently came upon a newspaper article (*Metro*, November 6, 2019, p. 6), describing similar conditions in England in a so-called dogs' home:

break. And then they fall out of the cage onto a conveyor belt which is halachically problematic because that's a question of *nefulah*,[22] and

---

Stacked on top of each other in cages so small they can hardly move, this was the sickening sight when RSPCA inspectors raided a home and found 54 dogs in unimaginable squalor.

The animals had matted fur, were covered in filth and some had no access to water. One inspector said: 'In the 12 years I have worked for the RSPCA I have never seen such appalling conditions and mental suffering inflicted upon such defenseless animals.'

On Monday, Kilmany O'Connor was banned from keeping animals for life.

But she escaped being caged herself – after Lancashire magistrates gave her a suspended 16-week sentence. The 57-year-old was arrested after police and RSPCA inspectors, along with Lancashire Fire and Rescue, environmental health, social services, county council dog wardens and a specialist vet, raided her home in Morecambe, Lancashire, on April 9.

Concerns had been raised about the welfare of a number of dogs at the address, magistrates heard.

A police spokesman said: "Within the address 54 dogs were located and found to be living in appalling conditions, the majority of which were cooped up in small cages."

Remarkably, all 54 dogs have made a full recovery and have been re-homed.

So if we are so concerned about dogs, why not about cows and chickens?

22. There is also the question of their transport from the farm to the abattoir. For the *Daat Kedoshim*, by R. Avraham David Warman, Lvov, 1871, 17:5, wrote concerning "the conveyance of geese from villages to the town, with their legs and wings bound and their heads bent downwards, that bring them to the city completely exhausted, and if they were slaughtered and there was no jerking around (*pirchus*), they are forbidden, because they may have already been dead, or almost dead, in which case they are categorized as *mesukanut*, in a dangerous state, close to death." So they need to be freed of their bonds, left a little to recover and only then could they be slaughtered. Such a procedure does not admit of rapid conveyor-belt *shehitah*. And of course, the same applies to all kinds of fowls. And see further *Simlah Hadashah*, by R. Alexander Sender Schor, Muncacz: 1901, 17:6, that since there is no clear definition of what constitutes *mesukenet* in a fowl, one must always rule stringently if one sees a sign of sickness, that it does not walk like a healthy one – if given the opportunity to walk – and so too the *Daat Kedoshim* as mentioned above. See *Shulhan Aruh Yoreh Deah* 17:1; *Darchei Teshuvah* by R. Tzvi Hirsch Schapira, Jerusalem, 1967, vol. 1, 58a, note 32, where he gives a detailed discussion of what constitutes *mesukenet* and requires *pirchus*, with a rich bibliography; *Daat Torah*, by R. Shalom Mordechai ha-Cohen Schwadron, Lvov, 1891, to *Yoreh Deah* 17, sect. 14, citing to the *Ittur* on the question of broken limbs, which always require examination (*bedikah*). So too *Hamudei Daniel*, by R. Daniel be

they are slaughtered one after another automatically so that sometimes they are not even alive when they are being slaughtered.[23] We know

---

R. Yaakov, Horodna: 1810 (cited by *Darchei Teshuvah* ibid., sect. 16), ruling that if the fowl is swollen, so that there might be a gap (*hefsek*) between the skin and the flesh, a *bedikah* is required. All of the above, and much more, is virtually impossible in rapid conveyor-belt style *shehitah*.

In addition, the practice was not to slaughter fowls before, i.e., in the view of, other fowls, and there is an opinion that the reason is because this would constitute *tza'ar ba'alei hayyim*; see R. Efraim Zalman Margaliot, *Beit Efraim*, Lvov, 1810, sect. 26.

And while we are speaking of the distress of chickens, we may note that R. Tzvi Pesach Frank, in his *Har Tzvi, Orah Hayyim*, ed. 1, Jerusalem, 1977, sect. 205, pp. 204–205, permitted removing chickens manually from the hen-house on Shabbat, even though they are *muktzeh*, if they are being pecked by other chickens, and not because they may lose their monetary value by being bitten, and perhaps becoming *tereifah*, but because of their distress.

23. See David Karen, *Prisoned Chickens, Poisoned Eggs*, Book Publishing Co., 1997. A definitive book on the chicken and egg industry.

According to Sears, p. 82, Empire Poultry Corporation, the largest producer of kosher chickens in the world today (written in 2003) slaughters between 100,000 and 110,000 birds per day four days a week, at its plant in Middletown, PA. Rubashkin and Sons, in Postville, IA, slaughters some 40,000 chickens a day, while Vinland Poultry, of Vinland, NJ, slaughters approximately 20,000 chickens a day.

He, however, when describing these large kosher operations, suggests that they are carried out with considerable care, involving quite a labor intensive system. He writes that:

> At least two attendants assist the *shochet:* the first removes each hen from the crate and passes it to a second attendant, who holds the bird during *shechitah*. After the *shochet* plucks away the neck feathers and slaughters the bird, he inspects its throat; then the attendant transfers the carcass to a cone in a conveyor. All this takes a matter of several seconds. A *mashgiach* (rabbinic supervisor) periodically checks the slaughterers' knives for knicks, a task which the *shochtim,* too, perform regularly. (Due to the high quality of modern steel knives, knicks are found relatively infrequently.) Kosher slaughter disallows the use of scald tanks, requiring that birds be defeathered by a cold-water process. Several *mashgichim* (supervisors) inspect the slaughtered birds for *treifos* (disqualifying signs), and still other *mashgichim* oversee the washing and salting process. From the standpoint of *tza'ar ba'alei hayyim,* the main problem is that the greater percentage of kosher chickens, like other food animals, must be purchased from the same factory farms that rule the industry.

Taking into account that these companies slaughter over 160,000 chickens a day, that there was such a case in Zoglobek,[24] and there was yet another scandal in the United States with a large abattoir.[25] So the fact that they are treated so badly, which is a question of *tza'ar ba'alei hayyim*, also

---

I am skeptical as to whether all procedures are stringently adhered to.

See also his note 64, ibid.:

> It must be acknowledged that not all factory farms are equally problematic. All broiler hens are "free-roaming," i.e., floor raised; however, spaciousness and sanitariness of the coops vary widely. Most "broilers" are fed a mixture of corn and soy treated with growth hormones and steroids, although certain growers do allow the chickens to develop naturally. Empire Poultry states that their chickens are not treated with growth hormones. However, given the size of such operations and the high probability of disease, the use of antibiotics is virtually ubiquitous.

Furthermore, slaughtering such vast numbers in so short a time would surely be tiring for the *shochtim*, and their hands would presumably tremble on occasion. (See below note 30.) So let me relate a story I learned concerning my grandfather, R. David Sperber, a great scholar and a recognized *gadol be-Torah*. When he was the rabbi of the town of Brashov in Rumania, he would regularly examine the local slaughterers and their knives. Once he heard that a certain *shochet* (slaughterer and butcher), who had grown old and whose hands were trembling, continued to slaughter animals and fowls and sell them in his shop. My grandfather instructed him to cease slaughtering, and when he refused to do so, grandfather declared his products to be *treif* (not kosher). The butcher was infuriated and came to my grandfather's house, and before all who were present began to berate him and curse him. In a calm voice my grandfather replied, "*Solst hoben a schwartzer jahr*" – "You should have a black year."

Everyone present was astonished. This was not in keeping with his character or his manner of conduct. The butcher was terrified. Never once had the Rabbi cursed anyone. He never grew angry. He was always calm and controlled, even in the most heated arguments. "Please, Rabbi, forgive me my insolence," he begged. My grandfather smiled at him and said, "My son, I wish you "*a schwartzer jahr*." He was referring to the priestly blessing in *Numbers* 6:25, "*Yaer ha-Shem Panav Eilecha vi-Yehunecha*" – "May the Lord cause *His countenance to shine* (*Yaer*) upon thee, and be gracious unto thee," meaning, since you will require a new profession, you should become a *sofer*, scribe, and may the letters you write in the Torah be truly black, as is required by the law, and thus God will cause His countenance to shine (*yaer*) upon you, and He will be gracious unto you, so that you will need not fear that you have lost all hope for supporting yourself in the future.

24. See *Haaretz*, December 7, 2001, *Yedioth Aharonoth*, July 13, 2001, etc.

25. I am referring to the Rubashkin family's company in Postville, OH, and other locations. See the horrifying report in *Associated Press*, August 5, 2008.

affects their halachic status. Hence, we have to see these issues at more than one level. *Tza'ar ba'alei hayyim* is forbidden, either rabbinically or biblically, as stated above. So animals have to be treated in a decent fashion. In addition to that, the sort of mass production requirement is such that in all too many cases the animals that reach the shops are really not kosher. Many prominent rabbis have pointed this out. So the question is not just *tza'ar ba'alei hayyim* from a *moral* point of view, but also from a *kashrut* point of view. Indeed, the late R. Aryeh Carmell wrote that:

> It seems doubtful that the Torah would sanction factory farming, which treats animals as machines, with apparent insensitivity to their natural needs and instincts," (*Masterplan: Judaism: Its Progress, Meaning, Goals*, Jerusalem, 1991, p. 69).

And let us consider the force-feeding of geese. In the latter days of their lives they are fed enormous quantities of food between two and five times a day. This is usually done by pushing a tube down the throat of the goose and forcing the food down beyond the point where it can be vomited out. The result of this process is a massive enlargement of the liver. The fact that a tube, or indeed, food of a rough quality, is forced down the gullet is liable to damage the esophagus, which immediately presents a halachic problem. And though the Rema, R. Moshe Isserles, permitted eating such fattened geese after checking the gullet for perforations (*Yoreh Deah* 33:11), a little later, R. Yoel Sirkis, the Bach, advised against it (*Yoreh Deah* 33, cited by Shach subsection 23).[26]

It took a while till this phenomenon was widely prohibited, but under the influence of great authorities like R. Alexander Sender Schor (*Tvuot*

---

26. Furthermore, in order to induce hunger to enable the force-feeding, the veterinary surgeons developed a chemical which when injected in the back of the chicken's neck in the form of two tablets just below the skin, dissolves in three to five days. They enjoin one not to inject deeply, but, nonetheless, at times one may perforate the gullet during such treatment. See the discussion of Rabbi A. Weinstein, in his responsum *Kuntres be-Inyan Ofot Petumot al Yedei Zerikah*, published under the auspices of the London Beth Din, London, 1957.

Schor, Yoreh Deah 33:5), the *Noda bi-Yehuda* (*Tzlach, Derush* 23:15), and R. Meir Eisenstadt (*Panim Meirot* 1:1) this became the accepted position among Polish Jewry, and so also in Galicia, Lithuania, Russia, and Rumania, etc. The matter remained a bone of contention among the various communities, and there is considerable literature on this issue in rabbinic responsa. And though the discussions were primarily halachic, i.e., the need to check the esophagus for perforations, or lack of them, or the outright prohibition against eating such geese, we cannot overlook the aspect of cruelty inflicted upon these fowl. Indeed, precisely because of the element of cruelty to animals, many countries have forbidden such force-feeding, so that such fattened geese are not so readily available, though there still are some European countries where this is practiced. However, contemporary decisors have cautioned against eating them (e.g., R. Tzvi Pesach Frank, *Har Tzvi, Yoreh Deah* 26, R. Ovadiah Yosef, *Yabia Omer* 9, *Yoreh Deah* 3, etc.).[27]

There is yet another very complex and serious kashrut issue concerning battery-fed fowls, including chickens, and that is that many factories are involved in genetically engineering the species in order to both save money in production and to produce a more sellable item, such as one that has more fat with fewer inedible inner parts, etc. This is often done by cross-breeding with species for which there is no known tradition as to their kashrut. And there is a well-known halachic principle that fowls are only eaten ([i.e., regraded as kosher for eating) when there is a tradition that they were indeed eaten (*Of tahor ne'achal be-masoret*, B. *Hullin* 63b, the formulation of R. Yitzhak) and the *Gemara* there concludes that the examination of the various *simanei teharah* in fowls is not in itself sufficient. All this has, of course, implications for the eating of eggs too.[28]

---

27. See the detailed discussion by R. Avraham Binyamin Meir Boim, in *Tzanz* 476, 2017, pp. 12–21.

28. There is considerable literature on this subject due to halachic controversies of the last century or so, collected recently in an anonymous pamphlet *Pitum Ofot ha-Petem ha-Metzuyim* (no date, but probably 2019), including a fine summarizing article by R. Yosef Wozner, *"Achilat Basar u-Beitzei Tarnegolim be-Yameinu," Paamei Yaakov*, Menachem Av, 2004, pp. 57–70. And most recently there appeared an anonymous pamphlet entitled *Kuntres ha-Of ba-Halachah u-ba-Metziut*, 2018, with an appendix

And now to give some indications of the rabbinic concern for the welfare of animals, I shall just list a number of examples, basing myself on Rav David Eigner's book, *Hilchot Gidul Tzon*, Ashkelon-Givataim, 2nd ed., 2013, which deals specifically with livestock.

> In the case of a likelihood of suffering to livestock, a number of prohibitions on the Shabbat may be waived (p. 11).
>
> Though milking cows and sheep is biblically forbidden on Shabbat, in the case of hand-milking twice a day, where not carrying it out would cause extreme distress, such milking is permitted on condition that its milk be thrown away *(le-ibbud)* (p. 25).
>
> A calf that was born outside *techum Shabbat*, in an open area where it might be placed in a life-threatening situation, may be carried into a safe place on Shabbat (p. 29).
>
> Certain kinds of medical intervention for a sick animal are permitted on Shabbat, if they do not contravene biblical prohibitions (pp. 33–34).

There are many more examples listed – with full source-references – and even more through the intervention of a non-Jew.[29]

Furthermore, there is an explicit halachah that one should not begin to eat before feeding one's livestock. And this was derived from the verse in *Deuteronomy* 11:15, "And I will give grass in the fields for thy cattle," and only afterwards, "and thou shalt eat and be satisfied" (see

---

by R. Mosheh Krauss, which discusses the questionable identity of many kosher fowls.

29.   As to feeding young puppies, or newly-born lambs and calves, see the responsum of the Rema, sect. 79, and A. Ziv, Jerusalem, 1971, pp. 328–329, who on Shabbat permits this because of *tza'ar ba'alei hayyim*, *Mishnah Berurah* 324, sect. 27 (*Magen Avraham* 305:12; but cf. *Beur Halachah*, ibid., citing authorities who forbid this, adding that the *Shiurei Berachah* is against force-feeding at any time, since it may perforate the gullet, as mentioned above).

We may further add that when horses drag a wagon and reach a steep hill or a dangerous path and find difficulty in dragging the wagon without further help, it is a *mitzvah* to help them get over their difficulties; see Steinberg, *Ha-Refuah ke-Halachah*, ibid., p. 232, no. 67, referring to *Shulhan Aruch ha-Rav, Hilchot Tza'ar Ba'alei Hayyim*, sect. 68; *Kitzur Shulhan Aruch* 191:2; and see additional examples (ibid., pp. 230–232), some of which we have discussed above.

B. Berachot 40a). And as a corollary of this ruling we read in the *Shulhan Aruch Orah Hayyim* 167:6 that after one makes the blessing over food:

> One must immediately eat, and not speak between the benediction and eating. And if he does so, he must repeat the benediction, except in the case that the talk was concerning matters related to the subject of the benediction, such as if he made the benediction over bread, and before he ate he said… Bring salt… give so and so to eat, *give food to the cattle*, and like; for in these cases he does not need to repeat the benediction.

Here, then, we see clear expression of rabbinic concern for the welfare of animals.

And my father, in a letter of congratulations to Prof. Aaron Bondi on his receiving the Israel Prize in 1984 for his work on animal husbandry, and specifically the feeding of animals, discussed whether the feeding of animals prior to one's own meal was a biblical or a rabbinic obligation, showing that according to some authorities it was indeed of biblical authority.

And such concern and, indeed, compassion for animals is already clearly indicated in the Bible. Thus *Deuteronomy* 25:4 forbids the muzzling of an ox while treading grain on the threshing floor, for the animal is entitled to enjoy food just as is a human laborer (ibid., 23:25–26), and rabbinic literature interpreted the term "ox" as a generic term incorporating all animals. Schochet (ibid., p. 58) quotes Carl Heinrich Cornhill[30] who comments with admiration:

> What a truly humanitarian sentiment finds expression in this law, *Thou shalt not muzzle the ox when he treadeth out the corn.* The brute should not perform hard labour and at the same time have food before its eyes without the possibility of eating therefrom. I remember some time ago to have read that one of the richest Italian real-estate owners, at the grape-harvest, fastened iron muzzles to his miserable, fever-stricken workmen, so that it might not occur to these

---

30. A prominent German Protestant theologian, 1854–1940.

poor peasants working for starvation wages under the glowing sun of Southern Italy, to satiate their burning thirst and their gnawing hunger with a few of the millions of grapes of the owner.[31]

Schochet continues (ibid., pp. 58–62) to show how expressions of compassion for the feelings of animals are to be found throughout biblical literature. Indeed, one of the descriptive characteristics of the righteous man is, inter alia, one "who regards the soul (*nefesh*) of his beast, but the tender mercies of the wicked are cruel" (*Proverbs* 12:10).

But even these somewhat random examples should serve clearly to demonstrate the care and attention that the halachah gives to the welfare of animals, and many of these rulings may be applied to fowls too (*Deuteronomy Rabba* 6:1, in the name of R. Berechiah in the name of R. Yitzhak).

"But surely, if it has a kosher label, it must be kosher!" was the next comment.

To which my response is: recently there have been a number of articles in the media on all the questions of *hechsherim* (kosher certifications). This is a very problematic issue.[32] The number of

---

31. See Schochet, ibid., p. 315, note 112 for the reference, and his additional comment there. (And cf. *Cor.* 12:10, and I *Tim* 5.18.)

32. One has to be completely sure of the honesty and integrity of the *shochet*. See Gedaliah Nigal, *The Hasidic Tales*, transl. by Edward Levin. Oxford and Portland, ORE, 2008, pp. 252–253:

> On one occasion the Ba'al Shem Tov stayed with the rabbi of a community for the sabbath. The rabbi's wife was distressed that she had no meat for the sabbath, nor did any of her neighbours. A slaughterer happened to pass by, and when asked by the rabbi's wife, he answered that only a few hours previously he had slaughtered a tender good animal.
> The Ba'al Shem Tov responded, saying, "I, too, very greatly love to eat the head, if it would be possible for it to be brought here in its entirety, and have *nikur* [removal of the sciatic nerve] performed here." The slaughterer concurred: "This is good!" and he arose and went quickly to bring the head to the rabbi's house. The Ba'al Shem Tov began to speak with the slaughterer: "The world [i.e. all Jews] says there is a distinctive sign in the teeth. Please count how many teeth it has." He opened the animal's mouth in order to count its teeth, and immediately shut its mouth, so that the slaughterer could not extract his hand. The animal pressed

on the hand, until the pain became unbearable, and the slaughterer cried out. The Ba'al Shem Tov asked: "Why are you screaming? There is no life in it!" The Ba'al Shem Tov then shouted at him: "Wicked one! Make your confession!" And he confessed to his sin, [namely] that he had never checked the lungs – "as you pleased, you pronounced kosher, as you pleased, you pronounced [organically] unfit [and therefore non-kosher]." He [the Ba'al Shem Tov] then prescribed for him a *tikkun* for his repentance.

Nigal adds on p. 324 the following note:

A similar story, disseminated by the pupils of R. Jonathan Eybeschuetz, is cited in Emden, *Beit Yehonatan ha-Sofer*, fo. 9a–b: "A certain butcher brought meat to sell. Eybeschuetz saw, and called to him, 'What is this meat?' He replied, 'It is kosher meat, that may be sold to Jews.' He told him, 'I order you to immediately bring the head of this animal to me.' He went and brought it. He told him: 'Stick your hand into the mouth of the beast,' and he did so. The head closed its mouth and held the butcher's hand with its teeth, and did not want to release it. The butcher sought to free his hand by force, but was unable to do so. He cried bitterly that it was improperly slaughtered ... Then Eybeschuetz commanded, the beast opened its mouth, and gave the butcher his hand back." For the slaughterer who rendered animals unfit because of his hatred of butchers, see Gemen, *Sifran shel Tsadikim*, "Ma'arechet" 36, 11.

For the motif of the slaughtered head closing its mouth and trapping the hand of the wicked slaughterer, forcing him to admit that he has slaughtered animals improperly, see also Emden, *Edut Be-Ya'akov*, fo. 44a; *ha-Shahar*, 5 (1874), 248.

33. See *B. Hulin* 17b that there are a number of different ways to check the sharpness of the *shehitah* knife. See further *Shulhan Aruch Yoreh Deah* 18, *Pri Meggadim – Siftei Da'at*, sect. 30, who wrote that:

halilah, that all the meat that comes into the shops is not kosher. But I
do think that a goodly percentage is not necessarily kosher, and that we
should be clearly aware of this situation. The fact that you have a sticker
on a wrapped-up item in a supermarket does not necessarily mean that
it has undergone the rigid examination and control that is halachically
required. For as long as the production business was small and limited
and almost personalized, a person would go with his chicken to the
local butcher whom he knew personally, and watch the actual *shehitah*,
so that he knew what was going on and had full confidence in the
shochet and his *shehitah*. But now that things are mass produced on such
a vast level, it is obvious there is going to be a certain amount of *treifus*

[R]eally one requires twelve different examinations of the knife, in three
directions, backwards and forwards on the skin of the finger and on the tip of
the nail, but what can I do, for among our many sins there is a laxity (*zilzul*) and
[the *shohtim*] do not do these examinations as they should [*bi-shlemut*], and may
the good Lord atone for us lest, God forfend, we stand accused... and I am not
speaking of the majority...

Nowadays such careful examination is rarely done. Furthermore, these examinations
must be done slowly (*Yoreh Deah* 18:9), and not in a cold place or with cold hands, or
a very hot place, or with sweaty hands, because in all such cases one is not sensitive to a
nick in the knife (*Kaf ha-Hayyim Yoreh Deah*, sect. 43). So, too, it should not be checked
by one who has just sharpened it (*Zivhei Tzedek Yoreh Deah* 18:90 and *Darchei Teshuva*,
ibid., sect. 61). Likewise, one must change fingernails every few checks (*Shulhan Aruch*,
ibid.), and the fingernail itself should be sharpened (*Kaf ha-Hayyim*, ibid., sect. 50).
And also, the knife should be rinsed off in hot water before it is checked, since on
occasions congealed blood fills a nick which will not be felt when it is examined.

There are numerous other rules involved but this should suffice to indicate that
when the slaughterers are involved in numerous *shehitot* and are pressed for time, they
can hardly fulfill all these requirements. (See also R. Yitzhak ha-Cohen Rabin's article,
"*Be-Din Bedikat Sakin Shel Shehitah*," apud *Sefer Tiferet Banim*, Jerusalem, 1999, pp.
56–67.)

As an aside, I recently came upon a curious pamphlet entitled *Daddy's Store: What
Makes Meat Kosher: A Children's Guide*, by Mary Glick, Forest Hills, 1986, and there –
the pages are not numbered – she writes:

The *shohet* must use a very smooth knife and must cut the throat of the animal
in a single stroke. The sharpness of the knife and the speed of the *shohet* prevents
the animal from feeling pain. Even though we must kill animals in order to eat
meat, there is a concern of Jews to prevent the suffering of the animal.

45

(non-kosher food) involved.

So am I then arguing that it is not possible to have mass-produced meat and fish which is kosher? The answer is: By no means.

The question we are dealing with is: is it possible to have, on the one hand, this sort of industrial production of meat and fish products, and at the same time to know that the results are strictly kosher. Yes, I think it certainly is possible; but I also think that the price of the product would be so prohibitively high that people wouldn't be able to purchase it, and therefore practically speaking it will never take place.

I was then asked how to respond to those who say that *tza'ar ba'alei hayyim*[34] is an instruction to tame our sadistic or violent cruel natures but does not necessarily have anything to do with the animals.[35]

---

34. It is interesting to compare the Jewish notion of *tza'ar ba'alei hayyim* with that of the Jains. For vegetarianism is a way of life for the Jain, having its origin in the concept of compassion for all living creatures, *jiva – daya*, so that any form of cruelty to birds, animals, and, of course, human beings, is a transgression against *ahimsa* (non-violence).

Jiya – daya means caring for and sharing the gift of knowledge and material well-being with all living beings, tending, protecting and serving them. It entails *maitri* – universal friendliness, *kshama* – universal forgiveness, and *abheya* – universal fearlessness. One of the most moving of Jain observances is the Day of Universal Forgiveness, the message of which is encapsulated as follows:

> *Khamemi savve jiva, savve jiva Khamanti me*
> *Miki me savva bhuye-su, vairammajjham na kenayi*
> I beg forgiveness of all living creatures as I forgive them all. I have friendship for one and all and have no ill-feeling or animosity for anyone.

See Padmanabh S. Jaini, *The Jaina Path of Purification*, Delhi, 1979, pp. 168–169, 170–173, 311–315, etc.

35. The Israeli law against cruelty to animals (*Hok Tza'ar Ba'alei Hayyim – Haganah al Ba'alei Hayyim*) was passed in the Knesset on January 11, 1994, with some additional comments on July 19, 1994. It consists of twenty-three clauses covering definitions of cruelty to animals, ministerial responsibility (Ministry of Agriculture – and, for certain purposes, the Ministry for Environmental Quality – *Eichut ha-Sevivah*), sanctions and punishments, institutional safeguards, etc., and was signed by Ezer Weizman, President of the State of Israel, Yitzhak Rabin, Prime Minister, Shevah Weiss, chairman of the Knesset, and Yaakov Tzur, Minister of Agriculture. See *Ha-Biosfera: Yarhon ha-Misrad le-Eichut ha-Sevivah*, 24/3–4, December/January 1994/1995, pp. 3–9. See also Y. Neril and L. Dee, Eco Bible, vol. 1: An Ecological Commentary on Genesis and Exodus

Consequently, so long as there is an element of human benefit to some practice –be it plucking the feathers of a live duck or having to raise these animals in really intensified environments in order to have enough to eat – it should be viewed positively.[36]

(Jerusalem) 2020, pp. 145–146.

36. This, indeed, was the opinion of R. Yisrael Isserlein in his *Terumat ha-Deshen, Pesakim ve-Ketavim*, sect. 108, who wrote:

> ... It would appear that there is no prohibition of *tza'ar b'aalei hayyim*, if it is done for one's needs and use, for the animals were created only to serve the needs of man (*B. Kiddushin* chapter 2). And know, that in *B. Baba Metzia* 36a *perikah* – un-burdening an animal – is because of *tza'ar ba'alei hayyim*. How then is it permitted to have an animal bear a burden from place to place ... and from this [and other evidence he cites] it would appear that under such circumstances (i.e. for one's benefit) there is no prohibition. But people are careful and desist [from causing discomfort to animals] for they do not wish to act with cruelty, fearing they will be punished for doing so ...

This is also the view of the *Hatam Sofer* (*Tinyana, Yoreh Deah*, sect. 10), who when asked whether one is allowed to hunt animals in the forest, or whether this comes under the prohibition of *tza'ar ba'alei hayyim*, or perhaps *bal tash'hit*, replied that if he kills the animal, there is no transgression of *tza'ar ba'alei hayyim*. And he only transgresses it if he inflicts pain upon it while it is alive. Likewise, there is no issue of *bal tash'hit*, since he can benefit from its skin, and as long as there is benefit it does not come under the category of *bal tash'hit*. He adds that since these are wild animals in a forest, not owned by anyone, hunting them will cause no loss to anyone – hence there is no *bal tash'hit*, and in addition, he gains benefit for the dead animal's skin.

However, he concludes, hunting is a non-Jewish occupation, entails potential danger, and one should distance oneself from such activity.

Moreover, it is surely significant that R. Pinchas of Koritz did not permit a *shohet* to act as the *shaliah tzibbur*, the cantor, as the cantor's duty is to bring people close to God and bring life to the soul, "while the slaughterer does the opposite," referring to Rashi's commentary to a passage in B. Hulin 27a. (See *Imrei Pinhas*, by R. Pinhas Shapira of Koritz, 2003, *Shaar Seder ha-Yom*, sect 64.) So, too, Responsa *Shut Hadar*, by R. Yehiel Michel Hibner, Lvov, 1894, sect. 29:200, states that R. Uri from Strelisk (1757–1826) would not permit the *shohet* to lead the services, "for there is a palatial hall (*heichal*) in the heavens which does not admit the prayers of a *shohet*." (See Z. W. Zichermann, *Otzar Plaot ha-Torah* to *Leviticus*, Brooklyn, 2016, pp. 291–293.) However, other authorities did not agree with this position, stating that the custom is otherwise. (See, e.g., *Sdei Hemed* by R. Hayyim Hezkiyahu Medini, Warsaw, 1891–1912, *Rosh ha-Shana* 3/11, and this seems to be indicated in the Rema to *Orah Hayyim* 53:25, Zichermann, ibid.).

My response would be to ask: how necessary it is for human beings to consume animal products? Obviously if it were absolutely necessary for health reasons,[37] then that might counter the prohibition of *tza'ar ba'alei hayyim* to some extent. That would mean that one has to be kind to animals as long as they are living with you, but when it becomes obviously necessary to eat for one's health, just like taking a medicine, one would be permitted to slaughter them. And while I believe that that is true, I also think it is true only if you say that it is really necessary to consume animal products. Now in the past, there wasn't the same quantity of food or variety of fruits and vegetables available to people. Let me illustrate this with a personal reminiscence. When I was a child during the war years in London, there was virtually no fruit available. There were apples and maybe pears. I remember that when I was a little boy I drew a picture of a barrow boy, and I drew two squares: in one square I did round circles and in the other square I did other round circles. And my brother, who was three years older, asked me, "What's this?" and I replied, "These are apples and these are bananas." "No," he said, "bananas are like [crescent] moons!" "No," I replied, "all fruits are round or almost round (referring to pears)." For I had never seen a banana, nor even an orange for that matter. We just had a bottle of orange juice concentrate once a month which was allocated on the basis of a ration-card for children.

However, this was not a universally accepted position. Thus, R. Yaakov Weil relates (*Hiddushei Dinim ve-Halachot le-Mahari Weil*, sect. 37) that when a person wears new leather clothing or shoes, one does not wish him *tithadesh* ..., since one had to kill an animal to get this leather, and the verse states that "His mercy is for all creations." (However, see *Rema, Orah Hayyim* 223:6, who sees this as a weak reason, but agrees that this is the accepted custom.)

R. Moshe Feinstein, *Igrot Mosheh, Even ha-Ezer* part 4, sect. 92, in discussing force-feeding of animals, concludes:

> A person is not permitted to inflict pain on an animal in all circumstances, even if it is to his personal gain.

So he would not agree with the ruling of R. Yisrael Isserlein. See also the discussion of R. Yishayahu Stoker, apud *Ha-Svivah ba-Halachah u-ba-Mahshavah*, pp. 152–155.

37. See *Sefer ha-Hinuch*, sect. 187, cited below at the end of this section.

Now obviously that was in a time of war. Going back to the nineteenth century and even earlier in history, the sort of healthy, wholesome food that is now available to most people was just not obtainable. But now we have everything we need. And we can take vitamins too! Moreover, excessive meat-eating is medically harmful (see below note 67).

A further issue of which we should be fully aware is that in mass egg production, male chicks are immediately killed because they are of no benefit in the production of eggs, so that the egg farms weed out the little chicks in the initial days of their lives. Eytan Halon writes in the *Jerusalem Post* of December 26, 2019, p. 13, that:

> Considered worthless by the egg and poultry industry, a staggering seven billion day-old male layer chicks are systematically culled worldwide every year.
>
> While both male and female broiler chicks can be grown quickly for meat production, unwanted male layer chicks are perceived as serving no commercial purpose and are destroyed en masse.[38]

---

38. In his article, ibid., he continues:

Faced with both economic and increasing ethical pressure, finding an effective and efficient way to determine or engineer the gender of all chicks prior to hatching has become an industry priority. Gene editing has proved unfeasible due to restrictions on GMO produce reaching consumers, and hormone checking, while effective, has proved costly and prohibitively time-consuming.

An alternative solution is being developed by Israeli bio-tech company LIVEgg, headed by engineers with decades of experience in the poultry industry and electro-optics.

To avoid the killing of day-old male chicks and eliminate manual sorting procedures, LIVEgg's ChickMale Saver solution uses sophisticated electro-optical technology and machine-learning algorithms to convert electrical signals and convert them into biological characteristics. The company expects to launch the solution next year.

"The technology is still under development but we believe this will be the solution as this is very cheap and can deal with 50,000 to 60,000 eggs per hour," LIVEgg CEO Alon Blum told *The Jerusalem Post*.

"There is a major focus on how to prevent the killing of those day-old chicks, for both welfare and economic reasons, and predict what will be the gender of the egg as soon as possible, so we can dispose of them before they hatch. Even if

So only the female ones that can lay eggs are kept alive, and the males are thrown out. Usually, they don't even kill them, they don't even twist their necks. They just throw them on a rubbish heap. I've seen this in various places. In fact, once, when we were on holiday in Kibbutz Hafetz Hayyim, we found a few of these little ones, nice fluffy little yellow chicks, and we took them home. And they grew, and we had chickens that lived on our roof for ten years! But most of them were not females. However, one of them was, and she laid an egg once every two days or so. We called her "Kapparah." So I think that this sort of treatment obviously goes strongly against the laws of *tza'ar ba'alei hayyim*, and I think it's even worse when you leave an animal to die

_____

we give layer chicks a lot of feed to eat, they will never grow to be broilers due to their genetic design."

LIVEgg was established in 2015 by parent company Baram Group, a leading Israeli poultry producer. Given the centralized nature of the poultry industry, the company is targeting pilot programs with leading industry operators.

Last year, LIVEgg brought its first product to market, a real-time embryo monitoring system called CrystalEgg. The company's non-invasive technology enables hatcheries to monitor embryo development, fertility rates and how many chicks are going to hatch.

"We are not bringing the data in a better-organized way. We are bringing a completely new set of information that was previously unavailable," said Blum.

"Research has shown that our technology can increase hatchery production by about 1–3%, which is quite a lot in our business. The chicks we produce are also of better quality because incubation is optimized and the hatch is optimized. Talking about food security, the fastest growing protein from livestock is chicken."

A further application of the technology, currently in an advanced stage of development, is to identify the fertility of eggs at day zero. Hatchery operators currently do not know whether eggs are fertile or infertile, leading to large quantities of costly biological waste after several days in the facility.

By identifying egg fertility as early as possible, Blum says, hatcheries can save space and increase profits.

"We believe the way to go to market is from top to bottom. Rather than going to small operations, we are going to the big companies and explaining how it affects their operations financially, and even how it affects their share of the market," Blum said. "Once they apply the technology, we know the small ones will come anyway and be part of it."

This, though not a vegetarian solution, and partially motivated by commercial considerations, should, nonetheless, be welcomed by all animal lovers.

rather than if you kill it quickly.

And then, of course, in the chicken industry they keep them all squashed in small cages so that they can hardly move, and they feed them with all sorts of chemicals in order to make them fat. They don't really have lives of their own, and I think animals should have lives of their own. And just to give an additional example of how the halachah relates to the suffering of chickens, we may call attention to the discussion of R. Tzvi Pesach Frank in his response *Har Tzvi, Orah Hayyim*, vol. 1, Jerusalem, 1977, sect. 205, pp. 204–205. He was asked whether one could actively remove chickens from their pen on Shabbat, if one sees them biting one another and pecking at each other' innards, or whether, since they are *muktzeh*, one may not remove them. He argues that if it were only out of concern for their monetary loss of value, it would not be permissible (see *Magen Avraham, Orah* Hayyim 334, sect. 3). But if out of concern for the animal's suffering, it would be permitted. He bases his ruling, inter alia, on a statement of R. Yishaya di-Trani the Elder, in his *Shiltei Gibborim* to Shabbat chapter 18, who writes, concerning a certain issue, that:

> *Tza'ar ba'alei hayyim* is a biblical prohibition, and rabbinic prohibitions are waived in the face of a biblical one.

He brings a number of proof-texts to bolster this ruling, among them what we find in *Shulhan Aruch Orah Hayyim* 305:18, namely that one may not ride an animal on Shabbat; but if one does so willfully one must dismount because of *tza'ar ba'alei hayyim*. And for this reason one may remove a burden from upon it on Shabbat, even though it is *muktzeh*.[39]

People don't seem to realize that chicken are living, sentient creatures. People have pets; they have dogs that they look after, and they spend money to buy special food for them, and some even take them to expensive hairdressers to have fancy hairdos. Others have cats that live with them and they buy them Friskies food, which is costly, and they stroke them and talk to them. They never think that there will

---

39. Cf. *Mishnah Berurah* ibid., sect. 64, p. 192.

come a time when, because they are hungry, they will cut their throat, peel their fur off, and eat them. That, of course, is also a question of kashrut, but I'm not talking from a kashrut point of view. I'm talking from a humane, a human, point of view, an emotional point of view. It wouldn't occur to them to act toward them in such a fashion. But with a chicken, one doesn't think about that; similarly with a fish; one doesn't think about whether it feels. (My children did not even know that an "*of*" was the same as *tarnegolet*!). One doesn't think about them as being living creatures. Children that have a tiny goldfish in their little aquarium and put little bits of food in it, get a little sad when sometimes they fall out and die. But they don't think of what they're doing when they eat a fish.

"What then do you mean when you say that animals are sentient beings?" I was asked. "*Beresheit* talks about them having a *nefesh* [soul] (*Genesis* 1:20, 21, 24, 30).[40] What does that mean?"

My response is that every child has seen a cat crying when it's hungry or after a fight when it has an eye scratched out. They've seen dogs moping when their owners go away, or when they are waiting to be stroked and cuddled. They know that they have feelings! They're sentient! They know that they have degrees of intelligence. They know that blind men can move around due to their dogs' intelligence. Cats know how to find their food. So they may not be human but they do have feelings and a degree of understanding, and if you hurt them, they'll cry, they'll squeal, they'll fight back to protect themselves.

And here we should take cognizance of what R. Saadia Gaon said over eleven hundred years ago (882–942) in his *Book of Beliefs and Opinion* (*Emunot ve-Deot*), transl. Samuel Rosenblatt, New Haven and London, 1948, pp. 175–176:

> Fourthly, one might think frivolously of the Bible on account

---

40. Note that the term *nefesh hayyah* in *Genesis*, ibid., used to describe aspects of animals and fish, is also the term used with regard to humankind (ibid., 2:7).

Recently there has been much discussion on this subject. See most recently David Mevorach Seidenberg, *Kabbalah and Ecology: God's Image in the More-Than-Human World*, Cambridge, 2015, pp. 130–131, 139–142, section entitled "Animal Souls in Rabbinic Literature," pp. 354–356, Excursus I, entitled "*Nefesh* and related terms."

of the precepts pertaining to the sacrifices, either because they order the slaughtering of beasts or the shedding of blood and [the offering up] of fat. I might make this a little more comprehensible by saying that the Creator had decreed that every human being must die. Accordingly, he apportioned to every human being his allotted lifetime, whereas the period of life of the beasts was made by Him to extend until the time when they would be slaughtered, setting up slaughter in their case in place of death. *Should their slaughtering, however, entail pain over and above that which is experienced in natural death, God would be fully aware of it and He would, of course, in such an event compensate the beasts in accordance with the excess of the pain.*

But this, we say, applies only if it could be proved by means of reason, not by prophecy, that there exists such an excess of pain. As for the endurance of pain [resulting from slaughtering] and the shedding of the animal's blood and [the offering up] of its fat, the purpose of that, as is made clear in the Torah, was to make us pensive. For the blood is the dwelling-place of our souls, as Scripture says: *For the soul of the flesh is in the blood* (*Lev.* 17:11). Seeing that, then, we would repent, saying: "We shall not sin again lest our blood be shed and our fat be burned as, alas, we see it happen" [My emphasis – D. S.].

Though Saadia is, as is to be expected, fully committed to the biblical laws of sacrifice and the slaughter of animals, he is also fully aware of the attendant pain and suffering involved, raising the question of *the excess pain they may be forced to endure.* So animals, and fish too (see above), are both sensitive and sentient, and though this may seem to be obvious, it has to be both stated and stressed[41] [My emphasis – D. S.], and there is no doubt as to the existence of "excess pain" even in the preliminary stages before *shehita.*

---

41. See further Schochet, ibid., p. 262, who refers us to R. Hayyim Bachrach (1638–1702), in his responsa *Havat Yair* no. 191 ad fin, who "theorize[s] that animals are all the *more* sensitive to pain precisely because of their paucity of intellect!" He also refers us to R. David ben Zimra, Radbaz, 1479–1573, Responsa, part 1, no. 728, who, he suggests, holds the same view, but I'm dubious as to whether we should adduce this from that responsum.

And having said all that, I cannot restrain myself, dear reader, from indulging in an interjection, in the form of a sort of literary interlude relating to my memories of our cat. Her biography began in Manchester in about 1943, when my father was teaching in a Modern Orthodox type yeshivah called *Mercaz Limmud*. One day the institution's cat had a litter of kittens, and my father, thinking it would be good for the children to have a pet, brought one back home. When we moved to London, I remember her sleeping peacefully in my mother's shopping bag on the train seat next to me.

At home in London, during the summer she would sleep on the kitchen window overlooking the small courtyard, and in winter, she curled up under the fireplace, an iron contraption standing on small squat legs.

The kitchen had a pantry attached to it, a small room with shelves on all sides, in which we kept all our food products. We did not have a fridge during those days. Between the fireplace and the pantry was the "warming cupboard" in which towels, sheets, and other laundry was stored. And between the fireside and the warming-cupboard there was a small space in which was daily placed a saucer with milk and a plate with leftovers from our food, for the cat, which we called "Pussy."

Once, I remember, something went wrong when cooking a piece of chicken, and it was declared by my father to be *treif* – i.e., not kosher. So we put it into Pussy's plate for her to eat, but she refused to touch it. From that time onwards we knew that she would only eat kosher food.

One day we found some mouse droppings in the pantry and some half-nibbled food. So we knew that there was a mouse living in our pantry. We installed a mousetrap with a piece of cheese in it, hoping to catch the mouse, but much to our surprise, we regularly found the cheese eaten away but no mouse in the trap.

So we decided one evening to put a piece of cheese on a plate in the pantry and lock Pussy up in it, hoping she would catch the mouse. Next morning, to our total surprise, when we silently opened the pantry door, we saw an amazing sight: Pussy eating one edge of the cheese on one side of the plate, and the mouse eating likewise on the other side. Truly a Messianic event (see *Isaiah* 11:6)! So from then on, I was completely convinced that both Pussy and the mouse were sentient creatures, and we'd have to feed the mouse just as we did the cat.[42]

---

42. Pursuing my lack of restraint, I wish to cite a story related by J. E. Hanauer in his *Folk-Lore of the Holy Land: Moslem, Christian and Jewish*, London, 2nd ed., 1935, pp. 198–199:

> A town cat, having destroyed almost all the mice and rats in the place, found itself forced, for lack of prey, to go into the fields and hunt for birds, mice, rats and lizards. In this time of need it thought of the following ruse. It stayed away for some weeks from its usual haunts, and, returning, lay down in front of a mouse and rat warren, with a rosary round its neck; then, with its eyes closed, fell to purring loudly. Soon a mouse peeped out of a hole, but, seeing the cat, hastily returned. "Why do you flee?" said pussy gently. "Instead of showing pleasure at the return of an old neighbour from the pilgrimage you run away as soon as you see him. Come and visit me; fear nothing." Surprised at hearing itself thus addressed, the mouse again ventured to the door of its hole and said, "How can you expect me to visit you? Are you not the enemy of my race? Should I accept your invitation you would surely seize and devour me as you did my parents and so many others of my kindred?"
>
> "Alas!" sighed the cat, "your reproaches are just; I have been a great sinner, and have earned abuse and enmity. But I am truly penitent. As you see from this rosary round my neck, I now devote myself to prayer, meditation and the recital of holy books, the whole of which I have learnt by heart, and was just beginning to repeat when you happened to look out of your hole. Besides this, I have visited the Holy Places, so am a Hajji as a Hafiz [one who knows the whole Koran by heart]. Go, my injured but nevertheless generous and forgiving friend, make my change of life and sentiments known to the rest of your people and bid them no longer shun my society, seeing that I am become a recluse. Whilst you are absent I shall resume my recitations. Purr, purr, purr."
>
> Much surprised at the news he had just heard, the mouse made it known to the rest of the tribe. They were at first incredulous; but at last, after one and another had ventured to peep from the mouth of its hole and had beheld the whiskered ascetic with the rosary round his neck apparently oblivious of earthly things, and steadily repeating his purr, purr, purr, which they supposed to be the contents of holy books, they thought that there might be some truth in the matter and they convened a meeting of mice and rats to discuss it. After much debate it was judged right to test the reality of the cat's conversion, but to be prudent at the same time; and so a large and experienced rat was sent out to reconnoitre. Being a wary veteran, he kept well out of the cat's reach, though he saluted him respectfully from a distance. The cat allowed the rat to prowl about unmolested for a long time in the hope that other rats and mice would come out, when his prey would be easy to catch and plentiful. But no others came, and at last the pangs of hunger made him resolve to wait no longer. The rat, however, was on the

Returning to our main theme, the verse in *Proverbs* 12:10 says, "A righteous man is reactive to the life (*ha-nefesh*) of his beast." Indeed, I believe this is the true meaning of the blessing we make after eating vegetables, beverages, or certain fruit, that is the *Borei Nefashot* benediction, which runs as follows:

---

alert and darted off the instant he noticed, from a slight movement of the cat's muscles, that the pretended saint was about to kill him. "Why do you go away abruptly?" mewed the cat; "Are you tired of hearing me repeat scripture, or do you doubt the correctness of my recitation?" "Neither," answered the rat as he peeped from the hole in which he had taken refuge. "I am convinced that you have indeed committed the holy books perfectly to memory, but at the same time I am convinced that, however much you may have learnt by rote, you have neither unlearnt nor eschewed your habits of pouncing upon us."

Of course, our Pussy never really went hungry.

And again, as further evidence of my lack of self-restraint, I shall quote an amusing passage on mice from Sven Hedin's *Trans-Himalaya: Discoveries and Adventures in Tibet*, vol.1, London, 1910, pp. 435–435. He is describing his visit to a remote Tibetan monastery:

We now ascend, as if the mountain itself were not high enough, two steep pitch-dark flights of steps, where it is easy to break one's neck, into the entrance hall of the Pesu temple. In a smaller room the flame of a butter lamp struggled vainly with the darkness, casting its dull light on some idols. Pesu is the hall of the gods *par excellence*, with innumerable statuettes of metal, very old, artistically worked, and certainly very valuable. Some figures were of medium size. I stood in front of the altar rank and inspected the gods. *Tankas* and long narrow scarves in many colours hung from the ceiling. On the right was the small, dark room, and on the left was a shutter creaking as it banged to and open in the wind. Before the gods stood a row of bowls with barley, wheat, maize cobs, and water. I asked a monk who had come up with me how long it took the gods to eat it all. He smiled, and answered evasively that the bowls must always be full; but on entering I had caught sight of some mice which quickly scuttled away in the darkness. What cruel irony what a picture of self-satisfied vanity and religious humbug! The serving brother has been in the Pesu, has filled the bowls and said his daily prayers, has descended the steps and locked the door behind him. When all is quiet the mice come out of their holes. They climb upon the altar table, stand on their hind-legs, curl their tails round the votive bowls, and consume the nectar and ambrosia of the gods.

Perhaps the monks were also concerned with the welfare of the mice.

Blessed are You, Lord our God, King of the Universe, who created many kinds of souls [*nefashot rabot*] and their needs. For all You have created to sustain the souls [*nefesh*] of all living creatures. Blessed be He, life of the worlds.

Surely this is a clear indication that all forms of living creatures have a *nefesh*, a soul, or perhaps a spirit?

So the beast (mammal) surely has a *nefesh*, a soul (*nefesh hayyah* – *Genesis*, ibid.),[43] and chickens too can feel. Break the leg of a chicken

---

43. It is interesting to note that some Greek philosophers believed that animals had a rational soul (*nefesh*?). See Richard Sorabji, *The Philosophy of the Commentators 200–600 A.D.: A Sourcebook*, vol. 1, Psychology, sect. 11b, "Is there a rational soul in animals?" Ithaca, NY, 2005, pp. 249–250.

(i) **Yes**: Porphyry [3 cent. C.E.] argues at length for the rationality (*logos*) of animals in *Abstinence* Book 3, translated by Gillian Clark [CiC] in the series *Ancient Commentators on Aristotle* (cf. *Sentences* 10 and 11), distinguishing external reason, i.e. speech, from internal reason, i.e. thought (3.2; 3.3; 3.7) and arguing that animals have both. With regard to external reason, Porphyry argues that animals even understand Greek, that if we do not understand them, this is no more significant than our not understanding Indian and that when he brought up a tame partridge in Carthage, it responded with human sounds. Porphyry also reports Theophrastus [3–4 cent. B.C.E.], in disagreement with his mentor Aristotle [4 cent. B.C.E.], ascribing reasonings (*logismoi*) to animals.

Here are some relevant passages from CiC.

Porphyry *Abstinence* [*De Abstinentia*] 3.3.4
And if we do not understand them, so what? Greeks do not understand Indian, nor do those brought up on Attic understand Scythian or Thracian or Syrian: the sound that each makes strikes the others like the calling of cranes.
Ibid., 3.4.4
But when animals speak to each other clearly and meaningfully, even if not all of us can understand, and are even seen to imitate us and learn Greek and understand their owners, who would be so brazen as to deny that they have language *(logos)* just because he cannot himself understand what they say?
Ibid., 3.4.7
We ourselves reared, at Carthage, a tame partridge which had flown to us, and as time went on and habit made it very tame, we observed it not only making up to us and being attentive and playing, but even speaking in response to our speech

and, so far as was possible, replying, differently from the way that partridges call to each other. It did not speak when we were silent; it only responded when we spoke.

Theophrastus cited by Porphyry, ibid., 3.25.3

Thus also we posit that all human beings are kin (*sungeneis*) to one another, and moreover to all the animals, for the principles of their bodies are naturally the same. I say this not with reference to the primal elements (*stoikheia*), for plants too are composed of these: I mean, for instance, skin, flesh and the kind of fluids that are natural to animals. We posit this the more strongly because the souls of animals are naturally no different, I mean in appetite and anger, and also in reasoning (*logismoi*) and above all in perception.

And cf. ibid., p. 243 v 1; referring to Plotinus (3 cent. C.E.) 4:3 [27] 8 (1–5). See further pp. 369–370 (18a), that:

Porphyry tried to persuade his fellow Platonists that, if you understand animals, humans and the gods, you will not think it right for humans to sacrifice animals to them. He did not succeed; Iamblichus replied that sacrifice is appropriate, even though by some Neoplatonists, the meat-eating, which for pagans went hand in hand with sacrifice, is indulged only to the extent that piety is thought to require.

Porphyry cites Theophrastus' rejection of three possible reasons for animal sacrifice, and goes on to expand the third point that sacrifice will not secure us benefits. For the gods have no needs (*Abstinence* 2.33; 2.37; *Letter to Marcella* 18; *Philosophy from Oracles* in Augustine *City of God* 19.23), and will not change their character (*Abstinence* 2.39; 2.41,).... Moreover, the gods cannot be affected (*Letter to Anebo*, pp. 4–5 Sodano), and they are not angry with us (*Letter to Marcella* 18, despite *Abst* 2.61.8 below, "complaining" – *skhetliazein*). The right sacrifice is that of a pure mind, which meat-eating impedes. One should come either in silence to the immaterial gods, or with hymns to the divine heavens. Animal sacrifice merely attracts evil demons. Porphyry makes some of the same points about invocation of the gods.

Porphyry's views are put in several works, including the fascinating *On Abstinence from Animal Food*, and the now fragmentary *Letter to Anebo*, whose respectful questioning of Egyptian religion is described by Augustine, *City of God* 10.11 [cited ibid., pp. 406–407].

This position is somewhat similar to that found in the Indian *Mundaka Upanisad* 1:2–16, 2:7–13, according to which some earlier Upanisadic teachers substantiated a sort of "spiritual" or "inner sacrifice" for the "maternal" or "external" one.

This is the Upanisadic text as found in *Sources of Indian Tradition*, vol. 1, New York and London, 1958, pp. 26–27:

This is that truth. The sacrificial rites which the sages saw in the hymns are manifoldly spread forth in the three [Vedas]. Do you perform them constantly, O lovers of truth? This is your path to the world of good deeds.

When the flame flickers after the oblation fire has been kindled, then, between the offerings of the two portions of clarified butter one should proffer his principal oblations an offering made with faith....

Unsteady, indeed, are these boats in the form of sacrifices, eighteen in number, in which is prescribed only the inferior work. The fools who delight in this sacrificial ritual as the highest spiritual good go again and again through the cycle of old age and death. [That is, they are reborn again and again in the phenomenal world. The doctrine of transmigration or reincarnation was probably unknown to the Brahman ritualists, but in the Upanishads, man's salvation from this cycle of rebirths became a matter of great concern. It is suggested that the Vedic sacrifices could bring only a temporary respite in the abode of a god, not permanent release from the cycle.]

Abiding in the midst of ignorance, wise only according to their own estimate, thinking themselves to be learned, but really hard-struck, these fools go round in a circle like blind men led by one who is himself blind.

Abiding manifoldly in ignorance they, all the same, like immature children think to themselves: "We have accomplished our aim." Since the performers of sacrificial ritual do not realize the truth because of passion, therefore, they, the wretched ones, sink down from heaven when the merit which qualified them for the higher world becomes exhausted. Regarding sacrifice and merit as most important, the deluded ones do not know of any other higher spiritual good. Having enjoyed themselves only for a time on top of the heaven won by good deeds [sacrifice, etc.] they, re-enter this world or a still lower one.

Those who practice penance [tapas] and faith in the forest; the tranquil ones, the knowers of truth, living the life of wandering mendicancy – they depart, freed from passion, through the door of the sun, to where dwells, verily, that immortal Purusha, the imperishable Soul [atman].

Having scrutinized the worlds won by sacrificial rites, a Brahman should arrive at nothing but disgust. The world that was not made is not won by what is done [i.e., by sacrifice]. For the sake of that knowledge he should go with sacrificial fuel in hand as a student, in all humility to a preceptor [guru] who is well-versed in the [Vedic] scriptures and also firm in the realization of Brahman.

Unto him who has approached him in proper form, whose mind is tranquil, who has attained peace, does the knowing teacher teach, in its very truth, that knowledge about Brahman by means of which one knows the imperishable Purusha, the only Reality.

and see how it reacts. Fish flap about when they are taken out of water though they don't know how to talk. If you don't hear them, you think that they don't feel. But they do have nerves. (See above what I quoted in the name of Dr. Donald Broom.) They know how to swim in what for them is the right direction; birds fly across oceans, animals travel far to their breeding grounds. They know how to avoid being attacked; little fish try to avoid being eaten up by big fish like sharks. They do have intelligence of some sort.[44]

Furthermore, rabbinic literature attributes certain pragmatically positive characteristics to animals and insects, suggesting a degree of sentience. Louis Ginzburg in his *The Legends of the Jews*, vol. 1, Philadelphia, 1909, pp. 42–46, sums this up so elegantly:

All Things Praise the Lord

"Whatever God created has value." Even the animals and the insects that seem useless and noxious at first sight have a vocation to fulfil. The snail trailing a moist streak after it as it crawls, and so using up its vitality, serves as a remedy for boils. The sting of a hornet is healed by the house-fly crushed and applied to the wound. The gnat, feeble creature, taking in food but never secreting it, is a specific [cure] against the poison of a viper, and this venomous reptile itself cures eruptions, while the lizard is the antidote to the scorpion.

Not only do all creatures serve man, and contribute to his comfort,

---

Here we strayed somewhat far afield.

44. This is expressed in a somewhat lyrical style in an ancient mystical (?) Jewish text called *Pirkei* (or *Perek*) *Shira*, the date of which is unknown, but probably Byzantine, which in chapters 3, 4 and 5 describe what the insects, birds, and animals sing, in their praise of God. See, e.g., J. D. Eisenstein, *Otzar Midrashim*, New York, 1915, vol. 2, pp. 523–525. For further bibliographic information on this tantalizing source, see M. M. Kasher and Y. D. Mandelbaum, *Sarei ha-Elef*, Jerusalem, 1979, p. 61, no. 66. A critical edition was produced by Malachi Beit Aryeh, Jerusalem, 1967. See also Y. Tamar, *Alei Tamar* to Y. *Hagigah* 2:1, Jerusalem, 1991, p. 248, where he comments on the passage there that describes how "all the trees opened their mouths and declared in song (*ve-amru be-shirah*), that this suggests that *Perek Shira* was already in the time of R. Yohanan ben Zakai, first century C.E., see also below notes 45, 95, 171.

but also God "teacheth us through the beasts of the earth, and maketh us wise through the fowls of heaven." He endowed many animals with admirable moral qualities as a pattern for man. If the Torah had not been revealed to us, we might have learnt regard for the decencies of life from the cat, who covers her excrement with earth; regard for the property of others from the ants, who never encroached upon one another's stores; and regard for decorous conduct from the cock, who, when he desires to unite with the hen, promises to buy her a cloak long enough to reach to the ground, and when the hen reminds him of his promise, he shakes his comb and says, "May I be deprived of my comb, if I do not buy it when I have the means." The grasshopper also has a lesson to teach man. All the summer through it sings, until its belly bursts, and death claims it. Though it knows the fate that awaits it, yet it sings on. So man should do his duty toward God, no matter what the consequences. The stork should be taken as a model in two respects. He guards the purity of his family life zealously, and toward his fellows he is compassionate and merciful. Even the frog can be the teacher of man. By the side of the water there lives a species of animals which subsist off aquatic creatures alone. When the frog notices that one of them is hungry, he goes to it of his own accord, and offers himself as food, thus fulfilling the injunction, "If thine enemy be hungry, give him bread to eat; and if he be thirsty, give him water to drink."

The whole of creation was called into existence by God unto His glory, and each creature has its own hymn of praise wherewith to extol the Creator, Heaven and earth, Paradise and hell, desert and field, rivers and seas – all have their own way of paying homage to God. The hymn of the earth is, "From the uttermost part of the earth have we heard songs, glory to the Righteous." The sea exclaims, "Above the voices of many waters, the mighty breakers of the sea, the Lord on high is mighty." ....

Every plant, furthermore, has a song of praise. The fruitful tree sings, "Then shall all the trees of the wood sing for joy, before the Lord, for He cometh; for He cometh to judge the earth"; and the ears of grain on the field sing, "The pastures are covered with flocks; the valleys also are covered over with corn; they shout for joy, they also sing."

Great among singers of praise are the birds, and greatest among them is the cock. When God at midnight goes to the pious in Paradise, all the trees therein break out into adoration, and their songs awaken the cock, who begins in turn to praise God. Seven times he crows, each time reciting a verse. The first verse is: "Lift up your heads, O ye gates; and be ye lift up, ye everlasting doors, and the King of glory shall come in. Who is the King of glory? The Lord strong and mighty, the Lord mighty in battle." The second verse: "Lift up your heads, O ye gates; yea, lift them up, ye everlasting doors, and the King of glory shall come in. Who is this King of glory? The Lord of hosts, He is the King of glory." The third: "Arise, ye righteous, and occupy yourselves with the Torah, that your reward may be abundant in the world hereafter." The fourth: "I have waited for Thy salvation, O Lord!" The fifth: "How long wilt thou sleep?" The sixth: "Love not sleep, lest thou come to poverty; open thine eyes, and thou shalt be satisfied with bread." And the seventh verse sung by the cocks runs: "It is time to work for the Lord, for they have made void Thy Law."

The song of the vulture is: "I will hiss for them, and gather them; for I have redeemed them, and they shall increase as they have increased" – the same verse with which the bird will in time to come announce the advent of the Messiah, the only difference being, that when he heralds the Messiah he will sit upon the ground and sing his verse, while at all other times he is seated elsewhere when he sings it.

Nor do the other animals praise God less than the birds. Even the beasts of prey give forth adoration. The lion says: "The Lord shall go forth as a mighty man; He shall stir up jealousy like a man of war; He shall cry, yea, He shall shout aloud; He shall do mightily against his enemies." And the fox exhorts unto justice with the words, "Woe unto him that buildeth his house by unrighteousness, and his chambers by injustice; that useth his neighbor's service without wages, and giveth him not his hire."

Yea, the dumb fishes know how to proclaim the praise of their Lord. "The voice of the Lord is upon the waters," they say, "the God of glory thundereth, even the Lord upon many waters"; while the frog exclaims, "Blessed be the name of the glory of

His kingdom forever and ever!"

Contemptible though they are, even the reptiles give praise unto their Creator. The mouse extols God with the words: "Howbeit Thou art just in all that is come upon me; for Thou hast dealt truly, but I have done wickedly." And the cat sings: "Let everything that hath breath praise the Lord. Praise ye the Lord."

This poetic panegyric of all creations' praise of the Creator, encapsulates Jewish religious thinking not only on the function of all elements of nature, but also, of the as it were, active role in this functionality.[45]

---

45. The sources for this passage have been masterfully marshaled in Ginzberg's vol. 5, Philadelphia 1925, notes 191–194, pp. 60–62, which need not be repeated here.

And an incidental comment on the stork mentioned above, see Ginzberg, *Legends*, vol. 2, p. 287, on how the storks were used by Moses to devour the serpents (cf. ibid., vol. 5, pp. 407–408 note 80), and compare Josephus, *Antiquities* 2:10.2, line 246, Loeb ed., Vol. 1, p. 271, where they are ibes, not storks. But see Rudolf Wittkower, *Allegory and the Migration of Symbols*, New York,1977, chapter 1, pp. 16–44, 188–196, on the widespread motif on the eagle and the serpent, where the eagle overcomes the serpent. In the Jewish sources (not cited by Wittkower) the stork or the ibis apparently has replaced the eagle, just as in some sources the dragon has replaced the serpent. And see ibid., pp. 38–39, where other birds take the place of the eagle, such as the ichneumon, a swan-like creature, etc. (His article is a veritable treasury of information.)

See "*Divrei ha-Yamim shel Mosheh Rabbanu alav ha-Shalom*," apud A. Jellineck, *Beit ha-Midrash*, vol. 2, 2nd ed., Jerusalem, 1938, pp. 6–7; *Sefer ha-Yashar*, ed. Venice 1624, *Exodus* 133b–136b; *Yalkut Shimoni* 1, *Exod.* 168; etc.

The theme of birds – primarily eagles – killing snakes has been exhaustively treated by Rudolf Wittkower in his article "Eagle and Serpent," in his *Allegory and Migration of Symbols*, New York, 1987, pp. 15–44, showing the global range of this motif. But for our purposes we shall call attention to the Hindu myth concerning the mighty sun-god eagle, Garuda. And so it is related in Vettam Mani's *Puranic Encyclopaedia*, Delhi, 1975, p. 282 (s.v. Garuda 7):

Garuda approached the pot of nectar, and Visvakarma who attacked him first was felled to the ground. The dust storm raised by the waving of Garuda's wings blinded everybody. The Devas and Indra, nay, even the sun and the Moon lined up against Garuda, but he defeated them all, and entered the particular place where the pot of nectar was kept. Two terrific wheels were rotating round the pot and they would cut into mince-meat anybody who tried to lay hands on the pot and a machine circled the wheels. Below the wheels were two monstrous

Actually, I found a somewhat surprising plea for consideration of animals in a passage in Rabbi Hayyim Falagi's *Refuah ve-Hayyim* (Healing and Life), Izmir 1875, chapter 5 where he discusses the various means (amuletic and otherwise) of protection against plague. There (pp. 42–43) he writes as follows:

> Even though it is the practice to have recourse to *contamast* [protection against disease], and excellent [means of] protection, nonetheless it would appear that one is not permitted to kill cats and dogs and such like, as is the practice on the part of non-Jews (*ha-loazim*) in a time of plague – there should not be a twofold distress – slaughtering and killing cats and dogs etc., so that they will not come in contact with the clothes and their property. And I say that that it is not right to do so, because the verse says "and his mercies are on all his creatures" (*Psalms* 145:9), and just as the case of Rabbi Yehudah ha-Nasi who was saved from several years of suffering because he had

---

serpents with glowing eyes and protruding tongues like flashes of fire, and the serpents never closed their eyes. The very look with those eyes was enough to poison anyone to death. Garuda blinded those eyes by raising of dust, pierced them in the middle with his beak and through the hole, his body reduced to such a tiny shape, went nearer to the pot. … carrying the pot of nectar in his beaks rose to the sky shielding the light of the sun by his outspread wings. Mahavisnu, who became so much pleased with the tremendous achievements of Garuda, asked him to choose any boon. Garuda requested Visnu that he should be made his (Visnu's) amrta. Both the boons were granted.

Wittkower further relates this motif in the "Roc" theme, ibid., pp. 94–95, relating it to "the flight between the Indian solar bird Garuda and the Chthonic snake Nagu," mentioned in the two great Sanskrit epics *Mahabharata* 1:1353 and the *Ramayaha* 3:39, referring us also to A. de Gubernatis, *Zoological Mythology*, vol. 2, London 1872, p. 94. In the Jewish version of this popular myth it is the stork, *hassidah* (feminine), from *hasid*, a righteous one who has supplanted the eagle in her virtuous act.

And in Wittkower, ibid., pp. 38–39, yet other species of birds appear in place of the classic eagle, e.g., the ichneumon, and a swan-like avian creature, etc.

It may well be that the stork came to replace the eagle in this legend because of the storks' love of water (see de Gubernatis, ibid., p. 261), while the serpent is frequently an aquatic creature in world mythology (ibid. pp. 388–420). And see further ibid., pp. 180–206.

mercy for the offspring of a rat, as is related in *B. Baba Metzia* (85a). And our Sages already said (*B. Shabbat* 151b), "He who takes pity over *creatures*, the Heavens take pity over him." And if he behaved in this fashion even towards unclean animals, so every person should draw a conclusion – much more so – must one have pity over a fellow Jew, and it will be this *mitzvah* of mercifulness which will protect one not to be harmed by them (i.e. these animals). Nevertheless, we should take every precaution to keep one's distance from them … and the Lord will not prevent goodness [from reaching] those who walk [the path] of righteousness.

So even in a period of plague and pestilence, when people suspect that such pestilence is purveyed by animals, one must not persecute them, remembering always that they too are God's creatures.[46]

Furthermore, Jewish sources present an idea of animals and humans as being part of the same moral community,[47] a notion that perhaps for us is difficult to conceive. Thus, animals and birds are rewarded for their good deeds. So writes Seidenberg, ibid., p. 154:

The Rabbis also extend moral agency to animals by depicting them receiving reward for their good deeds. This is how *Tanchuma* [*Noah* 11] explains why the animals in the ark merit being saved:

---

46. See also R. Hayyim Palache in his *Ruah Hayyim, Orah Hayyim*, vol. 1, Izmir, 1877, 605:2, wrote that:

It would seem that if one throws food out onto one's roof in order to feed the birds, then for that reason "All who have pity over creatures, heaven has pity over him," (*B. Shabbat* 151b). Consequently, it is the practice of he who is sick and requests mercy [from heaven], one throws food for the birds onto the roof in order to be merciful to creatures, and as a result heaven will treat him with mercy.

And so too in his *Refuah Ve-Hayyim*, Izmir, 1875, chapter 12, sect. 74, that when there is a sick person in one's house… one shall feed… the birds of heaven.

See *Otzar Plaot ha-Torah*, by R. Zeev Wolf Zichermann, *Exodus*, Brooklyn, 2014, pp. 431–432.

47. For an interesting comparison, see Richard Sorabji *Animal Minds and Human Morals*, London and Ithaca, New York, 1993.

"'And Elohim remembered Noach and every animal' [*Genesis* 8:1] – If [God] remembered Noach, why also animal and beast? May the name of the Holy One be blessed, who never deprives any creature / *b'riyah* of its reward. [If] even a mouse has preserved its family (i.e. species), and did not mix with another species, it is worthy to get reward." According to *Tanchuma*, the animals on the ark merited to be saved because they had properly performed the mitzvah of procreation [See also *Tanhuma* Buber *Noah* 11; cf. *Tanchuma Noah* 17, 18]. They were not simply saved for Noach's sake, as one might conclude based on a superficial reading of *Genesis*.

Similarly, according to *B'rei'shit Rabbah* 22:8, because the birds and wild animals buried Hevel after Qayin killed him, they received the reward of having their blood buried when they are slaughtered.[48] Other *midrashim* focus on the righteous behavior of the dogs of Egypt, who were silent when the children of Israel left. Because of this, their descendants (i.e., all dogs) have the right to eat any meat that is not kosher, as it says, "to the dog you will cast it" [*Exodus* 22:30].[49]

---

48. See *Bereishit Rabba*, ed. Theodor Albeck, vol. 1, p. 215, note 1; parallel in *Tanhuma Bereishit*, sect. 10; *Pirkei de-R. Eliezer*, chapter 21, ed. R. David Luria, Warsaw, 1852, 49b, and editor's note 46.

49. Seidenberg expands this in his note 503 on pp. 154–155 as follows:

M'khilta reads:

"To the dog you will throw it / *lakelev tishl'khun oto*" [*Exodus* 22:30] – to teach you that the dog is more honored than the servant … to teach you that the Holy One does not cancel / wrest / *m'qapei'ach* the reward of any creature, as it is said: "and against all the children of Israel a dog will not sharpen / *yecherats* its tongue" [*Exodus* 11:7]. Said the Holy One: Give him his reward. (*Kaspa* 20, 321)

Similarly, *ShmR* [= *Shmot Rabbah*] 31:9:

Said the Holy One: You are indebted/obligated/*chayavim* to the dogs, for in the hour that I killed the firstborn of Egypt … the Egyptians were sitting all night and burying their dead, and the dogs barked at them, and at Israel they didn't bark … therefore … "to the dog you will throw it."

Ysh [= *Yalkut Shimoni*] 1:187 incorporates both passages, adding to them a vignette often appended to the last section of *Pereq Shirah* (see notes 41, 95, 121). According to this story, R' Yisha'yah (or Osha'yah) fasted eighty-five fasts

Likewise they are punished for their iniquities (whatever they may be). Thus *Jonah* 3:5–8 describes the atonement of the people of Ninveh as including their cattle having to fast and wear sackcloths and *M. Sanhedrin* 1:4 speaks of animals being tried in capital cases like humans, basing itself on *Exodus* 21:28–29, which deals with oxen held responsible for their goring. So according to this notion, just as animals have a responsibility towards humans, so, conversely, humans have a responsibility towards animals, and Bilaam was reprimanded for violently beating his donkey (*Numbers* 22:32). Hence, the righteous should be cognizant of the soul (*nefesh*) of his animal[50] (*Proverbs* 12:10).[51]

I was then asked whether in my opinion there is a spirit of halachah, an integrity or morality or a soul of halachah? Or is halachah simply the engagement with rules and the fulfilment of those rules without regard to the spirit? For it would seem that there are many in the observant world who check off their list and don't think about the consequences of their actions. With regards to *tza'ar ba'alei hayyim*, in the Yeshiva

---

to receive an answer to the question, "Why do dogs merit to sing a song of praise to God?" The angel who answers him cites *Exodus* 11:17, saying that dogs even merited that their excrement be used to tan parchment for *t'filin, mezuzot* and Torah scrolls. And then the angel admonishes the rabbi: "Turn yourself back (away from) what you asked and don't continue in this matter, as it's written: 'Who watches/*shomer* his mouth and his tongue, keeps / *shomer* his soul from trouble' [*Proverbs* 21:23]." Essentially, the angel tells Yisha'yah to behave at least as well as the dogs in Egypt. See also *TB Shabbat* 155b, which derives dogs' rights from *Proverbs* 29:7.

50. See Seidenberg, ibid., pp. 139–142, section entitled "Animal Souls in the Rabbinic Tradition," and index, p. 372. s.v. animals-souls cf.

51. See Bernstein, ibid., p. 104. And see also p. 105, ibid., where he refers to *Tanhuma Noah* 5, that Noah and Yosef both acquired their reputation as *tzaddikim* – righteous ones – for having saved animals in their efforts to preserve the world from natural cal amities. Thus Noah is called a *tzaddik* in *Genesis* 6:9, "because he provided sustenance to God's creatures," and so too Josef for having saved Egypt's livestock by storing grain in anticipation of the famine (Bernstein, ibid., p. 241, note 35). And Rebecca was deemed a worthy wife for Isaac because of her character as revealed in her treatment of Eliezer's camels (*Genesis* 24:14–20).

See also Seidenberg, ibid., pp. 17–21, on the concept of "Biodiversity," and ibid., pp. 54–59, on "The Chain of Being."

world there is this bravado about eating a lot of meat.[52] For those who are eating meat, which obviously is thought to be kosher, is there a legitimate argument that there is a spirit of halachah that gets trampled when we're just worried about the technicalities of kashrut?

Indeed, this is a very important issue, because it raises the question of the relationship between formal halachah and what we call meta-halachah. Meta-halachah is something that is a kind of overarching, all-embracing principle of morality and ethics into which the pattern halachah has to fall. There are biblical statements which are fairly clear on this issue. *Ve-asita ha-yashar ve-ha-tov*, "You should do what is right and good," (*Deuteronomy* 6:18) which is not clearly defined in any way. It means that all our actions, whatever they may be, have to be "right and good." So that if we were to do something that strictly speaking is permitted, or at any rate not explicitly forbidden, but not good, it would go against *ve-asita ha-yashar ve-ha-tov*. The halachic formulation of this

---

52. See, for example, *Shulḥan Aruch Yoreh Deah* 303:6:

He who takes an oath in order to ... rectify his behavior is ... praiseworthy. For example, one who is gluttonous and forbids himself to eat meat for a year or two, ... this is to be considered an act of worship before God...

See also Rambam, *Hilchot Deah* 3:2 (transl. Moses Hyamson, Jerusalem, 1965, vol. 1, 49b–50a):

A man should direct all his thoughts and activities to the knowledge of God alone. This should be his aim in sitting, rising and conversation...

So too, when he eats, drinks, or cohabits, his purpose should not be secure physical gratification, in which he would only eat and drink that which was pleasing to the palate, and cohabit for the sake of sensual pleasure, but he should have it in mind that he eats and drinks solely to maintain his body and its organs in health and vigour. He will then not partake of everything which the palate craves, like a dog or an ass, but will choose foods that are wholesome to the body, whether these be sweet or bitter; and will avoid eating things that are injurious to the body, even though they taste sweet. One, for instance, who is of a hot humour, will not eat flesh-meat or honey, nor drink wine, as Solomon said in a metaphorical sense, "It is not good to eat much honey." (*Prov.* 25:27). Such a person should rather drink an infusion of chicory, even though it is bitter. And so, since life is impossible without eating and drinking, he will be guided in his choice of food and drink by hygienic considerations, to recover and maintain sound health.

is called *Naval bi-Reshut ha-Torah*: a person who acts in an absolutely reprehensible fashion without actually going against any specific halachic instruction. (See below note 44, Ramban to *Leviticus* 19:1.)[53] I think this is something very important, very basic to a real understanding of halachah. And when we talk about *tza'ar ba'alei hayyim*, we should

---

53. A classic example of such behavior is to be found in the description of the activities of the antediluvians (i.e., those before the deluge), as described in *Genesis Rabba* 31:5, eds. J. Theodor and C. Albeck, Jerusalem, 1965, vol. 1, p. 279; *Y. Baba Metzia* 4:2, 9c:

> This is what the antediluvians used to do. When one of them would take out a basket full of vegetables, then one of them would come and take from it something worth less than a *peruta* (the minimum value coin). And yet another would take less than the value of a *peruta*, an amount [so small] for which one could not summon them to court [i.e. and this until he was left with nothing].

For the law is that theft of less than the value of a *peruta* cannot be brought before the judge. So in this way they cunningly impoverished him in a manner that the law could not touch them.

For yet another example of such reprehensible activity, see the story in *Y. Pe'ah* 8:8. The background to this tale is in *M. Pe'ah*, ibid., which rules that one who has (assets worth) two-hundred denarii is not liable to receive Gleanings, the Forgotten Sheath, *Pe'ah* or the Poorman's Tithe, i.e., the various kinds of communal (agricultural) charities:

> A disciple of Rabbi [Yehudah ha-Nasi] possessed two-hundred denarii less one, and Rabbi was wont to give him once every three years the Poorman's Tithe (Maaser Ani – given every third year). [And since Rabbi Yehudah ha-Nasi was wealthy, this tithe was worth a great deal.] Other disciples were jealous of him, and gave him another denarius [so that he now had two-hundred, and was no longer liable to their tithe]. When Rabbi came to him to give him charity, he said to him: "Rabbi, I now have the requisite amount" [i.e. two-hundred denarii, and can no longer accept this charity]. Rabbi explained, "This is a wound afflicted by the Pharisees (*makat Perushim*)," [i.e. injurious injustice done under the pretext of the letter of the law, in other words an act of hypocrisy]. He indicated to (other) disciples that they should enter his shop and eat at his expense to the value of a *karat* (a quarter of a *dinar*), and then he gave him what he was wont to give him.

On *makat Perushim*, see M. Jastrow, *A Dictionary of the Targumim, The Talmud Babli and Yerushalmi, and the Midrashic Literature*, New York, 1903, vol. 2, p. 781a, s.v. מכה, for reference to other such examples.

recall the story of Rabbi Yehudah ha-Nasi (*Genesis Rabba* 33:3),[54] who, according to the sources, suffered very greatly in the latter years of his life. And that was because he acted in an unacceptable fashion to an animal. An animal was bleating as it was being taken to slaughter, and all he said was "*le-chach notzarta*" [For this were you created]. He didn't express any sympathy towards the animal. Halachically he did nothing wrong. The animal was being taken to slaughter, and presumably it would be slaughtered in an admirably kosher fashion. But his lack of sympathy for the creature is the reason why he was severely punished.[55] And in

---

54. Parallels in *B. Baba Metzia* 85a; *Y. Kilaim* 9, 32a; *Y. Ketubot* 12, 34d. See *Genesis Rabba*, ibid., eds. J. Theodore and C. Albeck, vol. 1, p. 305, and notes ad loc. to line 5, where the different variants are noted. The tale relates he suffered for thirteen years from toothaches. One day an insect (variant version: a rat) came close to him and his daughter wished to kill it. He said to her, "Leave it alone." [The Lord is good to all] and His tender mercies are over all his works" (*Psalms* 145:9). And then he was cured of his pains.

The notion that God is merciful to all His creations is also expressed in *B. Baba Batra* 16b, in God's reply to Job:

> The wild goat is cruel towards her babies. Just before she gives birth she climbs to the top of a mountain in order that her babies will fall down and die. I prepare an eagle to catch the falling baby goat on its wings and set it down in front of the mother. If the eagle were to come a second too soon or too late the baby would die. … the deer has a narrow womb which makes birth difficult. When she is ready to give birth I prepare a snake which bites her and facilitates birth. If the snake were to bite a second too soon or a second too late the deer would die.

I shall not further elaborate on this fascinating subject, but merely refer the reader to Avigdor Aptowitzer's classic study on "The Rewarding and Punishing of Animals and Inanimate Objects: On the Aggadic View of the World," *HUCA* 3, 1926, pp. 117–156; Ephraim E. Urbach, *The Sages: Their Concepts and Beliefs* [Hebrew], Jerusalem, 1969, p. 247, etc.

55. In *B. Baba Kama* 71b we read how Rava asked a question of Rav Nahman, and received an answer. On the following day, he asked of him the same question and received an opposite answer. Rav Nahman then explained that the preceding day he had not eaten *bisra de-tora* – meat of a bull – which, according to the commentators, broadens one's heart and understanding, and therefore makes more likely a correct explanation.

Most commentators take the term *bisra de-tora* literally; however, Rashi ad loc. interpreted Rav Nachman's statement as meaning that on the previous day he had not

the late twentieth century, the Animal Rights Movement[56] sought to spread the message that one has to develop this sensitivity to the plight of animals. And at least one major rabbinic authority seems to have been influenced by this movement and its critique of cruelty in obtaining seal furs for women's coats by beating animals to death with clubs, or the inhuman procedures to be found in fur farms. Thus, the late Rav Chaim David HaLevy, Sefardic Chief Rabbi of Tel-Aviv, ruled that furs obtained by such means should be boycotted. In a 1992 responsum, Rav Halevy states: "If the killing of animals for the obtainment of their furs were accomplished by a quick, easy death, that would be one thing; but in actuality, this is not the case... The animals are caught in a kind of ring trap that causes them great anguish until they are released and killed and stripped of their furs. This constitutes actual *tza'ar ba'alei*

---

analyzed accurately the nature of the question. Yaavetz, that is R. Yaakov Emdin, in his notes ad loc., explains that *bisra de-tora* is understood by Rashi to mean "in depth learning." And *Tosafot* ad loc. suggest that Rav Nahman had been fasting and as a result he was not thinking clearly.

For us what is of interest is Rashi's non-literal interpretation suggesting that he did not see meat eating as something that encourages enlightenment and a depth of understanding. See further *Otzar Plaot ha-Torah*, by R. Zeev Wolf Zichermann, *Exodus*, Brooklyn, 2014, pp. 432–434. And in *Derashot ibn Shuaib*, by R. Yehoshua ibn Shuaib, the disciple of the Rashba (c. 1280–1340), Constantinople 1523, to *Parshat Shemot, w*e read that the forefathers were shepherds, and they would seek to be alone to contemplate on heavenly issues, for the air in the desert is pure and clean, and they would keep themselves apart from other people, and in order to train themselves to be merciful to creatures, as we learned from Jacob.

This is further amplified by the *Or Hahayyim*, R. Hayyim ibn Atar, on the verse in *Genesis* 33:17, "And Jacob journeyed to Sukkot, and built him a house and made booths for his cattle." The *Or Hahayyim* wrote:

> And should you ask, just because Jacob built booths [*sukkot*], should the place be called *Sukkot*? But perhaps this was because he did something new and novel, due to his feeling compassion for his cattle, something that no one before him had done to build booths specially for them.

56. The concept of cruelty to animals laws in the secular world dates to the 1800s, while animal rights laws began seriously to be discovered in the mid-twentieth century. See Bernard E. Rollin, "Animal Rights as a Mainstream Phenomenon," *MDPI* 1/1, January 2011, pp. 102–115.

hayyim; there can be no disagreement about it."

The same authority adds: "I have been informed that nowadays there are farms where animals are raised for the purpose of killing them and using their furs... However, as explained above, according to many authorities, even killing without *tza'ar ba'alei hayyim* is forbidden if there is no compelling human need *(tzorech hiyuni).* According to all views, it is clear that such acts are tainted by cruelty, which is foreign to the character traits of the children of Abraham, Isaac, and Jacob... Therefore, one should refrain from wearing furs." And this despite the well-known fact that the wearing of mink and other furs long ago had been an esthetic preference and a status symbol. Just as medieval Polish nobility wore fur-trimmed hats (possibly due to the influence of the Mongol hordes that invaded Eastern Europe during the 13th century), so did prominent rabbis and Jewish communal leaders. Most Chassidim still wear the traditional *shtreimel* made from tails of the sable or marten, an object widely perceived as the movement's cultural logo.[57]

---

57. See Sears, ibid., p. 88, who adds in note 79 that:

> R. Chaim ibn Attar, *Ohr HaChaim* on *Leviticus* 17:13, citing *Mishneh Torah, Ma'achalos Asuros* 8:17, as well as his *Sefer Pri To'ar,* sec. 117, which prohibit the trapping of non-kosher animals by Jews on the grounds of *tza'ar ba'alei chaim.* However, R. Halevy apparently objects to complicity in such acts even when performed by others.

See also R. Hayyim David Halevy, *Aseh lecha Rav,* vol. 1, Tel Aviv, 1976, no. 69, pp. 211–214. And in a lengthy note (80) on p. 89 Sears writes as follows:

> It is difficult to ascertain how many animals are killed for furs annually in the U.S. The Humane Society places the total number at approximately 30 million animals (www.hsus.org). However, if this figure once was accurate, it is probably considerably lower today. Based on information from the National Agricultural Statistics Service and the U.S. Dept. of Agriculture, the Humane Society states that the number of cage-raised minks killed for fur in the U.S. declined from 4.12 million in 1987 to 2.84 million in 1997. The number of cage-raised foxes killed in the U.S. fell from 100,000 to 20,000 over the same ten years. According to the International Association of Fish and Wildlife Agencies, an estimated 4 million fur-bearing animals are trapped annually, as compared to more than 17 million in the mid-1980s. This dramatic change is the combined result of public objection to animal abuse and the availability of less expensive alternative products.

According to the Fur Commission of the USA, approximately half the animals killed for their pelts are raised in confinement on "fur farms," where eventually they are euthanised by carbon dioxide, pure carbon monoxide gas, or lethal injection. The American Veterinary Medical Association and the Geulph University Research Facility in Canada deem these methods to be humane (www.furco mmission.co m). However, because the Industry ls for the most part self-regulated, a sizeable percentage of cage-raised animals are not killed by these methods, but by carbon monoxide generated by engine exhaust, anal electrocution, genital or ear-to-foot electrocution, or by having their necks broken.

Pressure from animal activists has led to the banning of the steel-jawed leghold trap in 89 European countries. In 1999, the U.S. House of Representatives banned the use of leghold traps and strangling snares on all National Wildlife Refuges. In 2001 H.R.1187 was introduced In the House of Representatives, which proposes to ban all uses of such traps in the U.S., as well as importing or exporting any article of fur obtained by such means. An alternative to these devices, the body grip or "Conibear" trap, was developed decades ago as an instant-kill trap; however, some studies indicate that as many as 85% of its victims may languish in agony for substantial periods of time with broken backs and other mortal injuries; see H.C. Lunn, "The Conibear Trap: Recommendations for its Improvement," Canadian Federation of Humane Societies, 1973.

The Humane Society states that for each trapped animal used in a fur coat, at least twice as many animals, including dogs, cats, and birds, are mistakenly caught and subsequently "trashed." Thus, to produce one 40" long mink coat, more than 150 animals of various species will spend a combined total of approximately 3000 hours in traps. One out of four trapped animals succeeds in chewing off its own leg to escape, and soon dies of sickness, exposure, or the inability to defend itself from predators (www3.sympatico.ca/taniah/animal/fur.tml). An average fur coat, depending on its type, variously requires 125 ermines, 100 chinchillas, 55 wild minks, 40 sables, 35 ranch minks, 30 muskrats, 30 rex rabbits, 27 raccoons, 25 skunks, 18 red foxes, 15 bobcats, 14 otters, 11 silver foxes, 9 beavers, or 8 seals (www.idausa.org).

We may also note that the Noda Bi-Yehudah (*Tinyana, Yoreh Deah* 10) cites the Mahari Weil as ruling that though generally a person who wears a new garment for the first time is customarily blessed with "May you wear it and acquire a new one," and may even himself make the blessing of "*she-heheyanu*," this is not done in the case of a fur coat, as it would appear that the killing of animals is not merely being condoned, but even encouraged as something desirable, as this would contradict the verse, "And His tender mercies are over *all* His works" (*Psalms* 145:9).

The continuation of his discussion is very relevant to the whole issue of *tza'ar ba'alei hayyim*, and I will therefore quote it albeit somewhat abridged (see Sears, ibid., p. 98):

It is true that the Rama (Rabbi Moshe Isserles) in his glosses on the *Shulchan Aruch* remarks that this reason is weak. However, the weakness lies only in the fact that putting on a fur coat does not necessarily imply that the animal was killed specifically for this purpose. The fur may have been taken from an animal that died a natural death, in which case [although the meat would not be deemed kosher] it is permissible to use the hide. Nevertheless, the Rama concludes that many people are particular [to refrain from offering the customary blessing to one who wears a new fur coat, in agreement with Mahari Weill]. Therefore: how could a Jew waste his precious time in the wanton pursuit of hunting and killing animals, without any legitimate need to do so?

Some have tried to justify the hunting of bears, wolves, and other wild animals because they are liable to injure human beings. These individuals base their view on the Talmudic statement [of Rabbi Eliezer]: "Whoever is first to destroy them is meritorious" *(Sanhedrin* 2a). This assumption, however, is mistaken for two reasons. First, the *halacha* does not follow Rabbi Eliezer's opinion. Even regarding a snake, Maimonides and the Ravad differ in their views *(Mishneh Torah, Hilchos Sanhedrin* 5:2). Second, even according to Rabbi Eliezer, we follow the view of Resh Lakish that this [mandate to kill a predatory animal] only applies to one that already has proven itself to be of murderous disposition (op cit.).

Another view has been advanced that [the prohibition of *tza'ar ba'alei chaim*] only pertains to animals that have been raised among people and therefore have become somewhat tamed, not to wild beasts. The latter are presumed to be dangerous at all times; therefore, it is permitted to kill them even on the Sabbath, at least in an indirect manner *(Shulchan Aruch, Orach Chaim* 316:14). This reasoning, too, is mistaken, and has nothing to do with our case. The above [mandate to kill wild animals] only applies when such animals are found in inhabited places, so that they constitute a menace to society, whereas we are discussing animals in the forests, etc. It is certainly no meritorious act to pursue them in their own habitat. Rather, it is an act of blood-lust.

As something of a curiosity I'd like to cite what I came across by chance in a local newspaper when I was recently in London:

> The Queen will no longer wear real fur, according to her senior dresser Angela Kelly.
>
> Her decision to "go faux" was revealed in MS Kelly's book about her close relationship with the monarch called *The Other Side Of The Coin.*
>
> She wrote: "If Her Majesty is due to attend an engagement in particularly cold weather, from 2019 onwards fake fur will be used to make sure she stays warm."
>
> Last night, the Queen was praised by animal rights campaigners. Humane Society International director Claire Bass said: "We are thrilled that Her Majesty has officially gone fur-free."

So obviously there exists a whole stratum of additional requirements which must not be trampled, in what we might call "the tunnel vision" of the technicalities of halachah.

Rabbi Neril then said: "As you're aware, in *Bereshit* 1:29, God tells people to eat plants, and in the following verse God tells animals to eat plants. Rav Kook talks about how *le'atid lavo* [in the future], that vision will return. How do you relate to that teaching of Rav Kook?"

My reply was: We know that the Nazir (R. David Cohen), who was the *Talmid Muvhak* of Rav Kook, wrote *Hazon ha-Tzimchonut ve-ha-Shalom*[58] [The Vision of Vegetarianism and Peace] in which he tried to develop the ultimate vision of vegetarianism. Rav Kook in *Olat Re'iyah*, his commentary on the Siddur, twice indicates that he, though not a vegetarian himself, saw that the ideal state would be one of vegetarianism, and that the sacrifices in the future would just be *menahot* and the *nesachim*, meal offerings and wine libations.

Furthermore, Rav Kook, in his own essay on vegetarianism and man's duty to the animals (*"Afikim ba-Negev,"* in *Ha-Peles*, Berlin, 1903–1904, *Talelei Orot* in *Tachkemoni,* Bern, 1910), wrote:

> The free movement of the moral impulse to establish justice for animals generally and the claim of their rights from mankind are hidden in a natural psychic sensibility in the deeper layers of the Torah. In the ancient value system of humanity, while the spiritual illumination (which later found its bastion in Israel) was diffused among individuals without involvement in a national

---

"Her decision is a perfect reflection of the mood of the British public, the vast majority of whom detest cruel fur and want nothing to do with it."

She added: "It sends a powerful message that fur is firmly out of fashion and does not belong with Brand Britain. We are now calling on the government to follow Her Majesty's example and make the UK the first country in the world to ban the sale of animal fur."

It is not known whether the Queen will still wear her ermine and velvet cape for future state openings of parliament.

(*Metro*, Wednesday, November 6, 2019, p. 7.)

58. Apud *La-Hai Ro'i*, Jerusalem, 1961. Rav Kook's position is discussed in Sears, ibid., pp. 159–161, 180–183.

framework, before nations were differentiated into distinct speech forms, the moral sense had risen to a point of demanding justice for animals. "The first man had not been allowed to eat meat," as is implied in God's instruction to Adam: "I have given you every herb yielding seed which is on the face of all the earth, and every tree in which is the fruit of a tree yielding seed – it shall be to you for food," [*Genesis* ibid.].[59] But when humanity, in the course of its development, suffered a setback and was unable to bear the great light of its illumination, its receptive capacity being impaired, it was withdrawn from the fellowship with other creatures, whom excelled with firm spiritual superiority. Now it became necessary to confine the concern with justice and equity to mankind, so that divine fire, burning with a very dim light, might be able to warm the heart of man, which had cooled off as a result of the many pressures of life. The changes in thought and disposition, in the ways of particularized developments, required that moral duty be concentrated on the plane of humanity alone. But the thrust of the ideals in the course of their development will not always remain confined. Just as the democratic aspiration will reach outward through the general intellectual and moral perfection, "when man shall no longer teach his brother to know the Lord, for they will all know Me, small and great alike" (*Jeremiah* 31:34), so will the hidden yearning to act justly toward animals emerge at the proper time. What prepares the ground for this state are the commandments, those intended specifically

---

59. Note also that R. (Meir Leibush) Malbim in his *Torah ve-ha-Mitzvah* to *Genesis* 1:29, states that:

Scholars have already explained that mankind was basically created not to be carnivorous, and this is evident from the formation of our teeth. And the most tame of animals live off vegetables and plants. And so too many of the tribes in India live off fruit and they are of a pleasant disposition. And so too Adam was born in East Asia, and there one finds numerous [edible] plants....

However, there are other authorities who disagree with him. See also Ibn Ezra to *Exodus* 8:22 on the vegetarianism of India. See also *Otzar Plaot ha-Torah* vol. *Leviticus*, by Zeev Wolf Zichermann, Brooklyn, 2016, pp. 603–604, quoting *Daat Shalom* by R. Shalom Moskowitz, *Maamar Shirat ha-Zeev*, etc.

for this area of concern (cited by Schochet ibid. pp. 293–294).

Schochet discusses Rav Kook's position stating that:

> Moreover, argues Kook, man's spiritual growth is an agonizingly gradual and torturous process, and seeking to accelerate it could prove to be dangerous. In other words, were the Torah to suddenly deny man the right to eat meat, the result might conceivably be his eating the flesh of other human beings, for he might be incapable of controlling his lust for flesh!
>
> When the animal lust for meat became overpowering, if the flesh of all living beings had been forbidden, then the moral destructiveness, which will always appear at such times, would not have differentiated between man and animal, beast and fowl and every creeping thing on earth. The knife, the axe, the guillotine, the electric current, would have felled them all alike in order to satisfy the vulgar craving of so-called cultured humanity.

Schochet concludes by summarizing his understanding of Rav Kook's position on vegetarianism (ibid., pp. 295–296):

> Scripture therefore permits man to eat meat, but it emphasizes that this is a reprehensible act, and the true meaning of the phrase "Because thy soul desireth to eat flesh" is, according to Kook, that when one's moral sensitivities vis-à-vis eating animals are as spiritually developed as those vis-à-vis consuming human flesh, one will undoubtedly abhor the eating of animal flesh as much as one would cannibalism! In the interim, however, one is permitted to eat meat, but only the flesh of certain animals slaughtered in accordance with the humane procedures of *shehitah*. One must cover the blood of certain animals to dramatize the sense of shame that prompts one to have to butcher innocent animals and consume their flesh. It is forbidden to eat *terefah*, for such an act places one in a league with those wild beasts which feed on small, helpless creatures; it would be as if man were sharing "spoils" with them. Likewise, it is not permitted to eat *nebelah*, for such an act would show a total lack

of compassion for the unfortunate animal, and a desire to gleefully benefit from its death.

Although Kook does not envision the ideal man-animal relationship as materializing until some future age, he exhorts his readers to put into practice acts of loving-kindness toward fauna. For example, a man should care for his old and weak working-animals long after their usefulness to him may have passed. Sheep-shearing and even milking a cow are, in reality, forms of robbery, and Kook cautions that such "gifts of nature" are not always ours for the taking.

Kook's central message is that man ought never to forget that meat-eating is but a temporary concession. The merciful God of Israel would never decree that man's survival should be eternally contingent upon his butchering animals. One day mankind will regain its true spiritual heights and recognize the deep kinship it shares with all of existence. Then the eating of meat will be abhorred, and man and animal will coexist in peace.

So both Rav Kook and his disciple distinguished between the present situation, which is non-ideal, and the visionary ideal situation where we would all be vegetarians. They saw the consumption of animal products as a situation which is *be-di'avad* [ex post facto], but not something which is in any way ultimately acceptable. I think that they would also have agreed that what you put into your body, what you eat, what you ingest and digest, and what actually becomes a part of your physical body, has not only an obvious physical effect upon you, but also a spiritual effect upon you. And kashrut already indicates this, in the sense that we only eat those things which we slaughter in the most humane manner possible. *Ever min ha-chai* (cf. *Deuteronomy* 12:23; *Exodus* 22:30),[60] ripping a limb off a live animal and eating it, is forbidden by law. Likewise, *oto ve-et beno* (*Leviticus* 22:28), namely you

---

60. See the Rambam, *Hilchot Maachalot Asurot* 4:10, 5:1; idem, *Hilchot Melachim* 9:10, that this is also one of the seven Noahide laws. See on this subject Aaron Lichtenstein, *The Seven Laws of Noah*, New York, 1981; David Novak, *The Image of the Non-Jew in Judaism: An Historical and Constructive Study of the Noahide Laws*, New York, 1983.

can't take a mother or a father and its child at the same time in order to slaughter them. *Shaleyah teshalah et ha-em ve-et ha-banim tikach lach* (*Deuteronomy* 22:7), when you take a bird out of the nest, you have to send away the mother bird. So the Bible indicates that animals are sentient and feel these things, and probably, if you are not sensitive to living creatures, you will not be sensitive to people either.

Indeed, the Rambam, in his *Guide for the Perplexed* (3:48, 599) explains *oto ve-et beno* as being "a precautionary measure in order to avoid slaughtering its young animal in front of its mother. For in these cases, animals feel great pain, there being no difference negating the pain between man and other animals." And ibid., 3:48, 600 he writes concerning *shiluah ha-ken*, "the law takes into consideration these pains... of beast and bird."[61]

So these halachot are there *le-zakek et ha-nefesh*, to purify the soul, in order that in human society we will be more positive individuals and relate to one another *ben adam le-havero*, in human interaction, in a more acceptable fashion.[62]

---

61. See Seidenberg's remarks on p. 148, note 479.
62. Recently, in an article published in the *Jerusalem Post*, December 8, 2019, p. 10, entitled "Self-righteous environmentalism doesn't work," Tzvi Bisk argued inter alia as follows:

> ... As for meat, do we really expect Brazilians, Argentineans, Texans and Australians to stop eating steaks, or the English their beef? Will 1.5 billion Muslims forego lamb? Will Hindu India cull its 200 million cattle and 100 million buffalo? Will those African peoples, for whom cattle are a vital part of their culture, eliminate 270 million cattle? Around 400 million of the poorest people in the world are pastoralists and small landholders who rely on livestock for food and livelihood. The largest portion of animal greenhouse emissions derives from these severely impoverished segments of the Earth's population – those least capable of forgoing any animal protein. The frontal attack on beef and lamb is as much of an ill-advised a strategy as attacking aviation.
>
> Interestingly, eating English beef in London causes less life-cycle greenhouse gas than eating avocados grown in Chile. Eating local would be a more rational battle cry than "Let's all go veggie." Also, according to the World Resources Institute, only 3% of United States greenhouse gas emissions are attributable to animal agriculture (factoring in pork and poultry beef constitutes less than 2%). No question it would be more environmentally responsible to get one's animal

Therefore, if we have to eat animals, we slaughter them with "the aim to kill them in the easiest manner possible, and it is forbidden to torment them through killing them in a reprehensible manner." See also *Pithei Teshuvah* to *Yoreh Deah* 23, sect. 10, citing *Noda bi-Yehudah Tinyana*, *Yoreh Deah* 10, who inveighs against hurting animals for the sake of sport, seeing it as unacceptable cruelty (ibid., 3:48, 599). And we should also bear in mind that a person is forbidden even to feed himself before he has first fed his animals (*B. Berachot* 40a).[63]

To the above I would like to add that which is found in the Hatam Sofer's responsum (*Orah Hayyim* 54):

> After He, may He be blessed, permitted us to eat animal meat, He desired that we be not cruel to them, but be merciful towards them, to minimize their pain. And it is for this reason He commanded us to slaughter them for the meat, and to make a blessing, "Who has sanctified us with His commandments, and has ordered us to slaughter...", implying that "He has satisfied us with His commandments and ordered us to slaughter them in order to be merciful to these creatures," i.e. slaughtering being a merciful way to kill an animal.[64]

---

protein from pork (one fourth the life cycle emissions of beef) or poultry (one fifth) or properly managed farm-grown fish.

Be that as it may, our concerns are not merely economic and ecological, though clearly these are important considerations, they are also ethical, and of course, relate to the halachic issues of kashrut (factoring out pork!).

63. I am not unaware of the apparent contradictions between Rambam's statement in his *Guide* and what he wrote in his *Mishneh Torah* (*Hilchot Tefillah* 9:7, and commentary to the *Mishnah* on *Megillah* 4:7 and *Berachot* 5:3) that *shiluah ha-ken* [sending away a mother bird before taking her eggs] is not for reasons of divine mercy (*hemlah*) but a biblical decree (*gezerat ha-katuv*). But a discussion of this issue is beyond the limits of this study. See for example, Josef Stern, *Problems and Parables of Law: Maimonides and Nahmanides on Reasons for the Commandments (Ta'amei Ha-Mitzvot)*, New York, 1998, chapter 3, pp. 49, etc.

64. On the degree to which *shehitah* could be considered cruelty to animals, see *Edut Neemanah, Part 1: Responsa on Halachic Problems Arising out of the Defence of Shechita in Europe*, with a Review of the Medical Aspects of Shechita, Jerusalem, 1974 (Hebrew), this in response to attempts in various European countries to forbid *shehitah*.

"How, then, can we bring such a message to rabbinical seminaries," I was asked. "There is some resistance in administrations – they only have five years with their students, and teaching a course on *tza'ar ba'alei hayyim* and the realities of the industries dealing with animals is not something they would justify spending their time on. How can one respond that this *does* need to be an integral part of rabbinic training?"

To which I replied that when speaking about the educational difficulties in persuading institutions and parents in schools and in yeshivot to take a more positive attitude towards vegetarianism or animal care (which is not the same as vegetarianism), there is obviously a need for a variety of strategic approaches.

It is fairly clear now that too much meat consumption[65] has a

---

See also *Physiological and General Medical Aspects of Shehita*, by I. M. Levinger, Jerusalem, 1976, with a rich bibliography. S. D. Sassoon, *A Critical Study of Electrical Stunning and the Jewish Method of Slaughter*, Letchworth Herts. 1955. Of further interest is Yekutiel Yehudah Greenwald's *Ha-Shohet ve-ha-Shehitah ba-Sifrut ha-Rabbanit*, New York, 1955.

The European countries, such as Germany, Poland and Lithuania, which before the Second World War demanded that animals be electrically stunned before they were slaughtered, triggered off a halachic controversy – see above. R. Yehiel Weinberg, in his *Seridei Aish* (vol. 1, Jerusalem, 1961, pp. 9–176) ad init, came out strongly against it, including the supportive responsa of ten major halachic authorities. The arguments were that stunning may make the animal *tereifah*, and sometimes they collapse, thereby being *nefulah*, and on occasions their limbs are negatively affected (*risuk eivarim*), their appearance is changed (see *Beit Yosef Yoreh Deah* 43, and *Rema*, ibid., sect. 2, etc.) and there are additional reasons to forbid such practice.

65.　See, for example, Ramban's famous passage to *Parashat Kedoshim* (*Leviticus* 19:1), that though the Torah permitted the eating of meat and drinking wine, *overeating* and drinking comes under the category of *"naval bi-reshut ha-Torah."*

It is of interest to find in Yalkut Me'am Lo'ez, by R. Yaakov ben R. Machir Kuli (1685–1732), Parshat Noach. p. 30, an explanation why the earliest generations (mentioned in *Genesis*) lived so very long, close to a thousand years. He states:

> You should know that our master R. Mosheh ben Maimon (Rambam) already gave a fine answer to this query, [by pointing out] that they had fine practices in their diet. For then they ate no meat and nothing of the live, and they drank no wine, and were nourished only from what grows in the earth. And they drank water, and their meals were in moderation, for they did not fill their bellies with sweat meats. For such food brings sickness to mankind.

negative impact upon one's health. I assume that parents want their children to grow up healthy. They don't want them to be obese, they don't want them to have heart problems at an early age, or indeed at any age. So they should understand that in any case they have to reduce meat consumption to a much more limited level.

Now if they feel that halachically on Shabbat they are obligated to have *basar ve-yayin*, then once a week, *be-di'avad* I would say that that is reasonable. And that would reduce the degree of meat consumption.[66] One also has to take into account the halachic issues, which would have to be explained, and it can be shown from existing films and videos the sort of problems that do exist in the whole meat production business.

In the sort of yeshivot where I learned, Lithuanian yeshivot, there

---

And it is interesting to compare what the first-century Roman Stoic philosopher, Musonius Rufus, wrote in his *That One Should Disdain Hardships*, translated by Cora E. Lutz, Yale Classical Studies, 1947, chapter 18a (pp. 87–88):

> As one should prefer inexpensive food to expensive and what is abundant to what is scarce, so one should prefer what is natural for men to what is not. Now food from plants of the earth is natural to us, grains and those which though not cereals can nourish man well, and also food (other than flesh) from animals which are domesticated. Of these foods the most useful are those which can be used at once without fire, since they are also most easily available; for example, fruits in season, some of the green vegetables, milk, cheese, and honey. Also those which require fire for their preparation, whether grains or vegetables, are not unsuitable, and are all natural food for man. On the other hand he showed that meat was a less civilized kind of food and more appropriate for wild animals.

R. Shimon ben Tzemach ibn Duran (Rashbatz) in his *Magen Avot* (Livorno, 1785), to *M. Avot* 2:7, which states in the name of Hillel that "the more meat, the more worms," writes:

> ... that much meat will not help one to live a long life, and on his death his abundance of flesh [presumably his fatness] will cause him distress with the proliferation of worms.

See also comments of R. Zeev Wolf Zichermann, in his *Otzar Plaot ha-Torah*, vol. 4, *Be-Midbar*, Brooklyn, 2019, pp. 395–397.

66. See now R. Aaron Potek's article, entitled "The Case for Limiting Meat Consumption to Shabbat, Holidays, and Celebrations," apud *Kashrut and Jewish Food Ethics*, ed. Shmuly Yanklowitz, Boston, 2019, pp. 218–234.

were two types of *shiurim* given. There was a *shiur iyyun* (text-focused lecture) which was *le-hiduda*, in order to sharpen the mind, and there was a *mussar shmues* (a morality lesson) which was given once a week, not by the Rosh Yeshiva, but by a *mashgiah* (spiritual mentor). And though this is something of a diversion from our main theme, and somewhat off the beaten track, I cannot resist conveying a recollection I have from my year's study in Yeshivat Kol Torah in Jerusalem in the late '50s, under the great Rosh Yeshiva, R. Shlomoh Zalman Auerbach *zt"l*.

The Mashgiach, Reb Gedaliah Eisemann, was also a somewhat unique personality. A *yekke*, he would gently chide any student who came even a minute late to the Beit Midrash. His weekly *mussar shmuesen* – moral lectures – were not merely a string of ethical exhortations, but carefully crafted examinations of moral values as grounded in halachic sources. Anyone who carefully observed his behavior throughout the preceding week, would note that he was practicing upon himself the message he would impart to us in the following week's shiur.

At that time I would daven (pray) very slowly and, I believed, intensively. My *Amidah* prayer took longer than that of my neighbors. The rule is that as long as one person is standing and davening the *Amidah*, whoever is in front of him cannot end his *Amidah* by taking three steps backwards. So the whole line of *daveners* in front of me could only stay "stuck" until I ended my *Amidah* prayer. Reb Gedaliah noticed this, and one day, after *Shaharit* (the morning prayer), he took me aside, and covering his mouth with his hand in order that none of his spittle touch me – this was his standard practice – told me that even when engaged in spiritual devotion and prayer, one must remain aware of one's neighbors. The message was both gentle and clear, and I have never forgotten that very brief conversation which has such vast moral implications.[67]

---

67. The technical halachic term for this is *tircha de-tzibbura* – the discomfort of the congregation. And this is forbidden because of *kavod ha-tzibbur* – the dignity of the congregation. In a recently published book, *Sefer Yekara de-Tzibbura: Be-Inyonnei Torah Tzibbur u-Kevod Tzibbur*, by R. Shimon Amsalem, Rehovot, 2019, introduction and sect. 9, pp. 21–25, he relates many stories of great Rabbis who, while in private they would pray at great length, when in the synagogue with the congregation they would finish the *Amidah* prayer quickly in order not to inconvenience the congregation,

The *mussar shmues* dealt with ethics. It dealt with the relationship between man and his neighbor. It was aimed at trying to improve the moral and the ethical state of the students. That was its purpose. It may have started off with the *halachah* or with something related to the weekly Torah portion, but then it went on to discuss the spiritual and moral implications of the original source dealt with. It is, therefore, not difficult to suggest that, without making any sort of clear prohibitions or limitations on the recipes of the meals of the members of the yeshiva and its *talmidim*, the *mussar shmuesim* could put a greater emphasis on the whole aspect of the nature of life and its sanctity. And not just human life, but all manners of life, which, of course, leads one into the much broader issue of ecology, going beyond the animal kingdom into the plant kingdom. (See below Essay Two.)

I would also strongly advise them to study the classic responsum of that great Torah scholar, R. Eliyahu Klatzkin (1852–1932) in his *Imrei Shefer*, section 34, published in Warsaw in 1896, with an excellent introduction by R. Moshe Nahmani to its republication, Jerusalem, 2016, under its title *Derech Yesharah*. This is a brilliant all-embracing exposition, covering all aspects of the law of *Tza'ar Ba'alei Hayyim*, and demonstrates deep halachic sympathy for the well-being of animals.

It is much easier to comprehend life in an animal, but far more difficult to see it in a potato. You see it in a cat, in a dog, or in any other type of pet. When you go to a zoo and you see these naughty little monkeys,[68] obviously highly intelligent, who will snatch things out of

---

knowing that otherwise it would wait until they had finished to say the *Amidah*. On this halachic concept, see *Entziklopediah Talmudit*, Vol. 20, Jerusalem, 1991, pp. 662–678.

68. Apropos of monkeys and their intelligence, – yet another recollected vignette from when I was in Varanasi (Banares) India in 2011 with my wife. On that occasion we rented a room on the roof of a building overlooking the sacred ghats. Between the bedroom and the room with a bath and toilet was a short open space of the roof. But that space was generally occupied by monkeys. One afternoon, after we had bought ourselves a few bananas in the bazaar and brought them up to our room, my wife decided to be generous and give a banana to a mother monkey holding her child. This was a major mistake. For subsequently we were plagued with "requests" for bananas, and on opening the door of our room, to go to the toilet, we would be invaded by a swarm of monkeys. It took careful strategic planning to go to the toilet and to have a shower and not be attacked by the monkeys.

your hand if you give them a chance, and grin and laugh at you (!), then you know that they have both life and understanding. You don't eat them because, of course, they're not kosher. But were there not the restrictions of kashrut, why not eat them, like the Chinese do? Except that you realize that there's something stopping you from doing so, emotionally, psychologically, and that becomes an ideology. It is not an easy task to change people's eating habits, habits that have developed over so many generations. But we have made great progress in all sorts

---

W. Crooke, in his *Things Indian*, London 1906, pp. 330–331 writes as follows:

> The Macacus [monkey], "the incarnation of unfulfilled promises," as he has been called, is a decided nuisance in bazaars, owing to his pilfering habits and the destruction he causes to tiled roofs, which are only imperfectly protected by thorns laid upon them. Many years ago it is said that a Sepoy regiment, offended at the extortion of the corn-chandlers of Mathura, as they marched through the city flung handfuls of dried peas on the roofs. These the monkeys promptly recovered from beneath the tiles, and wrecked the bazaar. In the eighteenth century they became such a pest at Benares that the Raja of Bishanpur, a pious Hindu, petitioned the Government to send a guard of Sepoys to destroy them. He stated in his petition that they used to enter his house, carry off the meat from his table, and steal whatever they could find; while they terrified his girls, assembling round them if alone, and making the most odious noises. Nowadays, when monkeys become intolerable at Benares, it is the custom to deport them to a jungle on the other side of the river. Not long ago, when being removed in crates to a jungle in the Siwalik Hills, a consignment escaped at the Saharanpur Railway Station, which they occupied for some days, doing infinite damage in the goods sheds. At last a wily railway-man smeared some goods wagons with treacle. Most of the monkeys invaded the train, and, when they were all well aboard, the engine-driver started at full speed. The monkeys were too much alarmed to jump till the engine slacked speed in a jungle some miles down the line, when they hastily disembarked and were no more seen. Timur, in his Memoirs, tells how his camp in the Siwalik Hills was attacked by a multitude of monkeys, who not only stole the eatables of the troops, but carried off small articles and curiosities.
>
> They are much dreaded by native women, who say that they are liable to attack by these *semi-human beasts*, bears, and monkeys .... [My emphasis – D. S.].

Here we have drifted somewhat far afield, but the above does demonstrate clearly the intelligence and "semi-humanity" of these creatures however unpleasant they might be. (But humans can be as well!)

of areas, and there is no reason that we should not aim to do so in this area too.

And to a yeshiva student who has a habit of eating meat many times a week, I would suggest that he go and make a visit to an abattoir, to a *beit shehitah*, or that he go to one of the processing plants, like Zoglobek, or one of the other big industrial plants that produce eggs, and see what happens to the chickens.

Let me tell you a story. We have ten children, six of whom are vegetarian, and two of those six are actually vegans. The others found that it was very difficult to be vegetarian when they were in the army, and so they became "*ovrei aveira*," transgressors, as they would put it. Where we lived in Katamon, near the kindergarten, there was a place where on every *erev* Rosh Hashana, they used to do the *kaparot* ceremony. There were cages full of chickens, and the people used to come and take a chicken and wave it around their head, and there was a *shohet* on the spot, next to the kindergarten, who would slaughter the chickens. They would flop around until they were properly dead,[69] and then the people would take them home. The children would be spectators to this spectacle, and I think that probably this is one of the reasons that many of our children became vegetarians (besides the fact that they were never given any meat!). A person who sees these things gets a different perspective on what he is eating.

I was then asked, "If God were to look down and see how we are using animals, industrially, what do you think His reaction would be?"

"Well," I replied, "It's difficult to know what God's reaction is to our

---

69. The fact is that even cows, etc., after being slaughtered do not die immediately. It takes a little time till they are "bled out." See, e.g., *Shulhan Aruch Yoreh Deah* 27:1:

> If he cuts [out some flesh] from the animal after it had been properly slaughtered, and if it is still shuddering (i.e. still alive), he is prohibited from eating it until the animal dies.

The *Shach* ad loc. refers us to *B. Sanhedrin* 63a, that as long as the animal is still alive one may not eat of its flesh; but once it has finally died one may, based on *Leviticus* 19:26. See further *Shach* ad loc., sect. 2, *Hagahot R. Akiva Eiger*, ibid., sect. 1, *Ketzot ha-Hoshen, Hoshen Mishpat* 232:1, etc.

behavior. It was God who told us not to inflict pain on animals. It was God that told us *oto ve-et beno* (the prohibition against slaughtering an animal and its offspring together). It was God that told us *Shaleyah teshalah et ha-em* (send away a mother bird before taking the egg).[70]

---

70. This issue requires some further elaboration. The verses in *Deuteronomy* 22:6–7 read as follows:

> If a bird's nest chances to be before thee in the way in any tree, or on the ground, whether they be young ones or eggs, and the mother is sitting upon the young, thou shalt not take the mother with the young. But thou shalt in any wise let the mother go, and take the young with thee, and that thou mayest prolong thy days.

So we have here two different commandments, (a) a negative one forbidding taking the mother and her young, and (b) a positive one, constituting a means to avoid transgressing the negative one (see responsa of Rashba, vol. 1, sect. 18, vol. 3, sect. 283). The Rambam (*Guide to the Perplexed* 3:48) and Ramban (to *Deuteronomy* ad loc.) and the *Sefer ha-Hinuch* (*mitzvah* 545) all state that the injunction to send away the mother is in order to inculcate in us the characteristic of mercy, so that we do not take away the young before the eyes of the mother, an act of cruelty.

This subject is discussed expansively in the Talmud, and the Tractate *Hullin* has an entire chapter (12) dealing with it. And in the *Zohar Hadash* (*Ruth* 94b) we are told that:

> When that bird is sent away to fly off from her young, she cries and goes off… and then the spirit of compassion is awakened upon all who wander from place to place… and is compassionate to them and forgiven them their sins.

And similarly in *Tikkunei ha-Zohar*, Tikkun 6, 23a, we read:

> When Israel abide by that commandment, from then on from above they speak of their merit.

We see, then, the great importance attached to this *mitzvah*, which is one of mercy and compassion towards fowls.

Recently I noticed that there is a similar ruling in Islam. See Ameer Ali Syed, *The Spirit of Islam: A History of the Evolution and Ideals of Islam*, London, 1922, pp. 157–158:

> A man once came to him with a bundle, and said: "O Prophet, I passed through a wood and heard the voice of the young of birds, and I took them and put them

And I think the sources indicate to us that originally it was only *basar kodshim* (ritually sacred meat) that was eaten: only *kodshim kalim*, those parts of the animal that could be consumed by the owners, were eaten. But *shehitat hulin* (slaughter for everyday food) was not exactly something that was encouraged, as we can see from the earliest development of the halachah. So if I am asked what God sees when looking down on us, I would suggest that in general He is somewhat dissatisfied with us. Not just because of that but because of many other things that we do. And I'm certain He is not pleased to see the way that we are treating His creatures. He is the One that puts some element of life into them, some element of understanding into them, He is the One that created the nerves with which they feel pain.[71] I do not think that it's possible to think of an *El rachum ve-hanun* (*Exodus* 34:6), a merciful and gracious God, *al kol ma'asav* (cf. *Psalms* 145:9), on all the works of His creation, as being pleased when He sees the infliction of pain upon animals.

And ultimately it cannot be denied that slaughtering an animal, even in the most "humane" fashion, is cruel. This was clearly acknowledged by R. Yehuda Azsód (1773–1880) in his responsa *Yehudah Yaaleh* (also called *Shut Mahari Asad*), Lvov-Presburg 1873–1890, sect. 164, who wrote that the custom on Rosh ha-Shanah was not to slaughter chickens, since "we are all requesting (God's) mercy on this day, and therefore it is not seemly to practice cruelty by slaughtering living creatures." Admittedly R. Hayyim Eleazer Shapira, the Muncacze Rebbe in his *Shaar Yisaschar* (Muncacz 1928), did not support this

---

in my carpet, and their mother came fluttering round my head." And the Prophet said: "Put them down"; and when he had put them down the mother joined the young. And the Prophet said: "Do you wonder at the affection of the mother towards her young? I swear by Him who has sent me, verily, God is more loving to His servants than the mother to these young birds. Return them to the place from which ye took them, and let their mother be with them." "Fear God with regard to animals," said Mohammed; "ride them when they are fit to be ridden, and get off when they are tired. Verily, there are rewards for our doing good to dumb animals, and giving them water to drink."

71. See Sorabji, ibid., p. 360, sect. 17(h) on Porphyry's philosophical plea for justice to animals based on their feeling pain and terror.

custom in practice, nonetheless Azsód's statement reflects a clear truth.

And if one does have to eat meat on occasions and this requires slaughtering an animal, then, at least, one must do one's utmost to limit pain involved. So writes R. Moshe Cordovera, in his *Tomer Devorah*, Jerusalem, 1969, p. 16:

> [Therefore a person should] not upset a growing thing [see below section on ecology] except for need, nor kill any animal except for need. *And he should choose a good death* (*mitah yafah*) for them, with a carefully examined knife to show mercy however is possible…

The phrase *mitah yafah* for proper *shehitah* which Cordovera used, is, as Seidenberg (ibid., pp. 164–165) rightly pointed out,

> Especially poignant and significant, [since] it derives from a rabbinic dictum that one must choose a good and easy death for a person who is going to be executed by the court. In the *Tosefta* [*Sanhedrin* 9:3] and the Talmud [ibid., 45a, 52b, *B. Pesahim* 75a, *B. Ketubot* 37b] this principle is derived directly from the commandment [in *Leviticus* 19:18] "Love your fellow like yourself." By appropriating this terminology, Cordovera concretely extended the commandment to love one's neighbor to all animals, specifically with regard to slaughter.…

Seidenberg (ibid.) adds that:

> R. Yishayah Horowitz (1562–1630) …. Known as the Shlah …. In his work *Shney Luchot ha-Brit* (vol. 2:3, *Torah she-bi-Chtav, Parshat Re'eh* 82b) … quotes the Talmud's formulation … "choose a good death for him," and comments, "this means *shehitah* … with a mistake" (*pegimah* [perhaps better translated as flaw]).

We have seen above that this is hardly the case in most abattoirs.

And here, it might be suitable to take a look at a few statements recorded in *Sefer Hasidim*, attributed to the great medieval Ashkenazi sage, R. Yehudah he-Hassid (died 1217). For example, in section 776 we read:[72]

> Any action that causes suffering to a person is punished, and also if suffering is caused for no reason to an animal, or for example, if one places upon it a burden too heavy for him to bear, and he is unable to move with it and one hits him [in order to move him on] – [he who does this] is destined to pay for his action, since [causing] suffering to an animal is forbidden by biblical law. It is written concerning Balaam, "Why has thou smitten thine ass?" (*Numbers* 22:32), and, on the other hand [Balaam said], "I would have even a sword in mine hand, for now I would kill thee" (ibid.. 29), and therefore he was killed by a sword… One may not tyrannize slaves or animals if they have alone no worry, and we may not meaninglessly trouble them. For is it not said, "And He shall give you compassion, and have compassion upon thee" (*Deuteronomy* 13:17) – so long as you are compassionate, He will show compassion to you. A person who has no need to eat meat, and who knows that if he slaughters [an animal, the meat] will go foul if he does not make use of it, [i.e. consume it, he] should not slaughter [it]… "A righteous man is sensitive to the soul of his beast" (*Proverbs* 12:10); if it is sick, [and] he should not trouble it, and if the time comes for [such a beast] to give birth, so [then] one may not burden it… A dog that does not bite… should be quietly and gently sent away, and not through the use of a large stick.

And in section 44, ed fin., the rabbis interpreted the verse in *Zachariah* 12:4, "And in that day, saith the Lord, I will strike every horse with astonishment and his rider with madness" – because he [the rider] hit it with his boots and spurs. There he also inveighs against those who place too great a burden on their animals, and hit them when

---

72. Ed. R. Reuven Margaliot, ibid., p. 425; ed. Shimon Gutman, ibid., pp. 588–589 (with extensive explanatory notes).

they can no longer move, and those who pull at the ears of cats to hear them squeal in pain,[73] and so forth.

However, ibid., in the long section 589 (ed. Margaliot, pp. 384–386, ed. Gutman, vol. 2, pp. 385–386, 534–537), we read as follows:

> … And the Holy One blessed be He, created animals that devour other animals, so that humans should not complain saying, "How could it be that the Holy One blessed be He, permitted humans to slaughter animals, beasts and birds, and was not concerned at the pain of His creatures." For this reason it is that He created other animals that devour one another. And if one was to argue that only beasts of prey were created to eat other animals of their own volition, one may answer that since we have found only those birds and beasts of prey eat other beasts of prey, while other animals and cattle that do not kill other animals, for we have observed that they are never beasts of prey, then we must assume that the Holy One blessed be He decreed it for humans too [i.e. namely that they may eat animals]. And should you argue that God should have decreed that all creatures eat only grass, and not other living creatures, the Holy One blessed be He knows that the Evil Inclination rules over all, and therefore He decreed that one should fear Him and that his needs be gotten by toil, so that he will pray to God, and direct his heart towards Him.

So, on the one hand our author justifies slaughtering animals to eat them, but on the other hand is cognizant to the fact that this is only due to the weakness of man (and beast) who are governed by lust and greed. Indeed, the consumption of meat in rabbinic parlance is called *basar ta'avah*, meat eaten to satisfy one's desire (*B. Hulin* 16b).

This concept is clearly formulated in Rabbenu Bahya ben Asher's (died 1320) *Shulhan shel Arba*, ed. H. D. Chavel, Jerusalem, 1969, *Kitvei* Rabbenu *Behaii*, p. 496:

> And one must consider that it would be preferable for humans

---

73. Ed. R. Margaliot, Jerusalem, 1957, p. 104 and editor's note 24; ed. S. Gutman, Brooklyn, New York, 2012, vol. 1, pp. 82–83, and his rich notes ad loc.

to have their food from which grows on the land, such as grains and fruit alone, and not animals. For animals have a soul activity (*nefesh tenuah*) somewhat similar to the activities of the intelligent souls (*nefesh ha-sechalim*) ... and the active soul should not be food for the human soul. And it was for this reason that Adam was instructed that his food be from grains and fruit, as it is written, "...Behold I have given you every herb yielding seed ..." (*Genesis* 1:29). But, during the period when all flesh corrupted its way, and all the animal kingdom was doomed to destruction [cf. *Genesis* 7:13 et seq.], and they were only saved through Noah's merit, [the consumption of] animals was permitted like that of the herbs of grass....

In this way he also explains the rabbinic statement in *B. Pesachim* 49b that an ignoramus [*am ha-aretz*] is forbidden to eat meat.[74] Since:

When we permit the killing of one soul [i.e. the animal one] for

---

74. Quite by chance I came upon the following passage in a volume entitled *Sefer Shulhano shel Adam: Al Inyanei Achila*, by an anonymous author, Jerusalem 2002, p. 287 (note). There he brings the following from Rav Zevin's *Sippurei Hassidim*:

When the Rabbi of Lubavitz was in Petersberg ..., one of his *hasidim* informed him that it was very difficult to get kosher meat. [He replied:] the Talmud says: "An ignoramus is forbidden [*asur*] to eat meat." *Asur* means bound – fettered. The ignoramus [feels] it is compulsory to eat meat. But one can survive without the lust for meat [*ta'avat basar*].

And on that same page (no. 7) he records the following passage:

R. Hanoch Henich ha-Cohen me-Alexander ... was the son-in-law of a rich man, and on occasion he would invite his friends, the *hasidim* of R. Bunim of Peshisha, to sumptuous meals at his father-in-law's. Once he declared, "Tonight, with the help of God, we will dine at my father-in-law's with a fine meal of meat, fish and wine." The Kotzker Rebbe who used to seek to be in the company of the Peshisha Rebbe, heard him, and cried, "Who needs meat and fish? Surely bread and a little borsht will suffice." The Rabbi of Alexander testified that from that time onwards he was unable to put in his mouth anything other than bread and borsht.

[the benefit] of the other [human] soul, it is only because the active soul is destroyed for the intelligent soul. But if he is an ignoramus, and has no intelligent soul, then, most certainly he is forbidden to eat meat, since we do not override and destroy an active soul for one which has no intelligent soul; and understand this.

But even without a full understanding of the philosophical conception underlying his argument, what is patently clear is that he sees vegetarianism as the ideal, and meat consumption as a concession to human (and animal) moral corruption.

Indeed, Rav Kook, in R. David Cohen's *Hazon ha-Tzimchonut ve-he-Shalom*, 1983, p. 28, explains the purpose of covering the blood of a slaughtered animal of a fowl (*kisui ha-dam*) is "to hide your shame [for eating meat] and your moral weakness" (see *Leviticus* 17:13).[75]

And see *Sefer ha-Hinuch*, H. D. Chavel, Jerusalem, 1952, sect. 187, p. 266, who wrote that:

> The Torah only permitted people to eat meat for the purpose of expiation of sins (*kapparah*), human necessities, such as food as medicine, or another that is a basic human need. But to kill animals with no benefit is considered to be mere destruction and murder ... though less so than the murder of a human being, but still regarded as murder (*shefichut dam*)....

See further the moving passage in *Exodus Rabba* 2:2,[76] on how Moses, when he was a shepherd, took loving care of his flocks. The midrash reads as follows:

---

75. See Seidenberg, ibid., p. 147, note 476, for another explanation of the *mitzvah* of *kisui ha-dam*, as a form of honorable burial – *kavod la-dam* – respect for the blood. Also ibid., p. 154, note 502, referring us to R. Yaakov Hayyim Sofer's *Kaf ha-Hayyim, Yoreh Deah*, vol. 1, sect. 28, subsect. 1 (correct Seidenberg's reference, and, moreover, the *Kaf ha-Hayyim*'s reference is to *Midrash Rabba Bereishit*). For different reasons for covering the blood, see *Entziklopediah Talmudit*, vol. 31, 454, note 13. See further Seidenberg, ibid., p. 349.

76. Ed. Avigdor Shinan, Jerusalem, Tel Aviv, 1989, pp. 105–107, with references to parallels and variant readings.

> When Moses was herding the flocks of Jethro in the wilderness, one of the sheep ran away. He pursued it until he found a rocky ledge. After discovering the ledge, he came upon a stream of water beside which the lost sheep stood drinking. At this he said, "I didn't know that you ran away because of thirst. You must be tired." So he carried it back on his shoulders. The Holy One, blessed be He, declared, "You have shown compassion in tending the flock belonging to mortal man. Thus shall you tend My flock [Israel]."

Similar characteristics are attributed to David (ibid., 2:3). Thus:

> David was tested through tending sheep, and found to be a good shepherd. He would restrain the larger sheep for the sake of the small ones. First, he would let the small ones graze on the soft grass, and then let the old sheep graze on the grass that was more difficult to chew, leaving the tough grass for the young bucks. He led them only to the wilderness, in order to distance them from theft. Therefore, the Holy One, blessed be He, told him, "You have proven yourself to be faithful with sheep. Now go and shepherd My flock [Israel]."

It is for this reason that he was considered to be suitable to serve as leader of his people.

We see, then, the sympathy and sensitivity revealed by this great rabbi, and the cautionary words of the Midrash, in the treatment to those animals that probably eventually he himself would eat. He was convinced that such compassionate sensitivity towards them would engender God's compassion towards us.

Finally, I think that all the statistical evidence on the sort of ecological damage that we are inflicting upon the earth, through animal production, farming, methane exposure, etc., is well known. How much less deleterious to the atmosphere, and to the world in which we live, would it be if we ate more grain and less meat? Indeed, the fact that we're damaging the ecology is actually something that is contrary to the notion of *pru u-revu* ("be fruitful and multiply") (*Genesis* 1:28), because by doing so it becomes more difficult for us to populate the world in a positive fashion.

There are, of course, other very serious problems such as the uneven distribution of population in the world,[77] the great concentration in some

---

77. Regional overpopulation is a subject that troubled people throughout time and place, and is one of the reasons, and even justifications, for the "quite impenetrable mystery of death," as demonstrated brilliantly by Haim Schwarzbaum in his essay "The overcrowded earth," (apud *Jewish Folklore between East and West*, ed. Eli Yassif, Beer-Sheva, 1989, pp. 127–142):

> Earth becomes overcrowded, some check has to be put on mankind increasing to an alarming rate. Thus the only solution is Death. A Bhuiya myth from Nagira, Pal Lahara State (Middle India), expresses the same idea: ... "No one died, no one could die. People increased in number so much that there was no room for them to live. Mahaprabhu thought in his mind: "Everyone is being born and no one is dying; where will there be room for all these people?" Mahaprabhu avails himself of the good services of a Centipede (=Death) and thus "Death entered the world," [V. Elwin, *Myths of Middle India*, Madras 1949, pp. 416 nos. 5, 6, and 7]. This vindication of death, expressed both in ancient literary texts and in oral folk literature, is, of course, much more reasonable and logical than the numerous, sometimes very trivial reasons and incidents current among aboriginal peoples accounting for the origin of death. This *economic* justification of death clearly testifies to the fact that in some parts of the world primitive man has quite realized the vast importance of instituting some order, or some equilibrium in the world of men, "that as many men as died so many should be born," as a Gond myth of Barangel, Ganjam District (India) says [Elwin, *Tribal Myths of Orissa*, Bombay 1954, p. 510 no. 4], or as the Eskimo of Greenland emphasize that the First Woman who brought Death said: "Let these die to make room for their posterity" (Schwarzbaum, pp. 128–129).

He notes (p.130) that a modern Yiddish folk tradition recorded among Polish Jewry expresses this notion quite adequately (in conformity with Midrashic and Agadic sources), "As soon as a new soul is brought into being an old one has to pass away," (H. Hayes, *Gleibungen un Minhagim in Varbindung mitn Toit*, Vilna 1928, vol. 1, p. 287c).

Hayes (ibid., p. 286) cites "a modern Jewish folk tradition ... that at first the Angel of Death was quite reluctant to accept the task imposed on him .... Only after the Lord had visited upon mortals all kinds of diseases, thus showing to man the real causes of death, did the Death Angel consent to carry out his duties" (ibid., pp. 132–133).

One of the most dramatic myths narrated in the *Mahābhārata* is one accounting for the origin of Death Personified as a woman. The story seems to have been quite popular and widespread in Ancient India. The Indian epic relates it even twice (*Mahābh.* VII 52–54 and XII 256 ff.), and we shall see later that even nowadays it is widely diffused among many aboriginal tribes of India, whose mythology is quite saturated with old Hindu ideas, notions and motifs kept alive for centuries. The gist of the myth is: Men created by Brahma increase incessantly and multiply to an alarming extent on the face of the earth. Overcrowded Earth lodges a complaint with Brahma of being unable to bear such a tremendous burden of throngs of people. Brahma is rather perplexed. He cannot conceive of any adequate measure by means of which he might considerably diminish and reduce the number of people on earth. In a vast fit of rage he is about to destroy the whole of mankind. Shiva intervenes on behalf of mankind, asking Brahma to mitigate his wrath and to withdraw the fire of his indignation. At last a woman goes forth from Brahma's body, a rather beautiful, black-eyed lady whom Brahma appoints as Goddess of Death, and whose function will be to annihilate people, the young and the old, the stupid and the clever, the rich and the poor alike. When the Goddess of Death learnt about this nomination she burst into tears and cried bitterly, imploring her Creator to release her from this disgraceful job of killing innocent people. She is afraid that she will be cursed and hated by mortals whose tears will consume and burn her flesh forever. Brahma promises to create all kind of assistants who will facilitate Death's task. He creates the various Messengers of Death in the shape of numerous, wasting Diseases, Hatred, Greed, Violence, Jealousy, Envy, etc. All these are instrumental in the annihilation of mankind. The Goddess of Death will thus not be blamed by people, on the contrary, they will welcome her with much pleasure, because she releases them from all sorts of trouble [A. Essigmann, *Sagen und Marchen Altindiens*, Bedin 1915, pp. 3 et seq; P. Deussen, *Vier philosophischen Texte des Mahabharatam*, pp. 404–413] (Schwarzbaum, pp. 130–131).

Schwarzbaum (pp. 140–141) also seeks to relate this to what we read in *Genesis* 6:1–3:

> And it came to pass, when men began to multiply on the face of the earth, and daughters were born unto them, that the sons of God saw the daughters of men that they were fair; and they took them wives, whomsoever they chose. And the Lord said: "My spirit shall not abide in man for ever, for that he also is flesh; therefore shall his days be a hundred and twenty years."

He also cites a passage from *Pirkei de R. Eliezer*, chapter 3 [ed. Gerald Friedlander, London, 1916, chapter 12, pp. 86–87], from Louis Ginzburg's *Legends of the Jews*, vol. 1, New York, 1909 (p. 65, and cf. idem, vol. 5, New York, 1925, pp. 86–87, note 38), as follows:

> When Earth heard that man was to increase and multiply, to replenish the earth and to subdue it (*Gen.* 1:28) it started to shudder and quake crying before its Creator: "Sovereign of all Worlds! I have not the power to feed the multitude of mankind." The Lord allayed Earth saying: "I and thou together will find food for

areas and lesser concentration in others. And likewise there is an uneven distribution of food which is a very serious issue. There are some countries which are glutted with food, and they actually destroy great amounts of grain either to keep the price up or because they have no way of making use of it. There is a cost for storing it, so that it's cheaper to burn it. Human population issues have to be worked out, at a global level. There are very serious problems as to how to deal with the great increase in population and the great inequalities in the conditions of those populations. And this is partly due to the uneven distribution of the natural resources, an issue which requires a careful examination of all aspects of nature, but that moves us into the area of ecology,[78] which is the subject of the next Essay.

---

the throngs of people." Accordingly, time was divided between God and Earth; God took the night, and Earth took the day. Refreshing sleep nourishes and strengthens man, while Earth brings forth produce with the help of God, who waters it.

And this he compares with what is found in the *Apocryphal Fourth Book of Ezra* 5:43 [*Liber Assiri Salathielis*, Hebrew transl. by A. Kaminka, Tel-Aviv, 1936, pp. 31 et seq., R. H. Charles, *The Apocrypha and Pseudoepigrapha of the Old Testament*, Oxford, 1913, vol. 2, p. 573]:

Where the Seer asks the Lord: "Couldst thou not have created all generations of men at once – those who have been, those who now exist, and those who are to be?" In reply he is told "that the world could not hold at once all those created in it."

He summarizes (p. 142) thus:

All the above-mentioned origin of death myths testify to the fact that the problem of an Overcrowded Earth plays a prominent part in mythology, folklore and legend.

The problem of (regional) overpopulation and the need for redistribution of overly dense population areas is too vast a subject to be dealt with here. I only wished to point out the fact that world folklore reflects the awareness of the problem.

78.   See most recently Mel Gottlieb's article "Ethical Eating and the Impact on Our Environment," apud *Kashrut and Jewish Food-Ethics*, ed. Shmuly Yanklowitz, Boston, 2019, pp. 235–243, who touches upon some of these issues, such as: fertilizer and pesticides, slaughterhouses and pollution, water consumption for animal production, etc. And see what I wrote in *BIU Today*, 2008, "The Mandate to Preserve and Conserve"; *Milin Havivin* 5, 2010–2011, pp. 6–7, "*Bal Tash'hit*: Waste Not Want Not."

ESSAY TWO
Ecology: New Areas of Religious Responsibility[1]

I would now like to call attention to some new fields with which the contemporary rabbi has to acquaint himself and to learn their challenges and the possible approaches to giving them solutions. The obvious one is, of course, technology which progresses with startling speed, presenting situations that never before confronted us. There is a huge literature on this subject, as is the case with medical ethics, business ethics, and so forth. But the one area that I feel has been somewhat neglected is that of ecology. It may not really be new, but has hitherto been too little emphasized. Close to twenty years ago, I wrote a short article in *The Edah Journal* (21, 2002), entitled "Jewish Environmental Ethics."[2] I began with a personal recollection based on changes that I

---

1. See "Introductory Note" on the history of the development of this chapter. See my article in *Conversations* 31, 2018, pp. 27–44, entitled "New Areas of Religious Responsibility." Here I have tried to create a sort of mosaic of those earlier elements, to give a broader and more composite picture of the subject I wish to address.

2. There is now a growing literature on the subject of Jewish environmentalism and ecology. To give just a brief sampling I will list the following items.

> David Kotler, *Human Ecology in the Ancient World: (Eretz-Yisrael, Greece and Rome)*, Jerusalem and Tel-Aviv, 1976 (Hebrew with English summary).
> *Eichut ha-Sevivah (Ekolugiah) bi-Mekorot ha-Yahadut*, Israel, 1990.
> Nachum Rakover, *Eichut ha-Sevivah: Habeitim Raayoniim u-Mishpatiim ba-Mekorot ha-Yehudim*, Jerusalem, 1993.
> Manfred Gerstenfeld, *Judaism, Environmentalism and the Environment: Mapping and Analysis*, Jerusalem, 1998.
> Manfred Gerstenfeld, *Eichut ha-Sevivah ba-Masoret ha-Yehudit*, Jerusalem, 2002.

The Environment in Jewish Law: Essay and Responza, eds. Walter Jacob and Moshe Zemer, New York, Oxford, 1993.

Jeremy Bernstein, *The Way Into Judaism and the Environment*, Woodstock, VT, 2006.

Ha-Sevivah ba-Halachah u-ba-Mahshavah, 4, Jerusalem, 2008, etc.

Most recently David Mevorach Seidenberg produced an impressive volume entitled *Kabbalah and Ecology: God's Image in the More-Than-Human World*, Cambridge, 2015. In the section entitled "Jewish Ecological Thought," pp. 2–15, he gives a fine survey of the resent literature and different perspectives on this subject, with rich bibliographic references (pp. 7–9, notes 21–29), and a listing of the main Jewish ecologically oriental organizations (p. 10, note 33, pp. 11–12, notes 42–44). However, his interpretation of some of the rabbinic sources is often rather problematic (e.g., his understanding of B. *Bava Kama* 91b in p. 12, note 45). Similarly in the same note his interpretation of B. *Shabbat* 105b as idolatrous is highly questionable.

We may further note that in 1994 the Israeli Ministry for Environmental Quality (*ha-Misrad le-Eichut ha-Sevivah*), published (through *Tamar* Publications) a volume which collected all the laws and by-laws dealing with this issue.

Seidenberg, ibid., pp. 30–31, uses the term "ecotheology," which he characterizes as:

> ... limiting the human exercise of power through exercising responsibility, morally accounting for animal suffering and animal consciousness, internalizing the fact of our dependence on Nature and on other creatures, and these are questions about human responsibility and the right way to balance human needs and the well-being of our species.

See further ibid., pp. 317–333, part 3, entitled "Ecotheology."

And in 2020, Rabbi Yonatan Neril and Leo Dee published an interesting book, which they called *Eco Bible*, vol. 1: *An Ecological Commentary on Genesis and Exodus* – a second volume is due to appear covering the rest of the Pentateuch. It is a rich collection of comments by both classical and modern commentaries on the Bible with ecological messages. It also includes the editors' own insights and observations, and full bibliographic references. It is a valuable contribution to the field of Jewish ecological thought.

However, it should be noted that some have sought to put the blame for the damage caused to our planet on the Judeo-Christian understanding of the verse in *Genesis* 1:28, where God blessed mankind saying, "Be fruitful and multiply and populate [literally: fill up] the earth *and subdue it, and have dominion* over the fish of the sea, and over the fowl of the air and over every living thing that creepeth upon the whole earth." This was stated in a statement published by the prominent Japanese Zen Buddhist philosopher D. T. Suzuki in 1953 and afterwards reformatted by Lynn White in an article entitled "The Historical Roots of our Ecological Crisis" (*Science* 155, 1967, 1203, and see

Suzuki, "The Role of Nature in Zen Buddhism," *Eranos – Jahrbuch* 22, 1951, 291).

René Dubos, in his *The Wooing of the Earth: New Perspectives on Man's Use of Nature*, New York, 1980, pp. 70 et seq., vigorously refutes this thesis, "which has become fashionable even and perhaps especially among theologians," arguing that it is "so completely at odds with historical facts that I have read more than 100 articles and books on the subject by lay scholars and theologians to better its understanding and implications." And on pp. 163–165, in Appendix III he lists close to fifty articles and books which he hopes "will stimulate a more rigorous analysis of the influence that religions beliefs or doctrines have exerted a human attitude towards the earth," adding that a bibliography as this same topic has been published: "Questions of Christianity and Technology: A Bibliographic Introduction," *Science, Technology, and Society*, Lehigh University, November 14, 1979.

His counterarguments to this thesis may be summarized as follows:

1. Extensive and lasting environmental degradation occurred long ago in many places where people had not had any contact with biblical teachings – in many cases indeed long before the biblical writings.

2. Ruination of the land was usually the consequence of deforestation, exploitative agriculture, and ignorance of the long-range consequences of farming practices.

3. The early teachers of the Judeo-Christian-Moslem religions expressed great concern for the quality of Nature and advocated practices for its maintenance. In ancient Judaism, for example, it was a religious commandment to take fields out of cultivation every seventh year, a practice of great ecological value since it helped to maintain the fertility of the soil.

Similar recommendations can be found in the writings of many Christian and Moslem teachers.

4. People destroyed more of Nature as the centuries went by, not because they had lost respect for it, but because the world population increased and also because technological means of intervention became more and more powerful. The plains Indians lived in "harmony with Nature" as long as their impact in the hunt was limited to what they could do with bows and arrows, but they decimated the herds of bison once they could hunt them from horseback with fire-arms. As long as the Caucasians had only axes of stone and of metal, it took them centuries and even millennia to destroy a large percentage of their forests, but power equipment now makes it possible to clearcut immense areas in a very few years.

The historical origin of the present ecological crisis is therefore not in *Genesis* 1:28 but in the failure of people to anticipate the long-range consequences of their activities – consequences that have recently been aggravated by the power and misuse of modern technology.

He adds (p. 29) that:

had seen during a short part of my own lifetime. I wrote as follows:

> A little more than thirty-five years ago, I served as a rabbi in India.[3] When one went to India at that time, of course, one went to Nepal. So I took a week off and went to Kathmandu. It was an absolute paradise. From this ancient, beautiful city one could see the Himalayas covered in snow against pure azure skies. Running through the city was a pristine river called the Bagmati. It is a holy river, where people bathed. The waters were so limpid and pure, you could drink directly from them. The city was small and you could take a bicycle and ride eight or ten kilometers out to the surrounding, even smaller townships. These were ancient townships with gorgeous temples such as Badgaon (now called Baktapur). I thought then that if there is a *Gan Eden Alei Adamot* – a Garden of Eden on Earth – this would be it. Had I wished to live in a land or city outside of Israel, it would have been Kathmandu. I was offered very attractive

---

> The belief that we can manage the Earth and improve on Nature is probably the ultimate expression of human conceit...
>
> But I would qualify that statement by saying that we "can manage the Earth," indeed, we must do so, but *in harmony with Nature*, and this is what contemporary ecologists are seeking to achieve.

I may add that Dubos himself, an eminent microbiologist and experimental pathologist, a professor emeritus of Rockefeller University in New York, has demonstrated this in his use of germ-fighting drugs derived from microbes.

However, I must admit that that interpretation of the words "and have dominion..." in *Genesis*, ibid., was understood by some commentators in a manner supporting the claim of Suzuki, etc. Thus the Ramban (Nahmanides, 1194–1270), to that verse wrote as follows:

> He gave them [humans] the power and dominion of the world to do as they wish with animals and insects and all crawling creatures, and to build and plant (see *Ecclesiastes* 3:23), and to mine copper from its mountains (see *Deuteronomy* 8:9), and such like; and this is what is meant by on the whole earth.

However, dominion is not necessarily exploitative.

3. I describe my time in India in a forthcoming book *From Yeshivat Hevron to Delhi: A Partial Memoir* (working title).

jobs there. At that time, very few Europeans came to this part of the world.

A little over two years ago (in November 2000), my wife and I were invited to an international conference in Baktapur, Nepal, on conservation. It was planned by two organizations, the World Wildlife Fund, which is the largest and most experienced independent global conservation organization, and the Alliance of Religions for Conservation (ARC), which consisted of representatives of eleven major religions, each trying to demonstrate that its respective religion has a clear interest in conservation and ecology. It was not the sort of conference in which participants tried to persuade one another of the higher ethical principles inherent in their respective religions. Instead, we were united in our goal of dealing with the challenges and dangers to the planet that we all inhabit.

And what a shock this was for me. Finally, we were confronted by the crazy traffic situation on the badly rutted roads, when blaring vehicles of all sorts contend with animal-drawn-carriages. Furthermore, there seemed to be no clear distinction between a pedestrian pavement and the vehicular section of the road. So we too soon learned to negotiate our way between the traffic when crossing a road.

But what for me was most significant and became even more evident during the course of our visit was that with all the pomp and splendor of the "happening" for which we had come, I was keenly aware that I was in a radically different place from that which I had visited some forty years earlier. You could no longer see the sky. It was overcast, darkened by dirty, smelly clouds. The Bagmati was now a cesspool.[4] And the main square, Durbar Square, in the heart of

---

4. I might point out that in an ARC meeting, one of the "Sacred Gifts" offered to the planet was to the Sacred Bagmati River, Nepal. And this was the statement of offering (p. 38):

The Sacred Bagmati River in Nepal is not the rapid flowing waterway it once was. The river, short in distance, runs through the country's expanding capital, Kathmandu, and has suffered from overextraction, damming and effluent disposal. The Friends of the Bagmati Association was formed at the time of the celebrations of Sacred Gifts in Kathmandu, 2000. The group is developing exciting new initiatives to turn the river's

old Kathmandu, bordered on all sides by the old Royal Palace and a variety of Temples, triple-roofed such as the Shiva temple, called the Maju Deval, in Nepali pagoda-style and covered in sensuous erotic carvings, was deafeningly bubbling with raucous life. The streets leading into the square were lined with open sewers. Buffalos pulling wagons filled with rice moved slowly and sedately alongside cows, cars, rickshaws, taxis and skinny barefoot children, whose hands were held out for "Rupees." The square itself was filled with street vendors huddled around their variety of wares, calling out loudly for attention. Sadhus crouched in ragged blankets in the dirt, half naked and smeared in dust and ashes, their hair and beards heavily matted. Women and girls carried *dokos* on their backs, that is, large wicker-baskets, filled with anything from vegetables to firewood. The *dokos* were fixed to their bodies by means of a *namlo*, a strap around their forehead. The heat and the dust were suffocating, the noise ear-splitting and the stench nauseating. For me this was "paradise lost."

And when you walked through the streets, you could smell the kerosene being used for cheap fuels in cars. My wife bought a *pashmina* [highly decorative stole, draped over the shoulders][5] –

fortune around and restore its sacred dignity, as well as acting as a central focus for the individual and corporate schemes already underway to help the river.

As much of the pollution is caused through small-scale abuse by ordinary people, the group is seeking to promote the sacred traditions of the river through celebration and education. Recently they have begun a neighborhood watch scheme with a view to empowering local citizens to care for their river and its environs. Through their initiative, the development of local participation in clean-up schemes and other good practices will tie into and influence governmental management.

It may be of interest to note that the Ganga (Ganges), India's longest river, is also considered the sixth worst polluted river in the world. Recently a number of initiatives have been incorporated to clean it up, such as the National Mission for a Clean Ganga, established on August 12, 2011, but since then somewhat dismantled, and other organizational structures are trying to deal with this massive problem.

5. The word is derived from *pashm*, the wool of a certain Asian species of mountain goat, *capra hircas*. See Rutam J. Mehta, *The Handicrafts and Industrial Art of India*, Bombay, 1960, p. 102. See Jamila Brij Bhushun, *The Costumes and Textiles of India*, Bombay, 1958, p. 71:

It is conveyed from Tibet to Rudak on the backs of particularly large sheep.

which is apparently what one has to get when one goes to this part of the world – and it smelled of paraffin. It had to be vigorously rinsed out. You didn't realize that you were in the valley of Kathmandu, surrounded by the highest and the most beautiful mountains in the world, since you couldn't see the mountains at all.[6] Small wonder that the magnificent Mount Everest was thought to be the abode of five celestial nymphs who confer longevity and is usually identified with Gaurisankar, called after Śiva and his consort. It is a place of mysterious legends of the Rishis or Siddhas, the deified saints, while the valleys were the domains of sages and saints who could meditate upon the snow-clad peaks of the sacred Himalayas. But now you had to go out of the valley and climb another thousand meters or so in order to be able to see the actual mountain range.

The city is now a huge, sprawling metropolis of over two and one-half million souls. Over a quarter of the population of Nepal is now concentrated in this urban sprawl. Those little townships ten miles away that I used to visit on a bicycle are all a part of the same city. They are linked up with no boundaries to demarcate borders. The roads are rutted. People walk around with cloth masks around their faces. When I was first there, there was no fear of thieves and pickpockets. But now, we were told that there are gangs of thieves who run around going after innocent tourists. If there was an ideal venue for an international conference to discuss conservation and ecology, this was it. Kathmandu is now an example of how you can ruin the

---

Rudak is the principal rendezvous of merchants who convey it to Leh – the chief-town of Ladakh, where it is purchased by merchants of Kashmir. One quat yields 2 pounds of wool annually, and besides the distinction of quality the wool is sorted according to the colour of the animal, separating it into white and dark or ash-coloured, the former for plain and the latter for dyed fabrics. White wool is twice as expensive as the coloured kind.

Of course, there are "fake" *pashminas*, made of inferior material.

6. This is still the case over fifty years later, both in Nepal and in many Indian cities. I was recently in Rajasthan, and from a fort perched atop a mountain in Udaipur I could hardly see the city in the valley below. And in Jaipur I climbed up to the top of the Sargasul Irisartal tower, which is in the center of town and is 140 feet high, and the whole city was cloaked in a haze-like pall. Cf. below note 105.

house in which you live, the garden you are meant to be enjoying.

My wife and I took a short flight in a small plane to rise above all the smog and be able to see Mount Everest which we flew over. It was only in this way that I could again see something of the beauty and splendor of the Himalayas. I was reminded of the midrash which tells of a ship in which many people are sailing, and one passenger starts to drill a hole under his seat. The others protested loudly saying, "What are you doing? You are making a hole in the bottom of the ship." He replied, "Well, it's only under my own seat." I thought: The earth is, at least so far, the only home we have. How can we maltreat it so!"

So here too I saw the magnificence of royalty, alongside poverty and pollution. And I saw how the "Garden of Eden" had been turned into a polluted urban wasteland.[7]

---

7. And let us compare this with the situation in the "primitive" Nepalese villages of, for example, the Nuers, higher up in the Himalayan Mountains. This is how it is described in *Nepalese Culture: Different Dimensions*, ed. Ram Dayal Rakesh, Kathmandu, 2003, in an article by Tejeswar Babu Gangch, entitled "Newar Cultural Heritage," pp. 119–120:

> Along with the courtyard system, a dug-well could be found even these days [2003] as the water supply system. The deep dug wells were cleaned and even today continue the system once every year on the day of SITHI during the dry summer season falling in late May or beginning of June. The tradition... is yet being followed by the Newars in the Kathmandu valley without argument. The dug wells could be seen and found covered up by the slabs fitted in with the tube well pumps or even [an] electric one. Thus, change appears to be an inevitable feature of cultural enhancement in tune with the innovation made in the society.
>
> The other fact of the water supply system for the commoners' purpose had been met through the waterspouts. The RAJ KULO – the royal canal – was the strong support to keep the waterspouts intact for water supply for common good. The spouts dug deep down the level of roads and the open spaces could even now be seen here and there by the roadsides. As the Raj Kulo system is disturbed by the local settlers in the rural areas and also by the farmers en-route, the *waterspouts are not in running condition now*. But it does not look remote to the possibility of reviving again if the sources were tapped properly.
>
> The river systems were maintained neat and clean. No lavatory drainage was flown down to the river system and, hence, the holy water. People would take morning baths in the river water. No chemical soaps were used either in the

Already then in a document published for that occasion, entitled *Celebration of Sacred Gifts for a Living Planet* (Kathmandu, November 15, 2000), a section called "Recognition of the Threat" (pp. 12–13) brought a few examples of what threatens our oceans, forests, fresh water, atmosphere and biodiversity. In short, all of life:

The planet is warming faster than at any time in the last 10,000 *years, causing the melting of ancient glaciers; also causing fires and the spread of disease with suffering and misery to millions.*

Around 12 million hectares of forests and woodlands are disappearing each year; that amounts to 26 hectares lost every minute. A third of the world's population lives in countries with critically low levels of forest cover and this continues to grow.

At least 60 percent of the world's commercial fisheries are destroyed or fished to the limit.[8] Demand is expected to almost double worldwide in the next decade. Today more than half a billion people in 31 countries experience chronic water shortages and it is estimated that soon one-third of the human population will be in this condition.

Toxins pollute every Ocean and penetrate every food chain.[9] Creatures of the once pristine Polar Regions now carry dangerously high levels of toxins such as insecticides and flame retardants in their bodies – chemicals which disrupt their fertility and growth and could soon threaten humans.

Across the planet species are under threat. Three species of tiger have already become extinct. And extinction is a real possibility for many others – whales and rhinos, to thousands of plant species. Habitat loss,

---

river or in the swimming pools. Fish were abounding in the rivers and in the ponds. Rivers were wide and deep and so pleasant. People would roam about the riversides. The air used to remain fresh and fragrant. *There was no air pollution till after the 1960s.* People old and young would take holy baths early at dawn during December through February having had the group morning walk by and largely known as Ma Madha is the winter season's group morning walk generally observed by the menfolk at the daybreak.

8. See, for example, the state of fishery in Lake Malawi, the ninth biggest lake in the world, and the fourth deepest, in *Ekologiah u-Sevivah* 2/4, Dec. 1995, pp. 219–220.

9. And as to fresh-water lakes, see ibid., "*Mayyim Achurim – Al Matzavam shel Agamim ve-Yamot ba-Olam*" ("*Troubled Waters – Lakes and Inland Seas*"), by Tamar Achiron-Frumkin, ibid., pp. 213–223.

over-hunting, poaching and pollution are just some of the threats.

There are already estimated to be 25 million "environmental refugees" and the number is growing. These accumulated threats have reduced the natural wealth of our planet by about a third in the last 25 years.

And in that same year, two years after Baktapur, I attended a meeting organized by ARC, called "A Celebration of Creation," which took place at The Banqueting House, Whitehall Palace on November 13, 2002. It was in honor of the Jubilee of Her Majesty Queen Elizabeth II, who attended with her husband Prince Philip, Duke of Edinburgh.[10] The highlight of the gathering was the Duke's speech, which we present here as a significant historical document:

---

10. We may note in parentheses that already in 1970, Prince Charles, Prince of Wales, the Duke's son, at the age of twenty-one, in his first key speech on environment at a countryside conference in Cardiff, as the new chairman of the Welsh Countryside Committee, talked about the pollution of air, sea, and rivers, and also of over-population and the problems of waste.

In one particularly prescient passage he said,

> "When you think that each person introduces roughly 2 lb of rubbish per day and there are 55 million of us on this island [i.e. British Isles] using non-returnable bottles and indestructible plastic containers, it is not difficult to imagine the mountains of refuse that we shall have to deal with somehow."

Recently he initiated a new project, the Sustainable Markets Initiative, supported by the World Economic Forum, listing his concerns that,

> The destruction of everything, the uprooting of trees, the draining of wet places, the destruction of all the interesting habitats, the destruction of so much of the centre of our towns and cities, this sort of white heat of progress and technology [is being carried out] to the exclusion of nature and our surroundings.

In it he hopes to bring prominent individuals from both the public and the private sectors together to identify ways to decarbonize the global economy and make the transition to sustainable markets.

When he opened the National Automotive Innovation Centre at Warwick University, he stated that:

> If we want to keep travelling, then we really have no choice other than to decarbonize this essential industry as rapidly as possible.

(See *The Times*, February 19, 2020, p. 15, article by Valentine Low.)

There is a mountain of evidence to suggest that the continuing growth of the human population and its insatiable demands for resources is having a devastating effect on the natural environment. Our demands are simply not sustainable.

There are two basic reasons to campaign to conserve the environment. First because the natural world is there: we depend on it and destroy it at our peril. Second because it is full of interesting things which we ought to try and understand. The Alliance of Religion and Conservation has provided a third reason: that in very simple terms the natural world owes its origin to a sacred being and it is therefore the duty of believers to care for it.

The way the human psyche is constructed means that humans are also concerned about broader issues; about spiritual matters; about the past and future; about the rest of the universe; about why we are here; about how we came to be here. In considering these issues, humanity takes a step away from the purely rational, scientific explanations. It steps into the region of beliefs, convictions and emotions.

We desperately need the conviction of religious belief to guide us in the way we live on, and use, the planet. We have got to learn to balance the economic and scientific realities against the religious demands for responsibility and consideration for the created world. It is not going to be easy, but I am sure that belief and conviction are very powerful motives to care for our planet with all its diversity.

I hope that this event will arouse and disturb your feelings about the future of our planet. I hope it will encourage you to look at the future in a new light and to recognize that, because we are intelligent, we are expected to be more responsible for all life on earth and for everything that makes this life possible.

And all this some two decades ago.

However, very recently I revisited India (November 2019),[11] and,

---

11. In the year 2019 I revisited India four times with my son Yehuda, first to Rajasthan in February, then to Himachal Pradesh in July, and Sikkim in November, and once more, to Tamil Nadu and Kerala in January 2020. We produced photographic

when in Delhi, reputed to be the most polluted of capitals in the world, quite by chance came upon the following article in *The Times of India* (Tuesday, November 26, 2019):

> ## Why not compensate victims of bad air quality: SC asks states
> ### Seeks Details of AQI, Disposal of Garbage
>
> New Delhi: The Supreme Court on Monday asked all the States to explain within six weeks as to why they should not be made liable to pay compensation to persons affected by bad air quality saying it is their bounden duty to provide basic civic amenities, clean air and drinking water to citizens.
>
> The apex court also issued notices to all states seeking various details, including on *air quality index* (AQI), managing air quality and disposing of garbage.
>
> It took serious note of water pollution and asked the *Central Pollution Control Board* (*CPCB*) and other states concerned and their pollution control boards to place before it data on tackling the issue of pollution, sewage and garbage disposal in rivers, including Ganga and Yamuna.
>
> A bench of justices Arun Mishra and Deepak Gupta asked the Centre and Delhi government to sit together and take decision within 10 days with regard to installation of smog towers in Delhi-National Capital Region (NCR) which would help in combating air pollution.
>
> The bench said "right to life of humanity is being endangered" by the bad air quality and water pollution and the states have to deal with the situation as "life span is being shortened" due to this.
>
> "Time has come to require the state governments to explain why they should not be asked to compensate persons who are affected by bad air quality," the bench said and asked the states: "Why liability should not be saddled for the tortious act of government machinery for their failure in discharging their duties."
>
> The SC also took exception that the State and Centre were

---

albums with a running text for each of these trips.

indulging in "blame game" over crucial issue of air and water pollution and asked them to work in tandem for welfare of the people.

The SC said despite various orders being passed by the top court from time to time in the pollution matter, the situation has worsened over the years and authorities have to be blamed as they have not performed their duties.

Referring to various Articles of the Constitution, the bench said it is the duty of state to take care of citizens and their health but the authorities have failed to provide good air quality and pure drinking water to them. It termed as "alarming" the situation of stubble burning in Punjab, Haryana and Uttar Pradesh and said despite its order prohibiting it, burning of crop residues in these states have increased. The bench said "not only the State machinery is responsible but farmers are also responsible for this."

The bench pulled up the chief secretaries of Punjab, Haryana and Uttar Pradesh for their failure to prevent instance of stubble burning despite apex court's order. "Can you treat people like this and permit them to die due to pollution," asked the bench and said life span of millions of citizens has shortened and people are "suffocating" due to pollution in Delhi-NCR.

During the hearing, the bench told solicitor general Tushar Mehta: "Should this be tolerated? Is this not worse than internal war? Why are people in this gas chamber? If it is so then better finish them with explosives. If it goes on like this then it would be better to go rather than suffer from diseases like cancer."

"You open the door of your house and see the situation (of pollution). No State wants to take any measure which is anti-popular," an anguished bench said. The SC took *suo moto* cognisance of the controversy regarding supply of alleged unsafe drinking water in the national capital and said it is the duty of the State to provide drinkable water to the citizens.

Chief Secretary of Delhi raised the issue regarding governance in the national capital and division of power between the Centre and Delhi government. "The problem of governance, if any, cannot come in the way in dealing with such matter," the bench said and asked the concerned authorities to sit and work out together to find out how to improve air quality and how to provide safe drinking water to the people. The bench criticized the Centre and Delhi government for "politicizing" the issue of water pollution and said they cannot indulge in this any "blame game" as people would suffer in this situation.

The bench said that six cities in the country, out of which three are in UP [Uttar Pradesh], are more polluted than Delhi and issues like air quality, safe drinking water and garbage disposal was virtually affecting every part of the country. "It appears to be a case of lost priority," the bench said, adding, "In India, this can be done but there is lack of proper planning."

The bench asked the Delhi government to appraise it about the steps taken with regard to anti-smog gun which sprays atomized water 50 metres in the air to bring down pollutants.[12]

---

12. Apropos of "smog" (as opposed to "fog"), I remember distinctly the great "smog" of December 1952, which lasted in London for some three consecutive days, and during which between 4,000–6,000 people died, and over 100,000 required medical treatment. London, being in a sort of bowl, surrounded on all sides by hills, during a period of anticyclone and also a windless time, a heavy pall settled over all of London. I remember that looking out of the kitchen window onto our courtyard and coal-shed; just about two yards from the window, the coal-shed was not visible. Doors were locked, windows were shut down, no one could go on the streets. There were no shops open, no buses, and London was paralyzed. One could not see one's hand held out in front of one's eyes. The effect was one of grey darkness. Only after three days, when the "smog" receded, did life return to normal, and the government instituted new measures, which eventually eradicated "smog," which was caused by a heavy load of industrial pollutants settling over the city.

The Ralbag (he is R. Levi ben Gershom, Provence, 1288–1344), in his commentary to *Exodus* 10:21, describing the plague of darkness which also lasted three days, and was something that was palpably felt – *ve-yamesh hoshech* – writes as follows:

> ... and they were forced to stop up their nose and mouth so that the thick smokey (*av ha-kitori*) [air], which the Lord in a wonderous fashion initiated, should not enter their body which would kill them ....

This accurately describes smog.

There is a tradition that Abraham ibn Ezra (1089–1164), when he was jailed in India, experienced a *three-day* fog of such intensity that there was palpable darkness, and so he too explained the verse in *Exodus* ibid. And through it is extremely doubtful

And in the same newspaper, a few pages further we read:

"22% groundwater dried up or critical"
Govt Report Seeks Change In Extraction
Vishwa.Mohan@timesgroup.com

NEW DELHI: Almost 22% of groundwater (assessed units)

---

that he was ever in India, he does attest to having experienced extreme dense fog at sea on a number of occasions. He also mentions Indian vegetarianism in his commentary to *Exodus* 8:22. See his (R. Mosheh ben Nahman, 1194–1270, Catalonia) extended commentary to *Exodus* ibid. and that of the Ramban to verse 23 ibid.

See note 75 above, though the fogs encountered in India were not quite so thick.

The effect was somewhat similar to that of a sandstorm without the stingish whiplash effect. See *The Travels of Marco Polo*, Yule-Cordier ed., London. 1903, vol. 1, p. 98:

> And you must know that when these Caranoas wish to make a plundering incursion, they have certain devilish enchantments whereby they do bring darkness over the face of day, insomuch that you can scarcely discern your comrade riding beside you; and this darkness they will cause to extend over a space of seven days' journey. They know the country thoroughly, and ride abreast, keeping near one another, sometimes to the number of 10,000, at other times more or fewer. In this way they extend across the whole plain that they are going to harry, and catch every living thing that they are going to harry, and catch every living thing that is found outside of the towns and villages; man, woman, or beast, nothing can escape them! The young men and the women they sell for slaves in other countries; thus the whole land is ruined, and has become well-nigh a desert.

Yule (p. 105) explains this "enchanted darkness" as follows:

> The *Magical darkness* which Marco ascribes to the evil arts of the Karaunas is explained by Khanikoff from the phenomenon of *Dry Fog*, which he has often experienced in Khorasan, combined with the *Dust Storm* with which we are familiar in Upper India. In Sind these phenomena often produce a great degree of darkness. During a battle fought between the armies of Sindh and Kachh in 1762, such a fog came on, obscuring the light of day for some six hours, during which the armies were intermixed with one another and fighting desperately. When the darkness dispersed they separated, and the consternation of both parties was so great at the events of the day that both made a precipitate retreat. In 1844 this battle was still spoken of with wonder. (*J. Bomb. Br. R. A. S.* I. 423.)

Ours, though not magical and without sand, was no less disastrous.

in the country has either dried up or is in the "critical" and "over-exploited" categories,[13] Jal Shakti (water resources) minister Gajendra Singh Shekhawat said as he emphasised the need to focus on efficient use of water resources and noted that 10% of water saving in the agriculture sector now would make it available for all users for the next 50 years.

The "Dynamic Ground Water Resources of India" report of the

---

13.   During that same visit to Sikkim, I saw the following notice-board outside one of the monasteries. It advised as follows:

TEN WAYS TO CONSERVE WATER
IN YOUR AREA TO HELP THE ENVIRONMENT

1. Turn off the tap while brushing your teeth.
2. Fill up a bottle of water and put it in toilet cistern.
3. Fix dripping taps, and repair broken or leaking pipes.
4. Using a bucket to bathe rather than taking showers will save a lot of water.
5. Use water filters rather than bottled water.
6. Install a solar-run water filter to provide water continuously.
7. Fill the kettle only with the amount of water you need.
8. In dry areas, harvest rainwater.
9. In dry areas, water gardens in the early morning or late evening.
10. Reuse the water that is offered daily on all monastery altars.

May I be like the Earth,
providing the air, the ground, the water, and everything
she provides that is our sacred source of life.
– 17th Karmapa

His Holiness the 17th Ogyen Trinley Dorje Gwalwang Karmapa, born 1985 in the Lhatok region of East Tibet of a semi-nomadic family, is head of the Karma Kagy School, one of the four schools of Buddhism in Tibet. He developed a network of Tibetan Buddhist monasteries in India which stress environmental protection, and function as part of the World Wildlife Fund, Sacred Earth: Faiths for Conservation program.

In an interview in 2015, with Yale Environment 360, he stated that:

… the Environmental emergency that we face is not just a scientific issue, nor is it just a political issue, it is also a moral issue. And therefore all of us approaching this issue have to pick our share of responsibility to find and implement solutions….

Central Ground Water Board (CGWB) showed that 1,499 out of 6,881 assessed units (blocks/mandals/taluks) in 2017 came under "over-exploited" (1,186 units) and "critical" (313 units) categories. ... The report sought immediate change in extraction pattern of groundwater and surface water interventions.[14]

With annual extraction of groundwater in these units exceeding annual replenishment, Shekhawat told TOI on Friday that it was

---

14. Of course this is not only true of India, but the world over. Y. Neril and L. Dee, in their *Eco Bible*, vol. 1: *An Ecological Commentary on Genesis and Exodus*, pp. 101–102, write as follows:

PRECIOUS GROUNDWATER

Exodus 2:16 – *Now the priest of Midian had seven daughters. They came to draw water and filled the troughs to water their father's flock.*
Rashi (ad loc.) explains, "The troughs were channels of running water (that were] made in the ground." This description indicates a sustainable rainwater collection system built in the desert. (Deserts are not all sand.) Many ancient civilizations had advanced methods of rainwater captured in the desert providing a key source of water. By digging wells above an underground aquifer, people could draw water up with buckets. By digging channels, desert dwellers could direct local streams into the well system, to top up the groundwater when it ran low, (Brian Beckers, Jonas Berking, and Brig Schutt, "Ancient Water Harvesting Methods in the Drylands of the Mediterranean and Western Asia," *Journal For Ancient Studies* 2, Sept. 2013, pp. 145–164. [The Nabateans were, of course, masters in this field. D. S.]). Rashi seems to be alluding to these practices in this commentary.

Today, depletion of groundwater is a global concern. Many regions are experiencing recurrent water stress, including the Sahara, South Africa, Australia, India, Pakistan, and Northeast China. It is estimated that over two billion people, or 35 percent of the world population, suffer from severe water stress.

In these regions and others, people often use groundwater as an additional water source. As one study notes, "If groundwater extraction exceeds groundwater replenishment for an extended time, the resulting lowering of groundwater levels can have devastating effects on... ecosystems and lead to land collapse and saltwater intrusion. Current levels of groundwater depletion are more than 100 percent higher than 1960 and are contributing 0.8 mm per year toward sea-level rise" (Yoshihide Wada et al., "Global Depletion of Ground Resources," *Geophysical Research Letters* 37, no. 20, 2010. This is about 25 percent of total seawater rise.).

Humanity is extracting water unsustainably, and at some point, many regions will exhaust underground water supplies that have been a key source for millennia.

time to improve "demand side" management by taking multiple measures instead of only managing "supply side" of water resources.

"Agriculture sector consumes nearly 89% of available water resources in India. We really need to help farmers and create awareness among them so that they can move towards water use efficiency measures such as drip and sprinkler irrigation," he said.

The minister, who visited Israel last week to take part in the WATEC conference, said there were many things which India could learn from Israel's experience and replicate. He said works on aquifer (underground layer of water-bearing rock) mapping was going on at full pace to delineate and characterise groundwater aquifers and develop suitable management plans. "Aquifer mapping of all 256 water stressed districts (covering nearly 5,500 blocks) will be completed by March. It will help us make farmers and other users aware of water availability and tell them how they should use it," Shekhawat said.

And on the same page:

Forest cover in W Ghats to fall to 10% in 10 years: Study
Viju.B@timesgroup.com

Kochi: The evergreen forest cover in Western Ghats is set to decrease drastically and will touch an abysmal 10% in 10 years, a study reveals.

The study has come as a grim warning to Kerala, especially against the backdrop of the state facing floods and landslides in two consecutive years. The study conducted by T V Ramachandra, director, Centre for Ecological studies, Indian Institute of Science-Bangalore, and S Bharath, Centre for Sustainable Technologies, highlighted the urgent need to conserve the last remaining core forest areas in the region.

"The increase in monoculture plantations such as acacia, eucalyptus, teak, rubber, developmental projects and agriculture expansions are the major drivers of land-use changes. The result is that the edges of forest are becoming more prominent due to sustained anthropogenic pressure," Ramachandra said.

The researchers have made a detailed study on the change in forest cover over the past 23 years. The Western Ghats region had 16.21% evergreen forest cover in 1985, which was reduced to 11.3% in 2018. The region now has 17.92% plantation area, 37.53% agriculture and 4.88% mining and built-up area.

Large-scale changes in agriculture and built-up cover are noticed in eastern Kerala, Tamil Nadu and Maharashtra areas in the Western Ghats.... etc.

And just a few days later, when I got back to Israel, I found the following article in the *Jerusalem Post* (Monday, December 2, 2019), p. 12:

UN chief: War against nature must stop
By ISLA BINNIE

MADRID (Reuters) – The world must stop a "war against nature" and find more political will to combat climate change, UN Secretary-General Antonio Guterres said on Sunday, the eve of a two-week global climate summit.

Around the world, extreme weather ranging from wildfires to floods is being linked to manmade global warming, putting pressure on the summit to strengthen the implementation of the 2015 Paris Agreement on limiting the rise in temperature.

"Our war against nature must stop, and we know that it is possible," Guterres said ahead of the Dec. 2–13 summit.

"We simply have to stop digging and drilling and take advantage of the vast possibilities offered by renewable energy and nature-based solutions." Cuts in emissions of greenhouse gases – mostly from burning carbon-based fossil fuels – that have been agreed so far under the Paris deal are not enough to limit temperature rises to a goal of between 1.5 and 2 degrees Celsius (2.7–3.6 Fahrenheit) above pre-industrial levels.

Many countries are not even meeting those commitments, and political will is lacking, Guterres said.

President Donald Trump for his part started withdrawing the United States from the Paris Agreement, while the deforestation of the Amazon basin – a crucial carbon reservoir – is accelerating and China has tilted back toward building more coal-fired power plants.

Seventy countries have committed to a goal of "carbon neutrality" or "climate neutrality" by 2050.

This means they would balance out greenhouse emissions, for instance through carbon capture technology or by planting trees.

But Guterres said these pledges were not enough.

"We also see clearly that the world's largest emitters are not pulling their weight," he said, "and without them, our goal is unreachable."

Last year's U.N. climate summit in Poland yielded a framework for reporting and monitoring emissions pledges and updating plans for further cuts. But sticking points remain, not least over an article on how to put a price on emissions, and so allow them to be traded.

"I don't even want to entertain the possibility that we do not agree on article 6," Guterres said. "We are here to approve guidelines to implement article 6, not to find excuses not to do it."

Bank of England Governor Mark Carney has accepted an invitation to become U.N. special envoy on climate action and climate finance from January 1, Guterres said.

And most recently in Geneva the World Health Organization (WHO) discussed the numerous harmful effects of climate change. I quote from the *Jerusalem Post* report from December 8, 2019, p. 2:

GENEVA (Reuters) – Climate change is harming human health as more people suffer from heat stress, extreme weather and mosquito-borne diseases including malaria, the World Health Organization (WHO) said on Tuesday.

The U.N. agency, in a report issued a day after a climate summit began in Madrid, urged governments to meet ambitious targets to reduce heat-trapping carbon emissions saying it could save a million lives a year through lower air pollution alone.

"Health is paying the price of the climate crisis. Why? Because our lungs, our brains, our cardiovascular system is very much suffering from the causes of climate change which are overlapping very much with the causes of air pollution," Maria Neira, Director of WHO's Department of Environment, Climate Change and Health, told a news briefing.

Yet less than 1% of international financing for climate action goes to the health sector, she said, calling it "absolutely outrageous."

Global temperatures could rise sharply this century with "wide-ranging and destructive" consequences after greenhouse gas emissions hit record levels last year, international climate experts warned last week.

"WHO considers that climate change is potentially the greatest health threat of the 21st Century," said WHO expert Diarmid Campbell-Lendrum.

"The reason for that is that unless we cut our carbon emissions, then we will continue to undermine our food supplies, our water supplies and our air quality – everything that we need to maintain the good health of our populations," he said.

The same sources cause air pollution and climate change, Campbell-Lendrum said, adding: "So about two-thirds of the exposure to outdoor air pollution is from burning of fossil fuels."

"WHO estimates that over 7 million people a year die from indoor and outdoor air pollution.[15] That is where the big win is," he said.

Some 101 countries responded to WHO's survey about the risks from climate change – but not big players including India and the United States.

"Over two-thirds have assessed that they have increased risks from heat stress, from injury and death from extreme weather, from food, water and vector-borne diseases and those range from everything from cholera to malaria," Campbell-Lendrum said.

(Stephanie Nebehay)

And when speaking of health and pollution and costs involved, Tzvi

---

15. On some of the causes and effects of air pollution, see Zev Naveh, "*Hashpaat Mezahamei Avir al ha-Sevivah ve-al-Briyut ha-Adam*," ("*The Environmental and Health Effects of Air Pollutants...*"), *Ekologiah u-Sevivah* 4/4, May 1998, pp. 189–219 (with rich bibliographies).

Bisk, in the same issue, p. 10, writes as follows:

> The 2017 Lancet Commission on Pollution and Health reported the global cost of pollution as "$4.6 trillion per year – 6.2% of global economic output." Climate-change deniers and fossil-fuel interests argue against solar and wind power and electric cars because of subsidies. But these direct subsidies pale in comparison to the monstrous indirect security costs and pollution-damage subsidies to fossil fuels.
>
> According to Steve Cohen of the Earth Institute at Columbia University, "Between 1970 and 2017 the US invested about $65 billion in air pollution control and received about $1.5 trillion in benefits."
>
> According to futurist Ramez Naam, "Every dollar spent on increased efficiency of buildings saves three dollars in energy bills... efficiency investments could cut energy use in half... with a net savings of $400 billion per year."
>
> Buildings consume 40% of total energy and produce 36% of greenhouse emissions in America and Europe. Instituting a policy of government-backed mortgages to Retrofit America or Retrofit Europe would have greater environmental impact than eliminating aviation, meat and maritime pollution combined, and would benefit the economy. Retrofits raise a property's market value by 2%–5%, while energy savings pay for the mortgage. The Empire State Building retrofit lowered energy bills by 40%. The Sears Tower retrofit cut energy for heating by 50% and electricity by 80%.
>
> Retrofitting would create tens of thousands of well-paying jobs and billions in profits, satisfying both business and labor. Banks could develop retrofit mortgage products for existing home and business owners. R&D for energy efficient technologies would generate additional contributions to universities and research institutes. Massive grass roots support for greening America and Europe would be generated.
>
> In short, such a policy would make people richer not poorer. Environmentalism will have triumphed when environmental billionaires replace silicon-valley billionaires in the media and average

citizens perceive it as raising their standard of living and quality of life rather than having to "make sacrifices."

These are but random newspaper cuttings from various geographic areas around the globe which much by chance I came across, and which could be greatly multiplied. But these should suffice to make clear the point that air and water pollution, diminishing pure water sources,[16] deforestation, global warming and such are a global challenge of vast dimensions.

Obviously we could bring any number of additional statements from world leaders warning us of the ecological changes facing the globe if we do not radically change our modern behavior and lifestyle. But let us see whether our Jewish sources, even though they be of earlier millennia, in any way relate to our contemporary situation.

But first I would like to recall a pigmy legend of a little boy who finds a bird with a beautiful song in the desert. He asks his father to bring food for his bird, but his father does not want to feed a mere bird, so he kills it. And the legend says that the man killed the bird, and with the bird he killed the song, and with the song, himself. He dropped dead, completely dead, and was dead forever (Joseph Campbell, *The Power of Myth*, with Bill Mayers, New York, 1981). The story is an allegory of what happens when human beings destroy nature and their environment: they destroy their world, they destroy nature and the revelations of nature and they destroy themselves.[17]

But now returning to our Jewish sources, the book of *Genesis* records a series of ecological disasters. The Garden of Eden was the supreme example of ecological balance, with all elements of nature living in complete harmony. Nonetheless, even at this initial stage of humanity, Adam is warned by God:

Of every tree in the garden thou mayest freely eat. But of the tree of knowledge of good and evil thou shall not eat of it; for in the day

---

16. Such as the shrinking of Lake Baikal in Russia and Lake Mali in Africa, as random examples.

17. See Jash Raj Subba, *Mythology of the People of Sikkim*, New Delhi, 2009, p. 173.

| that thou eatest thereof thou shalt surely die (*Genesis* 2:16–17).

The mere fact that he was prohibited from partaking of one single element in the Garden of Paradise, was intended to indicate to him that he was not the master, the owner, of the Garden, but only enjoyed it by the grace of God. And when he and Eve transgress this prohibition, being seduced by the serpent who assures them that "God doth know that in the day ye eat thereof, then your eyes will be opened, and ye shall be as God, knowing good and evil" (ibid., 3:5), and thinking themselves of sufficient authority to gainsay the order of God, they are ejected out of the verdant Garden of Paradise, and driven into a land "cursed" with "thorns and thistles" (*Genesis* 3:17–18). Some time later due to mankind's evil practices, a great flood sweeps over the earth (ibid., 6:5–7:22).[18] And then, human hubris brought about what appears to have been an earthquake destroying the cities of Sodom and Gomorrah and others, as a result of the evil social practices of the local inhabitants (ibid., 19:1–30). In the days of Abraham there was a great famine (ibid., 26:19), and so too in the time of Isaac (ibid.), no doubt also as punishment for the people's lack of fear of God (ibid., 20:11). And these "ecological disasters," to use contemporary terminology,

---

18. In *Midrash ha-Gadol* to *Genesis* 6:7, ed. M. Margaliot, Jerusalem, 1947, pp. 142–143, we read:

> Said R. Yohanan: To what is this similar. [It is like unto] a king who had an orchard in which he planted all manner of edible fruit trees. He gave it over into the hands of a tenant that would [look after it and] enhance it. But that tenant was lazy, and not only did he not do his work, but he [actually] ruined it. Said the King: I gave over to you my orchard so that you would enhance it, [but surely not] to ruin it. What did the king do? He set it on fire. So too, the Holy One blessed be He created His world and included in it all manner of sources of pleasure, and handed it over to mankind to benefit from it and to enhance it. There arose the generation of the Flood and angered [God] and ruined [His world], and denied [His existence], saying, "What is the Almighty, that we should serve Him? (*Job* 21:15). Forthwith, the Holy One blessed be He said, "I will blot out man [whom I created] from the face of the earth" (*Genesis* ibid.).

This amply describes what we are doing in our own days, and what may well be the consequences if we do not mend our ways.

were, according to the Bible the result of humankind's unethical and flawed behavior.

Indeed, the Bible is replete with passages indicating the relationship between mankind's ethical and religious behavior and its effect upon nature. See, for example, *Leviticus* 26:3:

> (3) If ye walk in My statutes and keep My commandments and do them. (4) Then I will give you your rain in due season, and the land shall yield her increase, and the trees of the fields shall yield their fruit. (5) And your threshing shall reach unto the vintage, and the vintage shall reach unto sowing time; and ye shall eat your bread to the full, and dwell in your land safely....
>
> (14) But if ye will not hearken unto Me, and not do all these commandments. (15) And if ye despise My statutes, or in your soul abhor My judgements, so that ye will not do all My commandments, but ye break My covenant ....
>
> (31) And I will make your cities waste, and bring your sanctuaries into desolation, and I will not smell the savor of your sweet odors. (32) And I will bring the land into desolation .... (34) Then shall the land enjoy her sabbaths as long as it lies desolate ....
>
> (40) If they shall confess their iniquity, and the iniquity of their fathers .... (42) Then I will remember My covenant with Jacob, and My covenant with Isaac, and also My covenant with Abraham will I remember; and I will remember the land. (43) The land also shall be left of them, and shall enjoy her Sabbaths....

Or in *Deuteronomy* 29:21–24:

> (21) And that generation to come of your children that shall rise up after you, and the stranger that come from a far land shall say, when they see the plagues of that land, and the sicknesses which the Lord hath laid upon it. (22) And that the whole land thereof is brimstone,[19] and salt, and burning; that it is not sown, nor beareth,

---

19. See Levi Ginzberg, *Halachah ve-Aggadah*, Tel-Aviv, 1960, pp. 205–219, article entitled "*Mabul shel Aish.*"

nor any grass growth therein, like that overthrow of Sodom and Gomorrah, Admah and Zeboim, which the Lord overthrew in His anger, and in His wrath. (23) Even all the nations shall say, Wherefore hath the Lord done thus unto this land? What meaneth the heat of this great anger? (24) Then man shall say, Because they have forsaken the covenant of the Lord God of their fathers, which He made with them when He brought them forth out of Egypt....

And, of course, the second paragraph of the *Shema* (*Deuteronomy* 11:13–17):

(13) If you indeed heed My commandments with which I charge you today, to love the Lord your God and worship Him with all your heart and with all your soul. (14) I will give rain in your land in its season, the early and late rain; and you shall gather in your grain, wine and oil. (15) I will give grass in your field for your cattle, and you shall eat and be satisfied. (16) Be careful lest your heart be tempted and you go astray and worship other gods, bowing down to them. (17) Then the Lord's anger will flare against you and He will close the heavens so that there will be no rain, the land will not yield its crops; and you will perish swiftly from the good land that the Lord is giving you ...[20]

One could adduce plentiful additional such quotations from throughout the Pentateuch and Prophets, etc., but these quotes make the point manifestly clear.

In our days our societal "sins" are, perhaps, of a different nature. Nonetheless, they, too, are the result of short-term hedonism, pursuit of monetary gain – the capitalistic ideology justifying such attitudes – and other such characteristics of contemporary society.

Indeed, this "short-term hedonism" was dramatically described by the great second-century Palestinian sage R. Shimon bar Yohai in his

---

20. See George Foot Moore, *Judaism in the First Centuries of the Christian Era*, vol. 1, *The Age of the Tannaim*, Cambridge, MA, 1927, pp. 460–473, "Sin and its Consequences."

caustic criticism of Roman civilization. I quote the Talmudic source (*B. Shabbat* 33b) as it is formulated by Abraham Joshua Heschel in his inimitable style. It is part of his polemic discussion with his contemporary, colleague R. Yehudah:

> Rabbi Judah ben Ilai, Rabbi Jose, and Rabbi Shimon ben Yohai were sitting together, and with them was a man called Judah ben Gerim. Rabbi Judah opened the discussion and said:
>
> – How fine are the works of this people (the Romans)! They have made roads and market places, they have built bridges, they have erected bathhouses.
>
> Rabbi Jose was silent.
>
> Then Rabbi Shimeon ben Yohai replied and said:
>
> – All that they made they made for themselves. They made roads and market places to put harlots there; they built bridges to levy tolls for them; they erected bathhouses to delight their bodies …[21]

Thus, governments, in order to satisfy their constituents, seek the short-term betterment and the comforts of society, but also, all too often at a great ecological cost. The exhaustion of natural resources, be they mineral, such as coal and oil, or vegetable, such as the decimation of great forests, or the at times uncontrolled use of dangerous elements, nuclear and even solar, may all be considered the "sins" of our generation. So ultimately the sin is not only against mankind, but, even more fundamentally, against the earth, and the earth is, at least so far, the only home we have. I am again reminded of the *midrash* about a ship in which many people were sailing. When one of the passengers started to drill a hole underneath his seat, the others began to protest: "What are you doing? You are making a hole in the bottom of the ship." He replied, "Well, it's only under my seat." And so when I came to Kathmandu, I

---

21. J. Heschel, *The Earth is the Lord's and the Sabbath*, Cleveland, New York and Philadelphia, 1963, p. 35 and see his analysis, ibid., pp. 36–48.

This short polemic debate highlights the nature of the argumentation, also expressing a rational justification for this "short-term" approach.

came back to a completely different place.[22] You couldn't see the sky. It was overcast, darkened by dirty, smelly clouds.[23] The Bagmati was a cesspool and very much smaller that I had known it to be previously. It had shrunk to a size smaller than the Jordan, and it reeked.[24] You couldn't see the mountains at all.[25] You had to go out of the valley and climb another thousand meters or so in order to be able to see the actual mountains.

The city is now a huge, sprawling metropolis of over two and one-

---

22. I describe my visits to Nepal and Kathmandu and the great changes that had taken place in the interval between those visits – some fifty years – in my forthcoming book *From Yeshivat Hevron to Delhi: A Partial Memoir* (working title).

23. I was reminded of the verse in *Isaiah* 51:6, "…for the heavens shall vanish away like smoke…"

24. In Sikkim, at the entrance to a monastery I saw in a recent visit there, was the following signpost put up by the K. H. 17th Gyalwang Karmapa:

CONSERVE RIVERS, LAKES, AND WETLANDS

1. Don't throw garbage into rivers!

2. In areas near a water source, designate a boundary and keep the area clean of waste products.

3. Keep cattle and other livestock away from the actual water source.

4. Plant vegetation on the banks of rivers and lakes to protect them and to improve the quality of the waters.

5. If monastic grounds are used for farming, encourage organic farming using few pesticides and fertilizers.

6. Protect nearby wetlands from agricultural expansion.

7. Recreate wetlands.

8. If building a connecting road, don't place it over a river.

Regretfully, this message has made little impact on most Indian rivers, especially within an urban context.

25. This is still the case over fifty years later, both in Nepal and in many Indian cities. See above note 86.

Compare what Toni Hagen wrote in his *Nepal: The Kingdom of the Himalayas*, in the preface to his second edition (Oxford, 1971) comparing Nepal from his past visit from 1951 to 1961, and his second visit in 1968, where he describes how "Shangrila" to Kathmandu is vanishing fast as a tasteless forest of ugly concrete constructions along streets strewn with rubbish and hashish addicts.

half million souls. Over a quarter of the population of Nepal is now concentrated in this urban sprawl. Those little townships ten miles away that I used to visit on a bicycle are all a part of the same city linked up with no boundaries to demarcate their borders. The roads are rutted. People walk around with cloth masks around their faces.

> Traffic on the streets is a rumpus of pollution belching two, three and four-wheel vehicles wending their way around a mess of people and a variety of animals.... The collection of ancient vehicles, low-quality fuel and lack of emission controls makes the streets of Kathmandu particularly dirty and unpleasant. Traffic rules do exist, but are rarely enforced.... Consider bringing a face-mask to filter out the dust and emission particles if you plan to ride a bicycle in Kathmandu.

So wrote Stan Armington in Lonely Planet's *Trekking in the Nepal Himalayas*, 1994, p. 68, and this is much the same in the present day.

If there was an ideal venue for an international conference to discuss conservation and ecology, this was it. Kathmandu is now an example of how you can ruin the house in which you live, the garden you are meant to be enjoying.

But closer to home, in the aftermath of the collapse of a bridge over the Yarkon River on July 14, 1997, and the death from asphyxia of four athletes resulting from the high pollution of the river, a governmental commission and citizen groups initiated clean-up projects.

Dror Avisar, chief hydrologist for the Israel Union for Environmental Defense stated: "Almost every major river inside Israel is polluted" (*Los Angeles Times*, August 9, 1997).

The pollution was mainly due to untreated sewage, storm runoff, hazardous chemicals, industrial waste, and other pollutants (*Jerusalem Post*, May 10, 2009). Contamination levels in the Yarkon River are finally in decline thanks to the channeling of highly purified wastewater into the river from a newly opened purification plant.[26]

---

26. For a discussion on the problems of pollution and private or corporate responsibility in Jewish halachic sources, see Meir Tamari, *Kesef Kasher*, Jerusalem,

The Kidron Valley through which sewage is channeled from Jerusalem down to the Dead Sea is destroying the nature of the area, leaving the surrounding area with a terrible stench and also polluting other water sources in the area.

Haifa Bay remains to this day one of the most polluted places in Israel, such that about 900,000 people in the city and the surrounding metropolitan area are being exposed to carcinogenic pollutants.

These are but a few of the examples of the environmental dangers still facing us here in Israel, despite governmental "clean-up" projects.

The pollution I experienced in Baktapur and Kathmandu, and knowledge of our own environmental problems, reminded me of the many regulations in our halachic literature aimed at preventing such pollution and contamination. Let me quote here Moshe Zemer's article "Ecology as a Mitzvah," in *The Environment in Jewish Law* (above note 66) chapter 2, pp. 28–29, which summarizes several of these directives:

> It was forbidden to make a permanent threshing floor less than 50 cubits (28 meters or 30.6 yards) from the border of a town, so that the wind would not carry the chaff when the owner winnows, that is, clears away the chaff from the grain. Graveyards, carcasses and tanneries must be kept 50 cubits from the town. A tannery may be set up only on the east side of a town, because the east wind is mild and reduces the unpleasantness of odors produced by tanning the hides (Rambam, *Hilchot Shechenim* 10:2).
>
> If someone does construction work on a threshing floor or a privy on his property that raises dust or particles of earth or causes a stench, one must do so at a distance so that the dust and the stench will not reach his neighbors, even if an ordinary wind is carrying these damaging elements (ibid. 11:1).
>
> We see here that the builder must take every precaution to prevent harm to others, even though the work he is doing is at quite a distance and is caused in part by the wind, over which he has no control. We might apply this principle to the large factories of our day that are at a distance from centers of population, but nevertheless dump

quantities of toxic industrial waste that cause great damage near and far.

How much the more can this ruling be applied to nuclear power plants and their waste disposal? Here is a question of responsibility to one's neighbors, to society, and to natural resources like forests, mineral deposits, and rivers. The recently poisoned Danube, which may be permanently ruined, is a case in point.

The Talmud relates that ten regulations were ordained for Jerusalem (*B. Baba Kama* 82b). One was the prohibition to make garbage heaps [in the city], because reptiles are found in them. Another is forbidding the use of lime and pottery kilns because of the smoke which Rashi says, blackens the buildings around. This smoke[27] had a deleterious effect on the residents of the Holy City....

One may add Maimonides' ruling in his *Hilchot Shechenim* 11:1 (followed by the *Shulhan Aruch, Hoshen Mishpat* 155:34), which reads as follows:

He who is involved in ... work which causes dust, dirt and the like, has to distance it so that the dirt or the stench of a toilet, or the dust, not reach his neighbor, so that he will not be harmed by them. Even if there was a wind which aids him in his work, but carries dirt, or the chaff of flax, or husks, and the like, and carries them to his neighbor [i.e. this is not a direct result of his activities], he, nonetheless, is obligated to distance it so that it not reach [his neighbor] and do him harm. [And this distancing is mandatory] even [if the damage is caused] by a normal breeze, [even though in most cases a person is not held responsible for damage caused by a normal breeze...].[28]

---

27. But contemporary industrial "smoke" has many additional toxic chemical components in partical form which are damaging to the health of humans, animals, fish, and fowl. See W. E. Westman, *Ecology, Impact Assessment and Environment Planning*, New York, 1985, see below near note 163.

28. This is based on *M. Baba Batra* 2:1–3. See *Responsa of the Rashba*, 2:65, who writes in response to a question regarding the prevention of smoke causing damage to neighbors:

Furthermore, the Talmud tells us that it is difficult to live in a big city (*B. Ketubot* 110b). How did the sages reach this determination? Rashi (ad loc.) explains in his commentary: "Everyone comes to live there in overcrowded conditions. The houses are so close to each other that there is no air to breathe. But in small towns there are gardens and orchards next to their homes and they enjoy fresh air." Our sages in the thirteenth century considered urban living to be incompatible with maintaining quality of life.

But nowadays pollution is no longer limited to the big cities alone, and even the countryside is frequently covered over with a grey pall.

Philip J. Bentley (apud Jacob and Zemer, ibid., pp. 48–50) brings further evidence of rabbinic concern for the quality of air and the water supply in urban areas:

> Within residential areas there were limits placed on the operation of various trades and businesses. Some businesses were barred from residential areas and were required to operate where they would not pollute the air or the water supply of the city's residents.[29] These included tanneries,

---

The *hachamim* [sages] of the Talmud said that one has to remove a furnace which causes smoke and therefore damage to neighbours. This, however, refers only to constant or excessive smoke, such as that which is produced by industrial furnaces. [This injunction to remove a furnace that causes damage would seem highly relevant to the ecological problems caused by "smoke-stack" industries such as steel and coal.] It does not apply to the smoke created by the normal activity of a household. Were this not the case, nobody would be able to build a house and make a fire beneath his food.

Meir Tamari, in his *With All Your Possessions: Jewish Ethics and Economic Life*, New York/London, 1987, p. 286, explains:

In other words, there exists a concept of damage caused by the normal activities of people, without which it would not be possible to continue any kind of human activity. In such a case the property rights of other individuals will have to be abrogated.

29. Bentley, ibid., pp. 50–51, brings the following interesting question put before the Ri Migash (R. Yosef ibn Migash):

threshing floors, and kilns (*M. Baba Batra* 2:8–9; *B. Baba Kama* 82b). One excerpt from the Mishnah can serve as example of these restrictions:

> *None may dig a cistern near his fellow's cistern; nor may he dig a trench, vault, water-channel, or washer man's pool unless it is three handbreadths away from his fellow's wall; and he must plaster it with lime. Piles of olive refuse, manure, salt, lime or stones may not be kept within three handbreadths of his fellow's wall and he must plaster it with lime. Seeds or a plough or urine may not be kept within three handbreadths of the wall. The hand-mill may not be kept at such a distance that the wall is less than three handbreadths from the lower millstone or four from the upper millstone; and an oven may not be kept at such a distance that the wall is less than three handbreadths from the belly of the oven or four from the rim (M. Baba Batra 2:1).*

Regulations like these indicate that population density was much like that of modern cities. They also reflect the fact that many trades were carried on at home. It was necessary to set limitations on what could be done in a private home or shop. Hazardous materials, vibration – and heat-producing machinery, and installations were limited in order to maintain safety for a neighborhood community. Even noise pollution was considered (ibid. 2:3).

[He] was asked to decide a case between Reuben and Simon. Sewage from both of their buildings flowed into the same underground cistern, but Simon's building was downhill from Rueben's and was closer to the cistern. When the cistern filled Simon asked Reuben to share in the expense of emptying it. Reuben refused saying that the cistern was Simon's problem. Ibn Migash decided in favor of Simon on the basis of a Talmudic principle that says that people living on higher ground are obligated to help people living below them in clearing out sewers and storm drains [see *Baba Metzia* 108a]. The fact that the cistern both used was on or near Simon's property did not obligate him to deal with effluvia from Reuben's building. Everyone who benefits from a public facility holds a responsibility for maintaining it. If those on higher ground were to refuse to help clean the cesspool because it was not on their property, and those who lived over or near it could not manage it themselves or were unwilling to, eventually no one would have a place to drain their sewage. The entire community themselves therefore shares the responsibility and the burden of maintaining public works. Simon must allow Reuben's sewage to collect beneath his building, and Reuben must help pay for its upkeep.

Jewish tradition also emphasizes a love of trees.[30] The sages felt kindly towards trees and were concerned for their welfare.[31] Thus in *B. Sukkah* 29b the rabbis stated that among the four things that cause eclipses [which constitute ominous omens] is the "cutting down of good trees," upon which Rashi comments,

> For in destroying them they appear to be spurning the Holy One blessed be He, and His blessings, that generate His goodness.[32]

---

30. A fascinating book on how trees have changed the way we live and their profound effect on the planet and humankind, was released on February 17, 2020. It is *The Story of Trees* by Kevin Hobbs and David West (Lawrence King Publishing, RRP). It takes the reader on a visual journey from some of the earlier known tree species, beginning with the Ginkgo biloba fossils dating back to earliest prehistoric times. Trees being the lifeblood of environment can correct and combat the enormous damages caused by carbon emissions, which are also a severe health hazard, and according to the Bill and Melinda Gates Foundation threaten the future of all our children.

31. See, for example, Tanna de-Bei Eliyahu, chapter 16:1, Jerusalem, 2020, Vol. 1, pp. 400–401, where a parable is given in which the king plants vines, trees, and other plants, and warns his children to look after them well, but they uproot the vines, cut down the trees and destroy the shoots; and when the king sees this he punishes them. This is compared to the children of Israel in the time of the Judges (cf. Ruth 1:1) who was punished for their iniquitous behavior. And in B. Hagigah 14a we read concerning Elisha ben Abuyah that he "cut down the shoots" (*kitzetz be-netiyot*), i.e., left the true path of Torah.

32. In India, too, eclipses are seen as periods of crisis. See William Crooke, *Religion and Folklore in Northern India*, New Delhi, 1925, pp. 39–41:

> Eclipses of sun and moon play an important part in the public and family ritual, and there are many explanations to account for their occurrence. Gāros and some cognate tribes suppose that the evil spirit Nawang swallows the sun and moon, and when the first shadow falls on their surface they beat drums and blow horns to scare him, while the Lhota Nāgas think that eclipses are caused by a great dog in the sky which tries to eat these luminaries. An eclipse portends that great men will die, so no work is done next day. On the North-Western Frontier it is supposed that a snake coming out to eat the moon obscures it, or that an army of fairies is flying between it and the earth. Bhotiyas think it advisable to let off guns at an eclipse to prevent the blacksmith from seizing sun or moon.
>
> Among Hindus of the plains eclipses are attributed to the Daitya or demon Rāhu, 'the looser or seizer,' who drank some of the Amrita or nectar produced at the churning of the ocean: the sun and moon detected him and informed Vishnu,

who cut off his head and two of his arms. But as he had become immortal by drinking the nectar his head and tail were tranferred to the heavens, where the head wreaks its vengeance on sun and moon by occasionally swallowing them, and the tail, Ketu, 'brightness,' gave birth to a numerous progeny of comets and fiery meteors. Ketu is now a demon who brings disease, and Rāhu in Bengal is the tribal godling of menial castes like Dusādhs and Dhangars who propitiate him by a special fire sacrifice."

Hence an eclipse is a crisis, a time of danger because demons are abroad. It is one of the Brahman's privileges to receive gifts from the pious, but he must not accept such as are degrading, like those intended to avert the dangerous influence of certain stars, and in particular the Chhāyadan or 'shadow gift,' made at eclipses, which consists of a vessel of ghi or clarified butter, in which the donor observes his reflection and then from the menial and degraded tribes, may be at the root of the common belief about Rāhu.

No cooked food should be eaten for twelve hours before an eclipse of the sun and for eight before that of the moon. Frequent eclipses, particularly of the sun and moon nearly together, portend grave political danger. Before an eclipse begins all the house water jars are emptied lest a demon may enter them, and stores of pickles and other confections are locked up to save them from pollution. The family priest lays a blade of the holy Kusa grass (*Poa cynosuroides*) on the threshold, and it is wise to bathe one's person and the images of the household gods which share in the pollution. The Mundas bring every metal article outside the house and expose them while the eclipse lasts. The careful Hindu housewife sprinkles Ganges water on leaves of the Tulasi or holy basil, and puts them into the drinking water and cooked food as a protection. A pregnant woman is in special danger during an eclipse and is subject to many taboos. She must do no work lest her child may be born deformed, and this deformity bears some relation to the work she does: if she sews cloth the child may have a hole in its flesh, generally close to the ear; if she cuts anything it will have a hare-lip; if she uses a knife or scissors it will be born with a cut on its body, if she cuts anything it will be born mad. As a protection from such danger a circle of cow-dung is drawn round her waist; she is shut up in a dark room where no ray from the demon-haunted sun or moon may fall upon her, and pregnant cattle have their horns smeared with red lead. A Brahman must not sleep on a bed or cat on the day of an eclipse, and if the sun or moon happen to set while eclipsed he must fast next day as well.

Bathing in a sacred place is the most effectual way of relieving sun and moon from the attack of the demon, because bathing removes a man's pollution and renders him pure enough to recite the Mantras or holy texts which scare the demon While bathing the worshipper should be attended by a Brahman who recites the Gayatri hymn. During a lunar eclipse it is advisable to bathe at Benares; during a solar, at Kurukshetra, the scene of the battle in the Great War. Bernier gives a graphic account of the bathing at Delhi during an eclipse in 1666, and

They went so far as to say that if a tree is unhealthy restrictions against its fruit do not apply (*Tosefta Sheviit* 1:11):

> The tree may be pruned with a knife ... and neither the laws of the seventh year nor those concerning the customs of the Amorites are to constitute any hindrance.

And, so, one should paint a red mark on a sick tree in order to announce that its fruit is permitted, and one may do so even during the sabbatical year (ibid., 1.10). And the Babylonian Talmud (in *B. Shabbat* 67a and *B. Hulin* 77b) states that the reason one paints it with red paint is:

> In order that people should see it and pray that [God grant] mercy to it.[33]

And the Talmud continues likening this situation to what is to be found in *Leviticus* 13:45:

> And the leper in whom the plague is, his clothes shall be rent, and the hair of his head shall go loose, and he shall cover his upper lip, and shall cry: "Unclean, unclean."

From which verse we learn that one must publicize the leper's distress

---

similar sights may be witnessed along the holy rivers at the present day. In the lower Himalayas, on the occasion of an eclipse, offerings were placed in a brazen jar to an image of a snake deity stamped on a piece of metal, because these deities have general power of influencing the weather. In Ladakh ram's horns are fixed on the bark of apricot trees as a propitiatory offering during an eclipse, and such trees are expected to bear ever afterwards an unfailing crop of the choicest fruit. In the villages, however, the most usual remedy is for women to go about beating brass pans to scare Rahu from his prey.

I hope the reader will forgive me for indulging in one of my other areas of interest in this long note.

33. See in detail S. Lieberman, *Tosefta Ki-Fshutah Zeraim* 2, New York, 1955, pp. 492–494; cf. my *Netivot Pesikah*, Jerusalem, 2008, p. 153.

so that "the multitude will pray [for his recovery]." And so, too, with the sick tree.[34] And, indeed, also the Torah in *Deuteronomy* 20:19 draws this parallel between mankind and trees, in the formulation, "are trees of the field not human."[35]

And just like human beings have their own birthday[36] and New Year, so, too, trees have a birthday as we learn from *M. Rosh Ha-Shanah* 1:1:

> On the first of Shevat is the New Year for trees according to Beit Shammai. Beit Hillel say on the fifteenth of that month.

And, of course, the view of Beit Hillel was the one which was accepted (*Shulhan Aruch Yoreh Deah* 331:57, 125). Indeed, in Israel from the late eighties of the nineteenth century this day became a festival of planting saplings throughout the country, so much so that in 1949, the first prime minister of Israel participated in a tree-planting ceremony in the area approaching (*prozdor*) Jerusalem,[37] and Israel's first President Chaim Weizmann opened the first session of the newly established *Knesset* (Parliament) on that day.[38] And outside Israel, already in (the late sixteenth century, under the influence of the Ari ha-Kadosh), a special ceremonial meal (called *Seder Tu bi-Shvat*) was established in which the fruits of the Land of Israel were eaten in a ritual fashion with

---

34. See S. Lieberman, *Tosefta Sheviit*, New York, 1955, p. 168; idem, *Tosefta Ki-Fshuta*, ibid., p. 492 to line 35.

35. And in *The Lord of the Rings* by Tolkien, there are wonderful tree-creatures called Ents, who play a central role in the world of mankind. And see further *Pirkei Shira* (cf. above note 41) on this source, where chapter 2 (ed. Eisenstein, ibid., p. 524) lists the verses of praise to God that the various plants and trees sing. On *Pirkei* (or *Perek*) *Shirah*, see Seidenberg, ibid., p. 320, note 1032.

36. There is a Nepali Gurung statement that:

> Humans are just like trees: They thrive, grow to full size, bear fruit, and then stop growing. Their leaves fall and they die. But new ones grow up in their place.
> (See Broughton Coburn, *Nepali Aama: Life Lessons of a Himalayan Woman*, New York, 1982, p. 115.)

37. See in detail in Yom-Tov Levinsky, *Sefer ha-Moadim*, vol. 5, Tel-Aviv, 1954, pp. 459–492.

38. Ibid., pp. 488–490.

a whole series of liturgical statements and benedictions.[39]

Moreover, a special and unique prayer came to be formulated for the special *Tu bi-Shvat* meal. It just appears in (the anonymous) *Hemdat Yamim*, Livorno, 1763, part 2, chapter 3, 109a–b, and was subsequently publicized many times in a slender volume called *Pri Etz Hadar*, a sort of *Haggadah* for *Tu bi-Shvat*. It contains, inter alia, the following passage:

> … And trees and grasses You made bloom from the ground with the stature and the design of what is above, to cause the children of Adam to know *the wisdom and discernment that is in them*, to reach what is hidden …. [My emphasis – D. S.]

This passage suggests that even the trees and the grasses have wisdom and discernment, and this was enunciated in the *Tu bi-Shvat* prayer.[40]

And, interestingly enough, just two days after *Tu bi-Shvat* on February 13, 2020, I saw the following article in the *Jerusalem Post* by

39. Ibid., pp. 329–336.

40. See Seidenberg, ibid., pp. 357–359 for an abridged translation of the prayer, and some bibliographic information. And ibid., p. 212, note 691, where he mentions that *Hemdat Yamim* was thought to have been written by Natan of Gaza, a disciple of the heretical messiah Shabtai Zvi, and possibly this is why no author's name appears in *Hemdat Yamim*, nor in *Pri Etz Hadar*.

On *Hemdat Yamim* see A. Yaari, *Taalumat Sefer: Sefer Hemdat Yamim Mi Hibro*, Jerusalem, 1954. Yaari also published in *Kiryat Sefer* 38, 1963, pp. 97–112, 247–262, 380–400, bibliographic notes on this work. A new edition of this work was published in four volumes in 2011, by Machon Hemdat Yamim, Bnei Brak, with a lengthy introduction in vol. 1, pp. 35–249, which seeks to prove that it was written by R. Binyamin ha-Levy of Safed (1590–1676). They also published *Otzar Hemdat Yamim*, ed. D. S. Kosovsky-Shahor, Bnei Brak, 2009, collectanea on this book. Most recently Lior Holzer published a volume entitled *Sefer ha-Beriah le-Natan Me-Aza* (*Natan ha-Azati*), Jerusalem, 2019, with a long introduction (in both Hebrew and English) dealing with Natan's alleged Sabbateanism, with rich bibliographic references. For a (partial) bibliographic listing of *Pri Etz Hadar*, see Ch. B. Friedberg, *Beit Eked Sefarim*, vol. 3, Tel Aviv, 1954, p. 851, no. 777, with an addition in *Beit Eked Sefarim he-Hadash*, ed. M. Moriah, vol. 4, Safed, 1970–1976, p. 112 no. 852.

In this note we have, perhaps, gone beyond the confines of this study, and, therefore, I shall no more expand on this fascinating subject.

Valerie Volcovici, with the heading "Plant a trillion trees: Republicans over climate solution."

> Washington (Reuters) – Republican lawmakers on Wednesday will propose legislation setting a goal for the United States to plant one trillion trees by 2050 to fight global warming, a plan intended to address climate change by sucking carbon out of the air instead of by cutting emissions.
>
> The proposed legislation reflects an acknowledgment in the Republican party of rising voter demand for action on climate change, even as it seeks to preserve the economic benefits of an historic drilling boom that has made the United States the world's biggest oil and gas producer.
>
> President Donald Trump, who has repeatedly cast doubt on the science of climate change, had expressed support for the idea of a massive tree-planting campaign during a speech at the World Economic Forum in Davos last month.
>
> "I'm working on legislation that would do just this: plant 1 trillion trees by 2050, with the goal of sequestering carbon and incentivizing the use of wood products," said Arkansas Congressman Bruce Westerman, a member of the House natural resources committee, which is expected to unveil the bill.
>
> Other elements of the plan, which are being released in additional bills over the coming weeks, will focus on sequestering carbon from power plants, recycling plastics and boosting "clean" energy, including natural gas and nuclear, according to congressional staff.
>
> Democrats, including all the top presidential hopefuls in this year's election, have made proposals for a rapid shift away from fossil fuels to help the United States and other countries avoid the worst impacts of climate change.
>
> Environmentalists argue that focusing on planting trees while ignoring emission cuts from fossil fuels is counterproductive. An overwhelming majority of scientists believe emissions from the combustion of fossil fuels are the main driver of climate change.
>
> "Planting trees is good of course, but it is nowhere near

enough of what is needed, and it cannot replace real mitigation and rewilding nature," Swedish teen activist Greta Thunberg said in Davos last month [in 2020].

Nature-based carbon removal measures like tree planting have gained traction globally: In July of 2020, for example, Ethiopia set a world record by planting over 350 million trees in 12 hours as part of a green campaign by Prime Minister Aiby Ahmed.

James Mulligan, a senior associate at the World Resources Institute, said mass tree planting could reduce 180–360 million tons of carbon dioxide per year by 2040 if implemented correctly.

"Funding is key," he said, adding that the program needs, a "smart governance system."

On a recent visit to Sikkim I saw notice boards outside Buddhist monasteries of His Holiness the 17th Ogyen Trinley Dorje Gwalwang Karmapa, which had the following printed in black letters on a black background:

ACTIVITIES YOUR MONASTERY OF NUNNERY CAN LEAD WITHIN YOUR COMMUNITY TO PROTECT FORESTS

1. When a new monk nun joins Monastery or Nunnery, have them plant tree sapling as part of their commitment to serve the world.

2. Monastery that need timber for building materials should oversee the planting of at least twice the number of trees that are used.

3. Encourage people who put up many prayer flags (such as gyalhar) to string the prayer flags up instead of using one bamboo pole per flag.

4. Designate a sacred place on the Monastery grounds, which can bring you closer to nature.

5. Plant trees in severely degraded areas.

6. Work with the local forestry department and environmental organization to select the right kind of trees planting.

7. After selecting areas, plant tree saplings mixed with half-grown and fully grown trees.

8. Keep the area protected from livestock and minimize the

extraction of resources (fodder, thatch, medicine, etc.) for a few years.

9. Monitor the forested area over the long term and experiment with different combinations of saplings.

10. Use sacred occasions to carry out environmental activities such as tree planting.

11. Encourage community management of forests.

12. Speak out against illegal timber cutting and trade.

In yet another monastery a notice with the same signatory listed "108 things you can do" to benefit the earth, beginning with an introductory section that states:

Our world is facing an environmental crisis which is complex, overwhelming, and affects us all, but it is difficult to know where to begin and what we can do.

It is very important for all of us to change our behavior and we need to start taking practical steps. These "108 Things You Can Do" are a path that everyone can follow in order to make a difference.

In Hindu sources we also find such a sensitivity to trees. Thus:

The axe which is to cut the tree for the sacrificial post is invoked while it is employed: "O axe, hurt it not"; and prior to the fatal blow, a blade of Darbha grass with its point upward is laid on the tree after having uttered the words: "O herb, protect it" (the sacrificial post); (S. B., III. 6. 4. 10). Afterwards an offering is made above the cut surface, with the prayer that the tree may grow up again with a hundred branches. (*'Āpastamba Srauta-sūtra'* VII. 2. 4. and 8).

See Stella Kramrisch, *The Hindu Temple*, Calcutta, 1946, vol. 1, p.16, note 34.

But returning to our Jewish sources, *Tu bi-Shevat* is not just a festival with certain halachic-agricultural guidelines, but nowadays may be seen as an epic call for a global ecological solution.

And now returning to *M. Rosh ha-Shanah*, ibid., the Talmud ad loc. (14a) also explains the view of Beit Shammai as follows:

R. Eleazer said, citing R. Hoshaiah: Since most of that year's rain is past, and still most of the season ahead.

And when, in the eleventh century, Rav Hai Gaon was requested to explain this Gemara, he said (Benyamin M. Levine, *Otzar ha-Geonim le-Rosh ha-Shanah*, Jerusalem, 1933, p. 23):

The Rabbis over there – i.e. in the Land of Israel – give [the following] reason, namely that thus far the trees have been living off the water of the past year, henceforth they live off the water of the coming year....[41]

Adding:

This seems reasonable. For this season is called in the language of Ishmael *al jamra al-tariya* (the second ember), and at this time the sap begins to flow and the trees begin to drink and come alive, and it is said *gari al-ma fi al-ud* (the water has entered the tree).[42]

---

41. This according to *Y. Rosh ha-Shanah* 1.2.

42. For an understanding of what "the second ember" means, see what I wrote in my article "A Tree Comes of Age," 2/4/18, in *Opensiddur.org*. There I wrote as follows:

What did Rav Hai Gaon mean by saying that this time of year is called "the second ember"? This remark can be understood in the light of an ancient Arab legend, according to which people spend the rainy season closed up in their tents, wrapped in layers of clothing, dozing by the glowing fireplace. The flocks and herds are also gathered into their enclosures surrounding the tent, shivering with cold and waiting for sunny days and expansive pasture in the fields and hills. Then Allah is stirred by his great mercy to bring down for them three embers from heaven: one ember, *jamrat al-hawi* (the ember of air) comes down on the seventh of Shevat and warms the air, bringing tidings of the arrival of spring. Then the farmer wakes from his slumber, opens the enclosure and begins to send his livestock out to the fields. However they will not yet find good pasture, and the weather is still bitter cold. Then the farmer waits expectantly another seven days, until the fourteenth of Shevat, on which day Allah brings down another ember from heaven (*jamrat al-mayi* – the ember of the water), and then the water warms up, enters the trees and makes them blossom and bear fruit once more. This makes the farmer joyful, and he sends his livestock off to the hills to pasture. However the weather is still too cold and windy to go out and till one's fields. The farmer

The importance the rabbis attached to trees may be seen in a *Mishnah* in *Baba Batra* 2:11:

A tree has to be removed from the proximity of a water storage pit [since the tree, through its roots, extends into the neighbor's field and prevents him from digging wells for his water]. But Rabbi Yossi said that even when the pit [is dug] before the tree [is planted], it is not necessary to destroy the tree, since this one digs within his own property and another plants within his own property.

The *Shulchan Aruch* in *Hoshen Mishpat* 155:32 and other authorities ruled according to Rabbi Yossi. Meir Tamari, in his *With All Your*

---

counts another seven days, and then Allah brings down the third ember from heaven (*jamrat a'ard* – the ember of the earth). The soil gets warmer and begins to be covered by tender blades of grass. Then the farmer shakes off the laziness cast over him by the rainy season, and goes out to work in the field and in his garden until evening. [See Yom Tov Levinsky, *Sefer ha-Moadim*, part 2, *Yemei Moed ve-Zikaron*, p. 325]. Another variant of this legend about embers appears in the work of the 13th century Arab geographer, Al-Kazwini, in his *Cosmography* [Abu Yahya Zakariya 'ibn Muhammed al-Qazurini (1203–1283), *Marvels of Creatures and Strange Things Existing*, vol. 1, p. 176]. During the month of Shevat the farmers of the land of Israel gradually make the fire which warms them less. On the seventh of Shevat they remove one ember from the fire, because the air is beginning to get warmer. On the fourteenth of Shevat they take out a second ember, because the water is getting warmer, and on the twenty-first of Shevat, a third ember, because the ground is also warming up. The day after the second ember is removed, on the fifteenth of Shevat, they plant roses, Jasmine and narcissus [Levinsky ibid. p. 321].

So we see that Rav Hai Gaon meant to explain the view of the School of Hillel, that the New Year for trees falls on the fifteenth of Shevat, and brought as evidence what he had heard from Arab farmers, that the trees begin to drink the warming water of the coming year [*Otzar ha-Geonim* ibid.]. This legend draws a comparison between the farmer, sleepy in winter and awakening in the month of Shevat, and the trees, dormant in winter and awakening on their New Year.

So just like human beings have birthdays, trees have their own birthday and New Year but also a sort of Bar Mitzvah, marking them as no longer being *orlah* after three years (*Leviticus* 19:23–25) (their fruit forbidden because of the trees' young age). Trees are dormant in winter and awaken to drink the water that grows warmer from the second ember in the middle of the month of Shevat, so that they can produce their fruit in due season and enable us to recite a benediction over trees and the fruit they bear.

Possessions: Jewish Ethics and Economic Life, New York/London, 1987, p. 286, comments that:

> At first sight it would seem that Rabbi Yossi permits each person to do within his property whatever he wants, without considering the effects on others. This would absolve one from many liabilities that the halachah imposes on him, however, and therefore cannot be accepted. The commentators and legal authorities explained, though the Rabbi Yossi accepted that the matter of the others' welfare exists, but that in this case there is another consideration. The *Tosefta* [*Baba Batra* 1:8] explains that Rabbi Yossi's argument is based on the concept of the common good and its maximalization. The sages who insisted on the destruction of the tree argued that *Yishuv ha'Olam* – the development of the world – is based on the existence of water pits and therefore they have preference. To this Rabbi Yossi countered that *"just as in your case you consider the water pits essential to Yishuv ha'Olam, I regard the trees as essential to the welfare of the world."* In other words, it is not solely the personal benefit of the tree owner that is important here, *but the contribution of his tree to the general welfare which overshadows the right of the owner of the water pit.*[43]

In India, too, there is a deep love and appreciation of trees, as is evident in Rabindranath Tagore's beautiful "story," "Life and Mind," in his *The Golden Boat*, Bombay, 1956, pp. 59–64 (English translation by Bhabani Bhattacharya), parts of which I will cite here:

> ...So long as I was a wanderer I had no time to glance at the wayside tree; today I have left the beaten path and can chat with it.
>
> The banyan gazes at my face and suddenly becomes restless, as though it wants to say: "Can't you understand?"
>
> I console it, saying: "I have understood everything. Don't worry".
>
> For a while it is quiet. Then again it becomes uneasy; that same shivering, restless rustling of leaves.

---

43. See the continuation of Tamari's discussion, ibid., p. 287, and the responsum of the Rosh (Rabbenu Asher) 108:10.

Again I soothe it, saying: "Yes, yes; I am your playmate. For millions of years in this earthen playhouse I have drunk deep draughts of sunlight with you; and with you have I shared the milky sap from the breasts of the earth."

Then a windy voice comes from the tree. Three times it moans: "Yes, yes, yes."

Its rustling echoes the same voice, the self-same voice that beats upon my heart through the coursing of blood that vibrates from the soundless rotation of darkness and light. It is the common language of the universe saying "I live, we live."

There is joy in that message. Each atom of the world trembles at the touch of that joy.

With the tree I am talking in that tongue, and sharing that same joy.

The tree asks me: "Do you live?"

I reply: "I do live, my friend."

When in springtime I first started my acquaintance with that tree, its leaves were young and green.

Through them the fugitive light of the sky reached the grass and made friends with the shadows of the earth.

Then came the rains of July. The leaves began to turn dark with the passing clouds. To-day they are thick, like the ripened intelligence of the aged, and through them the sun's light can no longer pass. Once the tree was like a daughter of the poor: to-day it is like a rich housewife, every limb bearing the signs of abundance. It waves its thousand emeralds and says: "Why enclose yourself thus within brick and mortar? Why not come out like me into the open?"

"Because we men have to take care of two worlds - the inner and the outer."

The tree says: "Indeed! Where's the inner one?"

"Within myself."

"What do you do there?"

"I create."

"How do you create within such bounds? You talk like a mystic."

"Water flows through the bounds of its banks and becomes a river: Ideas flow through similar bounds and become creation. The same substance is caught within different bounds and turns sometimes into a gem, sometimes into a tree.

The tree wants to know more about my bounds.

I reply: "My mind is my bound. Whatever is caught in it becomes a thing of creation."

The tree continues: "How does that hedged little creation of yours compare with our sun and moon?"

"This creation of mine cannot be measured in terms of the sun and the moon, which are things of the outer world."

"Then how would you measure it?"

"By the measuring-rod of joy and of pain."

The tree says: "The west wind whispers into my ears and sets my soul a-quiver with joy. But I grasp naught of what you say."

"How else can I make you understand? As soon as I catch that west wind in the strings of my lyre it changes from one thing of beauty to another. I do not know across what unknown sky this new creation may blow: but I think there is a sky of pain – a sky that is beyond all measure."....

The banyan raises all her branches and says: "Stop awhile. You think too much and you talk too much. I know that the tree is right: "I come to you resolved to keep silent." I say, "but owing to evil habit I talk even in silence, as some people walk in sleep."

I gaze at the tree with listless eyes. Its smooth leaves are gliding rapidly over the lyre of sunlight, like the fingers of a harpist.

Suddenly my mind says: "Where is the link between what you've been seeing and what I've been thinking?"

I take it to task: "Another question? Can't you keep silent for a space?"

I sit without a word and see the day hurrying past.

The tree asks "Have you understood all?"

"I have."

Next day my mind asks me: "Yesterday, with your eyes fixed on the banyan, you said: 'I have understood all.' Tell me, what is it that you understood?"

I say in reply: "In me the life-spark has grown dim under the fumes of thought. So, to see its undarkened flash. I have to turn to the grass, to the tree."

"And what do you see?"

I see how this life-spark revels in itself; how it dresses itself in millions of patterns of leaves and flowers and fruits, full of sap, full of smell, full of colour. So I gazed at the banyan in silence and wonder, and said: "King of all trees, your twigs have caught that cry of joy which hailed the first birth of life in this earth. The simple laugh of that primeval age gleams in your leaves." In me I feel the stir of that early Life-spirit. It was lying inert under the smoke-screen of thoughts, but you have sent a call to it, saying, "Come out into the open to feel the sun and the wind, and bring with you your brush and paint."

My mind is silent awhile. Then sadly it says: "You always talk about life, but never about the materials which I gather with so much care for your use."

"Need I talk about them? They talk about themselves in the loudest voice. The earth groans under their volume and complexity. I find no end to them. To what dizzy height will they mount up layer by layer? The answer is writ large on the leaves of that banyan tree."

"Oh, really? And what is that answer?

"It says that so long as life is wanting, all is a ponderous volume, a mass of ugly substance. But at the touch of life matter combines with matter and becomes a thing of beauty. For proof look at the banyan tree."

Once upon a time, when history was yet unborn, Life awoke from slumber and set out for the unknown world of inert matter. Its body was without fatigue. Its princely garb was neither frayed, nor stained with dust.

In this July morning the banyan reveals to me a glimpse of that primal Life-spirit. It waves its twigs as though its Life-spirit says to me: "Hail to thee, friend."

I ask, "Prince, how goes your fight with the giant of the desert?"

"Of no import. Just cast your eye all around."

I look round. Some fields are green with grass. Some are covered with paddy sprouts; beyond, stretches a forest of fruit-laden trees screening the horizon from sight.

"Prince, you are courageous. Though young, you are fighting the giant who is strong and cruel. You are small in stature, your arrows are few in number; the giant is heavily armed and wears a shining mail. Yet, on all sides, I see your green flags flapping in the wind. You have put your foot on the giant's neck; even the stones have admitted defeat and dust is bowing before you like a slave."

The tree asks: "Where did you see all that?"

I say in reply: "Your battles have the appearance of peace, your actions have the semblance of repose, your victory has the guise of humility. Hence it is that the meditative come to you to learn the tactics of your invisible battles and the secrets of your victory. You have opened schools in the forests to show us how Life works: there the weary come to your shades and the dispirited seek a word from you."

The Life-spirit in the banyan is gladdened at my words, and says in ecstasy: "True it is that I fight the giant of the desert, but I have a younger brother, and I know not to which battle he has gone. Were you speaking of him a moment before"?

"Yes, we call him Mind".

"He is even more restless than I and never content. Could you give me some news of that venturesome one?"

"I can. You are fighting to live; he is fighting for gains and another fight is going on somewhere for renunciation. Your fight is with the inert, his with want, and another fight is going on against accumulation. The struggle has grown hot. Victory and defeat seem equally uncertain. In this uncertainty your green flags are putting heart in the fighters. 'Victory be unto Life,' say the melodies of Life rising to a higher and higher pitch till one fears lest they should break. But above the whirl of music your lyre cries. 'There is no fear! –And 'The keynote flows from my strings – the keynote of all life. All crazy tunes shall at last harmonize with my note and create an ever-lasting song of beauty. To give and to receive will then become as natural as the blossoming of flowers or the ripening of fruits.'

This remarkable parable of nature, expressed through the dialogue of the man and the tree encapsulate a deep understanding and appreciation of the relationship between man and nature and the "two worlds, the inner and the outer." Of course, the tree has a special status in Hinduism, especially the pilpal, the banyan, and the bhodi trees. See, e.g., Mala Bansi Lal, *Trees in Indian Art and Folklore*, 2000.

Here we should also call attention to tree marriage: see Alexander Porteous, *The Forest in Folklore and Mythology*, New York, 1928, pp. 181–183. But this subject is beyond the scope of this study.

Interestingly enough, Tagore, in another of his books, *Sādhanā: The Realisation of Life*, MacMillan India, 1913, pp. 3–5, in a chapter entitled "The Relationship of the Individual to the Universe," seeks to give a sort of socio-anthropological explanation for this special relationship to trees and nature in general, an explanation which is both provocative and perhaps historically questionable, but certainly fascinating and imaginative, as follows:

> The civilization of ancient Greece was nurtured within city walls. In fact, all the modern civilizations have their cradles of brick and mortar.
>
> These walls leave their mark deep in the minds of men. They set up a principle of 'divide and rule' in our mental outlook, which begets in us a habit of securing all our conquests by fortifying them and separating them from one another. We divide nation and nation, knowledge and knowledge, man and nature. It breeds in us a strong suspicion of whatever is beyond the barriers we have built, and everything has to fight hard for its entrance into our recognition.
>
> When the first Aryan invaders appeared in India it was a vast land of forests, and the new-comers rapidly took advantage of them. These forests afforded them shelter from the fierce heat of the sun and the ravages of tropical storms, pastures for cattle, fuel for sacrificial fire, and materials for building cottages. And the different Aryan clans with their patriarchal heads settled in the different forest tracts which had some special advantage of natural protection, and food and water in plenty.
>
> Thus in India it was in the forests that our civilization had its birth, and it took a distinct character from this origin and environment. It was surrounded by the vast life of nature, was fed and clothed by her, and had the closest and most constant intercourse with her varying aspects.

Such a life, it may be thought, tends to have the effect of dulling human intelligence and dwarfing the incentives to progress by lowering the standards of existence. But in ancient India we find that the circumstances of forest life did not overcome man's mind, and did not enfeeble the current of his energies, but only gave to it a particular direction. Having been in constant contact with the living growth of nature, his mind was free from the desire to extend his dominion by erecting boundary walls around his acquisitions. His aim was not to acquire but to realize, to enlarge his consciousness by growing with and growing into his surroundings. He felt that truth is all-comprehensive, that there is no such thing as absolute isolation in existence, and the only way of attaining truth is through the interpenetration of our being into all objects. To realize this great harmony between man's spirit and the spirit of the world was the endeavor of the forest-dwelling sages of ancient India.

In later days there came a time when these primeval forests gave way to cultivated fields, and wealthy cities sprang up on all sides. Mighty kingdoms were established, which had communications with all the great powers of the world. But even in the heyday of its material prosperity the heart of India ever looked back with adoration upon the early ideal of strenuous self-realization and the dignity of the simple life of the forest hermitage, and drew its best inspiration from the wisdom stored there.

The west seems to take a pride in thinking that it is subduing nature; as if we are living in a hostile world where we have to wrest everything we want from an unwilling and alien arrangement of things. This sentiment is the product of the city-wall habit and training of mind. For in the city life man naturally directs the concentrated light of his mental vision upon his own life and works, and this creates an artificial dissociation between himself and the Universal Nature within whose bosom he lies.

But in India the point of view was different; it included the world with the man as one great truth. India put all her emphasis on the harmony that exists between the individual and the universal. She felt we could have no communication whatever with our surroundings if they were absolutely foreign to Man's complaint against nature is that he has to acquire most of his necessaries by his own efforts. Yes, but his efforts are not in vain; he is reaping success every day, and that shows there is a rational connection between him and nature, for we never can make anything our own except that which is truly related to us.

And it is out of this "rational connection between [man] and nature," symbolized in the forests and the trees, that Tagore finds the "harmony that exists between the individual [man] and the universal [nature]."

For an artistic representation of this idea, see, e.g., the image, illustration no. 61, in Marilia Albanese, *Ancient India from the Origins to the XIII century A.D.*, Italy, 2001. The explanation is on p. 61:

> As nature is the manifestation of the sacred, water, trees, stones, caves and mountains are worshipped in the Hindu religion. Often the divine power of a place is displayed in anthropomorphic guise, as, for example, with the Yakshi or Shalabhanjiika, the dryads who live in trees and embody their vital essence. These beings are depicted as lithe as climbing plants and as soft as mature fruit. The example is from Rajasthan ... dated to the 10th century, and can be seen in the Guirner Museum in Paris.

See further ibid., p. 117 to illustrate, where the explanation is:

> Trees were thought to be inhabited by supernatural beings – tree sprites known as *Yaksha* or *Yakshini* – and were worshipped from ancient times. They were enclosed by a palisade to which partitions and columns were added in later times, forming a structure that seems to have become the proto-type for the first places of Buddhist worship.

But after this somewhat lengthy interpolation, let us return to the Jewish tradition, as much as Jewish tradition loves trees,[44] and even has a

---

44. Further, for a full discussion on the Jewish attitude to trees, see Rephael Patai, *Adam ve-Adamah: Mehkar be-Minhagim, Emunah ve-Aggadot Eretz Yisrael ve-Umot ha-*

special benediction to be declaimed when seeing a tree budding, namely, "Blessed art Thou ... who has withheld nothing from this world, but created in it beautiful creatures and trees for humans to enjoy" (see *B. Berachot* 43b and *Rosh ha-Shanah* 11b).[45]

From the ending of the benediction, "... trees for humans to enjoy," one may discern the deep appreciation of the rabbis of the divine gift of trees. There is, albeit, a difference of opinion among the decision as to whether this benediction is said over all trees that bud, be they fruit bearing or not, or only over fruit trees, the "enjoyment" being the edible fruit that will mature. The others argue that just to see "the rebirth of the plant kingdom so evident where the trees begin budding is a source of great pleasure and enjoyment. There is yet a further difference of opinions among the later authorities as to whether this benediction is of the category of *birkat ha-nehenim*, benedictions over pleasure incurred, i.e., for eating, drinking, smelling, or even seeing beautiful things, or of *birkat ha-hodaah*, benedictions of thanks, where there is not necessarily a physical benefit, just a wish to thank the Creator for blessing us with his wonderful works. Each position is bolstered by sources and arguments, but all these differing opinions reflect the very positive attitude of the halachah to nature.[46] This, however, does not contradict the fact that

---

Olam, vol. 1, Jerusalem, 1942, pp. 206–283. It was posted by the "17th Gyalmang Karmapa."

45.   On the blessing over trees, *birkat ha-Ilanot*, see Pinhas Zvihi, *Sefer Ateret Paz*, Jerusalem, 2008, a close to three-hundred page book (!) dealing with all aspects of this benediction.

46.   See the detailed discussion in *Sefer Ateret Paz*, pp. 31–34, where the author brings a wide variety of sources on these conflicting opinions, with great clarity. They also have their further implications, such as: if one mistakenly makes this benediction over a "sterile" tree, according to those who rule that one does not make a benediction, in such a case, is this benediction invalid (*beracha le-vatalah*) so much so that, if one then sees a *fruit* tree, one must make the benediction again, or perhaps the first benediction is nonetheless sufficient to serve for the subsequent viewing – obviously closely afterwards – of the fruit tree. Here, too, there are differing opinions, all of which are discussed by R. Zvihi. And according to those who see it as a blessing of praise and thanks, preferably it should be said standing (pp. 133–134).

And further on in his book (p. 117) he states that one should try to make this benediction in a quorum of ten (*minyan*), this further publicizing the occasion, giving an additional indication of its importance.

the damage that trees can do to property is also the subject of regulation as we have seen above.

Thus, the Mishnah in *Baba Batra* 2:7 rules that:

> Trees must be kept at a distance of 25 cubits from a town; carobs and sycamore trees 50 cubits. Abba Shaul says: All wild fruit trees must be kept at a distance of 50 cubits. If the town was there first, the tree is cut down and compensation must be given. If there is any doubt as to which was first, it is cut down and no compensation is given.

Although the Mishnah gives no reason for these rulings, Ulla (Eretz Yisrael, flor. c. 250–320 C.E.) explains that it might blemish the beauty of the city, constituting a nuisance, and therefore must be distanced or even uprooted.[47] However, it seems more likely that the reason behind the Mishnah's ruling was that the roots of the tree could damage the public water catchments outside the city and the public drainage system and fresh-water piping system within it, and any nearby graves.[48]

Similarly, they could not be planted closer than twenty-five cubits to cisterns (fifty cubits for some kinds of trees) because of possible pollution of the water supply caused by falling leaves and bird and animal droppings. Trees had to be planted at least four cubits away from a property's boundary and, if the branches came to overhang another's property or the public domain, they should be trimmed. If the root system spread into another's property, that could be cut away to allow for plowing, the digging of trenches, and other purposes (ibid., 2:11–14).

Kabbalists even believed that plants and trees have souls that may at times need redemption, and this benediction serves to draw mercy upon them (ibid., pp. 117–125, 129–130, 163).

47. See Shlomo E. Glicksberg, "The Tree as a Hazard: The Evolvement of a Halakhah," *Moed: Annual of Jewish Studies* 18, 2008, pp. 2–11 for an in-depth discussion on this ruling, and the many interpretations that have been offered. On the distinction between "nuisance" and "damage," see his PhD dissertation, Bar Ilan University, 2005, entitled *Ecology in Jewish Law: Preventing Nuisance*, p. 14.

48. See *Tosefta Baba Batra* 1:7, and Glicksberg, ibid., pp. 4–5. See further my *The Cities in Roman Palestine*, New York and Oxford, chapter 9, pp. 128–148.

On the other hand, the Jerusalem Talmud says, "It is forbidden to live in a city without greenery."

These Talmudic laws are codified and amplified works as Maimonides' *Mishneh Torah* and the *Shulhan Aruch*, and were operative in Jewish communities in the Diaspora as well as in *Eretz Yisrael*.

Indeed, Maimonides, who himself was a city dweller, having lived in Cordoba, Fez, and Cairo, wrote in one of his books on medicine:

> The quality of urban air compared to the air in the deserts and forests is like thick and turbulent water compared to pure and light water. In the cities with their tall buildings and narrow roads, the pollution that comes from their residents, their waste makes their entire air reeking and thick although no one is aware of it. Because we grow up in cities and become used to them, we can at least choose a city with an open horizon. And if you have no choice, and you cannot move out of the city, try at least to live upwind. Let your house be tall and the court wide enough to permit the northern wind and the sun to come through, because the sun thins out the pollution of the air.

As mentioned in the Introductory Note, I revisited this subject in an essay entitled *"Bal Tash'hit:* Waste Not Want Not," which I wish to cite here, with additions, because of its relevance to the field, adding some of the possible halachic implications.[49]

*   *   *

The biblical prohibition against wanton destruction is mentioned in two verses in *Deuteronomy* (20:19–20):

> When thou shalt besiege a city a long time, in making war against it to take it, thou shalt not destroy the trees thereof by

---

49. A fine exposition of this notion may be found in Eilon Schwartz's *"Bal Tash'hit: A Jewish Environmental Precept,"* *Environmental Ethics* 18, 1997, pp. 355–374 (reprinted in A. O. Waskow, *Trees, Earth, and Torah*, Philadelphia, 1999, pp. 83–106).

forcing an axe against them; for thou mayest eat of them, and thou shalt not cut them down,[50] for the tree of the field is a man('s) life[51]

---

50. It is interesting to compare the above with the Indian relationship to trees. This has been described in some detail by William Crooke in his *Religion and Folklore of Northern India*, Oxford University Press, 1925, chapter XVI, entitled "Tree and Plant Worship," pp. 400–418. There we read on p. 400 that the sacred groves:

> Have been described as the only form of temple known to them [most primitive tribes], and they are preserved inviolate by an effective sanction. They give shelter to a group of godlings who are held responsible for the fertility of the crops and people, an appeal is made to them in times of sickness, and if the trees be cut or injured the spirits show their displeasure by withholding the needed rain and in other ways.

And ibid., p. 401:

> The Maghs of Bengal believed that it was dangerous to fell trees except on the presence of Europeans on whom the blame the sacrilege would fall, but in their company they would advance fearlessly. When a large tree was felled one of the party was always provided with a green twig which he placed in the center of the stump as the tree collapsed. This was intended to give the tree a chance of sprouting again, and thus propitiate the spirit whose occupancy had been thus rudely disturbed…

And on p. 402:

> In the Central Provinces trees are believed to be animate and occupied by spirits; before a man cuts a tree he begs pardon for the injury he is about to inflict upon it, and Gonds must not shake a tree at night or pluck any of its leaves or fruit because the tree spirit is asleep and must not be disturbed.

See further idem, *The Popular Religion and Folk-lore of Northern India*, Westminster, 1896, vol. 2, chapter II, pp. 83–121. We cannot enlarge here on this fascinating subject, which is discussed in a considerable body of bibliographic literature.

51. This verse is, I would suggest, the ultimate source for the practice in the town of Beitar during Second Temple times to plant a tree at the birth of a child, and when that child got married, the tree would be cut down, and its wood used from for the bridal canopy (*huppah*). See *B. Gittin* 97a. I discussed this subject in detail in my *Jewish Life Cycle*, vol. 2, to be published shortly, chapter 10, entitled "A Tree was Planted when a Child was Born," with parallels in other countries and races. And see Alexander Porteous, *The Forest in Folklore and Mythology*, New York, 1928, pp. 181–183, etc.

to employ them in a siege.

Only the trees which thou knowest that they be not trees for food destroy and cut them down: and thou shalt build bulwarks against the city that maketh war with thee until it be subdued.[52]

This biblical prohibition of *bal tash'hit*[53] – "not to destroy," would appear to be quite limited, as it refers explicitly to trees the fruits of which are edible but not to fruitless ones, and this within the framework of siege warfare. Furthermore, in *B. Pesahim* 50b[54] we are told that one who cuts down good trees – *ilanot tovot* – presumably fruit-bearing trees, will see no blessing during his lifetime. However, the rabbis extended this prohibition to include fruitless trees under certain circumstances. Thus in *Piskei Tosafot* no. 132 we read that he who cuts down a tree, even a fruitless one will see no blessing (cf. *Shvut Yaakov*, by R. Yaakov Reischer, vol. 1, no. 159).[55] And on this my sainted grandfather, R. David Sperber, wrote in his *Afarkasta de-Anyah*, vol. 1, Brooklyn, 2002, sect. 35, that presumably this refers to a case where the tree was cut down for no good reason, the reason being that the rabbis in *B. Ketubot* 112b stated that there will come a time when even fruitless trees will bear fruit. And since, hopefully, the Temple will soon be rebuilt, those fruitless trees that he wishes to cut down will be fruit-bearing trees, which one is forbidden to cut down. He adds, that if, however, they are being uprooted for a valid purpose, such as to use the timber for building purposes,[56] or even uprooting an elderly fruit tree to replace

---

52. Compare this with the *Cairo Declaration*, article 3 b, relating to armed conflict:
    It is forbidden to cut down trees, to destroy crops or livestock, to destroy the enemy's civilian installations by shelling, blasting or any other means.

53. See R. Ovadiah Yosef, *Yabia Omer*, vol. 5, *Yoreh Deah* 12:1, 4, 7, on various aspects of this prohibition.

54. The source is in *Tosefta Bikkurim* 2 ad fin. See S. Lieberman's comments in his *Tosefta ki-Fshutah*, *Zeraim* 2, New York, 1955, p. 855 to line 71, cf. *Derech Eretz (Rabba)*, ed. Higger, Brooklyn, NY, 1935, p. 309; idem, *Masechet Kallah*, New York, 1936, p. 343. See further *B. Sukkah* 29a, *B. Baba Kama* 91a, *B. Baba Batra* 26a.

55. Lieberman, ibid., found the source of this statement in *Tosafot* MS. Oxford, and also refers us to R. Rabbinovitz, *Dikdukei Sofrim* to *Pesahim*, Munich, 1874, p. 146, note 40.

56. See *Eichut ha-Seviva (Ecologiah) bi-Mekorot ha-Yahadut*, Bar-Ilan University,

1990, pp. 18–23, for a discussion of when uprooting fruit trees may be permitted, referring, inter alia, to R. Yaakov Ettinger's (1798–1871) Responsa *Binyan Tziyyon*, 61, with reservations of R. Naftali Tzvi Yehudah Berlin (the Netziv, 1817–1893), in *Meshiv Davar*, vol. 2, sect. 56, etc. See *Sheilat Yaavetz*, vol. 1, sect. 76, who was asked if one could cut down trees to expand the space of a synagogue, and he seems to rule positively. See the detailed analysis of this complex responsum in R. Yishayahu Stoker's article in *Ha-Sevivah be-Halachah u-ba-Mahshavah*, pp. 156–161, with R. Shabtai Rappaport's remarks, and the continuation on pp. 161–165, for the discursions of R. Yair Bachrach in his *Havat Yair,* sect. 195, and the *Hatam Sofer*, vol. 2, *Yoreh Deah*, sect. 102, and R. Rappaport's interpretation ibid. And see *Yabia Omer*, ibid., p. 194, citing, inter alia, *Turei Zahav, Yoreh Deah* 116:6, who permitted cutting down trees in order to build a house on the "deforested" area.

Rav Shabtai Rapporport interprets the Hatam Sofer's position thus:

> The law of *bal tash'hit* is not based on the notion that one may not waste resources that are available to you. Rather it is based on the inherent right of everything in nature, the Holy One blessed be He created all nature, and in principle wished that everything remain as it is, not to be destroyed or moved from its place. Hence, one may not destroy nature without good reason, or waste resources with a reasonable justification. When it is of use, that is to say, nature is at our disposal, not to be destroyed but to serve a valid purpose, such as to make clothing or for food. But this use of nature must take into account the total balance. One has to be completely convinced of the valid necessity of the use of elements of nature in order to be permitted to destroy them, thus denying them their inherent right of survival. (See Stoker, ibid., p. 165.)

Perhaps this is how we should understand the passage in *Pirkei de-R. Eliezer*, chapter 34, translation Gerald Friedlander, London, 1916, p. 254:

> When people cut down the wood of a tree that yields fruit, its cry goes from one end of the world to the other and the sound is inaudible ... When the soul departs from the body, the cry goes from one end of the world to the other, and the sound is inaudible.

(On the latter, cf. *B. Yoma* 20b and *Genesis Rabba* 6:7.)

R. David Luria (RDL), in his edition, Warsaw, 1852. Fol. 79b, note 19, explains that this is probably based on the verse in *Deuteronomy* 20:19, prohibiting the cutting down of trees during a siege, "for the tree of the field is [like] a man" – *ki ha-adam etz ha-sadeh*, likening the tree to humankind. Cf. *Psalm* 128:3: "Thy wife shall be as a fruitful vine...," thus using the same kind of symbolic imagery. Then he also brings additional suggestions to clarify the inner meaning of this passage, also referring us to the *Recanati*, Jerusalem, 1961, 87b, to *Deuteronomy* 20:10.

it with a young healthier one, this should be permitted.[57] However, it would seem preferable to avoid such activity, as indicated by the Midrash in *Exodus Rabba* 35:2, on the verse in *Exodus* 26:15:

> "And thou shalt make boards for the tabernacle of *shittim* wood standing up." Why *shittim* wood? The Holy One blessed be He taught us something for all generations, namely that if one wishes to build one's home with wood from a fruit-tree, say to him: The King of Kings, who owns everything, when he commanded to build a tabernacle, said, "Bring only wood from a non-fruit-bearing tree." How much more so you.[58]

Furthermore, the biblical verse makes no mention of scorched-earth policies, blocking off water sources, and wanton destruction in general. And already the Midrash in *Ecclesiastes Rabba* 7:13 warns one of the irreversibility of some kinds of damage to nature:

> "See the works of God, for who can repair that which has been ruined?" (*Eccles* 7:13). When God created Adam, the first man, He took him to view all the trees of the Garden of Eden and said to him, "See how pleasant and excellent are My works. Everything that was formed, I created for your sake. Take heed that you do not ruin and destroy My world, for if you ravage it, no one will be able to repair it after you."

---

57. The responsum is long and detailed (pp. 111–115) and he again returned to the issue, ibid., sect. 121, pp. 293–298, bringing a wealth of sources from the whole spectrum of rabbinic literature.

58. See *Afarkasta de-Anya*, ibid., p. 113, etc. Cf. *Tanhuma*, ibid., sect. 9. And indeed all the tabernacle wooden apartenances were from *shittim* wood; *Exodus* 25:28; 30:5; 37:15, 28; 38:6, etc. See also R. Tzvi Pesach Frank's *Har Tzvi Orah Hayyim*, vol. 2, Jerusalem, 1977, sections 101–102, pp. 154–156, on whether one may cut down fruit-bearing branches to serve as *schach* for a *Sukkah*, and whether during the period of its *orlah* one may cut down such a tree to build a *Sukkah*. There he deals in detail with the parameters of the prohibitions of *bal tash'hit*. His rulings are rather ambivalent in both these cases.

And this, indeed, is the case with the so-far unsolved problem of what to do with plastic and other non-biodegradable refuse.

So it is understandable why the rabbis broadened the application of this original prohibition. Thus, in the *Sifre* to *Deuteronomy*, ibid., sect. 203[59] we read:

> Thou shalt not destroy the trees thereof by forcing an ax against them" (*Deut.*, ibid.) – Are we speaking merely of "an ax," or perhaps also [that one may not] draw away [from them their] water channel? Therefore we learn, "thou shalt not destroy the trees thereof – [meaning] in any way."[60]

---

59. Ed. Finkelstein, New York, p. 239.

60. On the relationship to trees in other cultures, see the very strange esoteric book called *Cultus Arborum: A Descriptive Account of Phallic Tree Worship*, anonymous author, but by Hargrave Jennings (the British freemason 1817–1890), privately printed, 1890, which, however, contains much interesting information. Thus, on pp. 8–9 we read concerning India:

> In a country like India, anything that offers a cool shelter from the burning rays of the sun is regarded with a feeling of grateful respect. The wide-spreading Banyan tree is planted and nursed with care, only because it offers a shelter to many a weary traveler. Extreme usefulness of the thing is the only motive perceivable in the careful rearing of other trees. They are protected by religious injunctions, and the planting of them is encouraged by promises of eternal bliss in the future world. The injunction against injuring a banyan or fig tree is so strict, that in the Ramayana even Rávana [the *rákshasa*], an unbeliever, is made to say "I have not cut down any fig tree, in the month of Vaisakha, why then does the calamity (alluding to the several defeats his army sustained in the war with Rámachandra and to the loss of his sons and brothers) befall me? [I have not found this reference in the Ramayana.]" As early as the Ramayana, the planting of a group of trees was held meritorious. The celebrated Panchavati garden where Sitá was imprisoned, has been reproduced by many a religious Hindu, and should any of them not have sufficient space to cultivate the five trees, the custom is to plant them in a small pot where they are dwarfed into small shrubs. Such substitutes and make-shifts are not at all uncommon in the ecclesiastical history of India. In Buddhist India, millions of miniature stone and clay temples, some of them not higher than two inches, were often dedicated when more substantial structures were not possible. The Panchavati consists of the *asvatha* [= fig tree] planted on the east side, the *vilva* [= bilva] of Aegle *marmelos* [= wood apple] on the north, the *banian* on the west, the *Emblica officinalis* [= lotus] on the south, and the *asoka* on the south-

Maimonides (in *Hilchot Melachim* 6:8) explains that they wish to cut off the water supply in order to dry up the trees, and his explanation is borne out by the reading in the *Sifre* MS London ad loc., "in order to dry up its trees."[61]

However, this expansion still remains within the context of siege activities. The rabbis further broadened its application to apply to all sorts of situations, not merely during a military siege. Thus, Maimonides (ibid.)[62] applies this not just to whole trees but to fruit in general, and

---

east. (Ancient Panchavati is identified with Nāsik, one of the sacred cities of India, as the scene of Rama's banishment, and of the incident where the nose [nāsika] of the ogress Sūrpenakhā was cut off by Lakhmana. See Benjamin Walker, *Hindu World: An Encyclopedic Survey of Hinduism*, London, 1968, vol. 2, p. 124, s.v. Nāsik. The *bilva* [*vilva, bal, bael*] tree has a triple leaf and is sacred to Siva as part of him resides in its leaves. It is forbidden to break its branches, and it is not to be used for firewood except by Brahmins [Walker, ibid., s.v. plants, p. 217]. The *asvutha*, also called pīpal is also a cosmological tree, mentioned frequently in the sacred writings, and has its roots in heaven and its branches on earth. The *aśoka*, "non-sorrow" [*sacra indica*] gives forth orange or scarlet blossoms when touched by the foot of a maiden. It was under this tree that Hanuman espied Sita as she sat, a prisoner of Ravana, mourning for Rama, and under this tree Mahaviva renounced the world. The lotus, or water lily, the national flower of Hindu India, is that mythical flower in the novel of Visnu from which Brahma springs [ibid., pp. 216–217].)

Of course, this is to be seen in the context of Indian belief in the deities residing in trees. See, for example, the following mantra cited in Jitendra Noth Banerjee, *The Development of Hindu Iconography*, Calcutta, 1956, p. 206:

Oh, thou tree, salutation to thee, thou art selected for (being fashioned into) the icon of this particular deity; please accept this offering according to rules. May all the spirits which reside in this tree transfer their habitation elsewhere after accepting the offerings made according to rules; may they pardon me today (for disturbing them); salutation to them.

But here we have rather strayed from our main theme into an area which requires its own examination.

61. *Sifre*, ed. Finkelstein, editor's note to line 2.

62. Rambam, ibid., writes: And not only trees, but whoever breaks vessels, tears garments, destroys a building, stops up a spring, and damages trees, transgresses *bal tash'hit*, and he is only punished by rabbinic law with lashes (*makat-mardut*). Cf. B.

not only to trees and fruit but to all manner of food, utensils, clothes, etc. (ibid., 10).[63] And, indeed, this is surely the thrust of the biblical commandment. For if in times of war, and during an extended siege – "When thou shalt besiege a city a long time" (*Deuteronomy* 20:19) – when the cutting down of trees serves a clear military purpose, such activity is forbidden, how much more so when there is less urgent a need, or no real need at all. Furthermore, even the barren trees may be cut down in order to serve as siege-engines to subdue the enemy and presumably reduce potential loss of life on the part of the besieging army – from which we may logically and persuasively infer that the wanton destruction of barren trees, serving no real purpose, would also be forbidden. An additional extension of this principle was the rabbinic prohibition against raising "small cattle" (*behemah dakah*), primarily goats, in Eretz Yisrael, since they crop grass close to the earth, leading to a denudation of the top-soil. (See *B. Pesahim* 50b, *B. Baba Kama* 796, *Shulhan Aruch Hoshan Mishpat* 409:1; also Tana de-Bei Eliyahu 15:18.)

Yet a further extension of the extended application of this principle is to be found in *Sefer ha-Hinuch* (sect. 529). The author writes as follows:

... So too [there comes] under [the category of] this [prohibition] not to cause any sort of damage, such as burning or tearing a garment or breaking a utensil, and any similar kind of destructive activity.... And this was the way of the righteous and the men of [good] deeds... who would not even destroy a single mustard seed, and who would feel grief over any kind of waste and destruction they saw, and if they were able to save anything from destruction, they would do so with all the strength....

We may recall what R. Aryeh Levine is credited with having related, as follows:

Bava Kama 91b. And see R. Hayyim Josef David Azulai [= Hidah], *Hayyim Shaal*, vol. 1, Livorno, 1892, no. 22.

63. Cf. *B. Shabbat* 129a. And cf. Maimonides, *Sefer ha-Mitzvot*, negative commandment no. 57.

I recall the early days, from 1905 onward, when it was granted me by the grace of the blessed Lord to go up to the holy land, and I came to Jaffa. There I first went to visit our great master R. Abraham Isaac Kook (of blessed memory), who received me with good cheer, as it was his hallowed custom to receive everyone. We chatted together on themes of Torah study. After the afternoon service, he went out, as was his custom, to stroll a bit in the fields and gather his thoughts; and I went along. On the way, I plucked some branch or flower. Our great master was taken aback; and then he told me gently, "Believe me. In all my days I have taken care never to pluck a blade of grass or flower needlessly, when it had the ability to grow or blossom. You know the teaching of the Sages that there is not a single blade of grass below, here on earth, which does not have a heavenly force above telling it 'Grow'! Every sprout and leaf of grass says something, conveys some meaning. Every stone whispers some inner, hidden message in the silence. Every creature utters its song (in praise of the Creator)." Those words, spoken from a pure and holy heart, engraved themselves deeply on my heart. From then on, I began to feel a strong sense of compassion for everything.[64]

---

64. Simcha Raz, *A Tzaddik in Our Times*, translated by Charles Wengrov, Jerusalem, 1976, pp. 108–109. Perhaps Rav Kook was referring to *Pirkei Shira* mentioned above. A similar tale is told of R. Shalom Dov Ber, the fifth Lubavitcher Rebbe, around 1896, when his son plucked a leaf off a tree (Sears. ibid.. pp. 224–225).

We are, of course, reminded of Naomi Shemer's wonderful song, *Shirat ha-Asabim*, The Story of the Grasses, which was undoubtebly inspired by one or more passages in the writings of R. Nachman of Bratzlav. The song goes (in part):

> Know that every blade of grass has its own song, and from the song of the grasses is born the shepherds melody.
> How beautiful and filling it is to hear this music.
> Good indeed it is to pray among them serving God in joy.
> As the heart, awakened with the grasses' song, fills with yearning…
> Then from the song of the grasses is born the song of the heart.

The source of this song appears to be a passage in R. Nachman's *Likkutei Moharan*, New York, 1965 (ed. R. Eliezer Breslover) 2:11, p. 44:

> Know that when a person prays in a field, then all of the grasses/plants together

come into the prayer, and they help him, and give him strength within his prayer. And this is what it means when prayer is called "conversation/*sichah*": it refers to "the growth of the field / *si'ach hasadeh*" [*Gen* 2:5], [meaning] that every shoot from the field gives strength and helps his prayer. And this is [what the verse means when it says,] "And Isaac went out to reflect in the field / *lasu'ach basadeh*" [Gen 24:63]: that his prayer (*sichah*) was made with the help and strength of the field (*si'ach*), that all the plants of the field gave strength and helped his prayer.

... And / or ibid., 2:16, pp. 68–69:

> Know that every shepherd has a unique melody/*nigun* according to the grasses and the place where he herds. For every animal/*beheimah* has a grass unique to her that she needs to eat, and also a shepherd isn't always in one place, and according to the grasses, and the place where he herds, so he has a *nigun*. For every grass there is a song/*shirah* which speaks ... and from the song of the grasses is made the *nigun* of the shepherd ... And this is the dimension of "From the edge/wing/*kanaf* of the earth we heard songs/*zemirot*" [Is 24:16] – [it means] that songs and *nigunim* come out from "the wing of the Earth," for by means of the grasses growing in the land a *nigun* is made. And since the shepherd knows the *nigun*, by means of this he gives strength to the grasses ... and there is pasture for the animals.

Seidenberg, ibid., p. 331, note 1071, comments as follows:

See also 2:11, which describes, "the strength of the grasses," rather than their song, entering into one's prayer. Embedded in this teaching is the recognition that each ecosystem or place might make its own unique contribution to human prayer and melody, and so uniquely reveal divinity.

He further explains that:

> Nachman seems to describe a lived experience, even if it is propped up by scripture. The difference between *shirah* [i.e. of *Pirkei Shirah*] or song and *nigun* or melody is that a song has words but a *nigun* may not. There is a paradox in this teaching: humans extract music from the song of the grass, but not the "verbal" part, whatever that may be. Elsewhere, Nachman teaches that song and prayer, encumbered by words, cannot reach the highest levels, but that *nigun*, without words, can even cross the empty space that separates the universe from God, reaching all the way to *Eyn Sof*, to the infinite, primordial source. Together, these passages describe a kind of ecosystem of language and song in which the human being is one organ of a complex cycle that nurtures life and divinity.

See further his various interpretations, ibid., note 1072. And though this is a long

And when he mentions "Every creature utters its song (in praise of the Creator)," we are reminded of the midrashic theme that every creature has a function in nature, and the subsequent danger involved in the threat of the extinction of any given species for a variety of reasons. Thus, in the *Second Alphabet of Ben Sira* 24a–24b, we read (in the formulation of L. Ginzberg, *Legends*, vol. 4, p. 90):

> On another occasion David expressed his doubt of God's wisdom in having formed such apparently useless creatures as spiders are. They do nothing but spin a web that has no value. He was to have striking proof that even a spider's web may serve an important purpose. On one occasion he had taken refuge in a cave, and Saul and his attendants, in pursuit of him, were about to enter and seek him there. But God sent a spider to weave its web across the opening, and Saul told his men to desist from fruitless search in the cave, for the spider's web was undeniable proof that no one had passed through its entrance.

And again (ibid., pp. 90–91):

> Similarly, when David became indebted to one of them for his life he was cured of his scorn for wasps. He had thought them good for nothing but to breed maggots. David once surprised Saul and his attendants while they were fast asleep in their camp, and he resolved to carry off, as proof of his magnanimity, the cruse that stood between the feet of the giant Abner, who like the rest was sleeping. Fortunately his knees were drawn up, so that David could carry out his intention unhindered. But as David was retiring with the cruse, Abner stretched out his feet, and pinned David down as with two solid pillars. His life would have been forfeit, if a wasp had not stung Abner, who mechanically, in his sleep, moved his feet, and released David.[65]

---

somewhat discursive note, it does cast some light on some additional mystical / Hassidic views on the nature of religious interaction between man and nature.

65. See Ginzberg's notes in vol. 6, p. 233, notes 47, 48, for additional references.

So just as the blade of grass serves a(n obvious) function in nature, so do the spiders and the wasps, and indeed all the creations of God. And this, no doubt, is the deeper underlying message of *Pirkei Shira*. (See above note 121.)

And I would suggest that this is also the inner meaning and message of a number of midrashim homiletically commenting on the verse in *Genesis* 2:20, "And Adam gave names to every beast of the field..." Again, in the words of Ginzberg, ibid., vol. 1, pp. 61–62:

> The wisdom of Adam displayed itself to the greatest advantage when he gave names to the animals. Then it appeared that God, in combating the arguments of the angels that opposed the creation of man, had spoken well, when He insisted that man would possess more wisdom than they themselves. When Adam was barely an hour old, God assembled the whole world of animals before him and the angels. The latter were called upon to name the different kinds, but they were not equal to the task. Adam, however, spoke without hesitation: "O Lord of the world! The proper name for this animal is ox, for this one horse, for this one lion, for this one camel." And so he called all in turn by name, suiting the name to the peculiarity of the animal. Then God asked him what his name was to be, and he said Adam, because he had been created out of Adamah, dust of the earth. Again, God asked him His own name, and he said: "Adonai, Lord, because Thou art Lord over all creatures" – the very name God had given unto Himself, the name by which the angels call Him, the name that will remain immutable evermore. But without the gift of the Holy Spirit, Adam could not have found names for all; he was in very truth a prophet, and his wisdom a prophetic quality.[66]

This theme finds further expression in a series of tales found in *Tanhuma Hukkat* 1, ed. Buber, pp. 98–99, *Genesis Rabba* 10:7, ed. Theodor Albeck, vol. 1, pp. 79–83, *Leviticus Rabba* 22:3, ed. Margaliot, pp. 498–502 etc. This passage in its various versions describes the roles played by fleas, mosquitoes, flies, snakes, frogs and crabs, all carrying out their functions as dictated by God.

66. There are numerous versions of this theme in rabbinic literature. See Ginzberg, ibid., vol. 5, p. 83, notes 29, 30, and cf. continuation of passage in vol. 1, pp. 62–64, and ibid., vol. 5, note 34. See also *Pirkei de Rabbi Eliezer*, transl. G. Friedlander, London,

In these sources, the "name," I believe, represents the *function* of the named.[67]

There is a wonderful tale ascribed to the Baal Shem Tov (R. Yisrael ben Eliezer c. 1700–1760):

> The Baal Shem Tov taught that when a piece of straw falls from a wagon loaded with straw, this has been decreed by Heaven. Similarly, when a leaf falls from a tree, it is because Heaven has decreed that this particular leaf at this particular moment would fall at this particular spot. Once the Baal Shem Tov showed his disciples a certain leaf as it fell to the ground and told them to pick it up. They did so and saw that a worm was underneath it. The Baal Shem Tov explained that the worm had been suffering due to the heat, so this leaf had fallen to give it shade.[68]

It requires a special sensitivity to nature to be able to make a statement of this nature. And it was just this sensitivity which led the rabbis to rule forbidding the raising of goats in certain regions, because their close cropping destroys the top-soil surface (see *M. Baba Kama* 7:7, and *B.* ibid., 79b).[69]

1916, p. 91, and note 8, ibid., the many versions are cited and commented on by R. M. M. Kasher, in his *Torah Shelemah Genesis*, vol. 2, Jerusalem, 1935, pp. 338–340, nos. 263–269. He compares the various sources discussing whether Adam also named fish (see the *Tosafot* to *B. Hullin* 66b). This theme is already found in pre-rabbinic sources, e.g., *The Book of Jubilee* 3:1–2 (here following the Scriptural source, adding however, "and everything that moves in the water," ed. R. H. Charles, *The Apocrypha and the Pseudepigrapha of the Old Testament in English*, vol. 2, Oxford, 1913, p. 16.).

67. See *Tikkunei ha-Zohar*, sect. 57, 91b: Adam gave each one a name according to its celestial powers. Ibid., He named each animal, angel and wheel (*ofan* – a mystical notion) in accordance with its form, function and watch (*matkonet, avodah* and *mishmeret*). I shall not enlarge upon this subject which requires a study in its own right.

68. *Sha'ar ha-Otiyot: Hashgahah Pratit*, cited in Sears, ibid., p. 42. Cf. *Jonah* 4:6–10.

69. For a full discussion of this ruling, see Tzvi Idlis and Eliezer Afarsmon, *Eichut ha-Sevivah: Hezeik Reiyah*, Hevron, 2009, pp. 13–19, section entitled "*Gidul Behemah Dakah.*"

On the (strange) interrelationship between human, plant and animal life, we find in the world of folklore the notion of men that grow on trees – *adnei-sadeh* (in *M. Kilayim* 8:5, and *Y.* ibid., 31a, 59–60, and, in Chinese traditions, sheep connected by their navel to the ground), a subject I dealt with in a chapter entitled "Vegetable-Men" in my *Magic and Folklore in Rabbinic Literature*, Ramat-Gan, 1994, pp. 21–25. To the above, we may add the following additional references: Fra Oderic, in *Cathay and the Way Thither*, by Henry Yule, Cambridge. 2010, p. 79, note 1:

> *"And here I heard tell that there be trees which bear men and women like fruit upon them. They are about a cubit in measurement, and are fixed in the tree up to the navel, and there they be; and when the wind blows they be fresh, but when it does not blow they are all dried up. This I saw not in sooth, but I heard it told by people who had seen it."* Here again we have a genuine Oriental story, related by several Arab geographers of the island of *Wak-wak* in the Southern Ocean (e. g., see Bakui in *Not. et Ext.*, ii, 399). Al Biruni denies that the island is called so, "as is vulgarly believed, because of a fruit having the form of a human heäd which cries *Wak! Wak!*" (*Journ. Asiat. S.*, iv, t. iv, p. 266). And Edrisi declines to repeat the "incredible story" related by Masudi on the subject, with the pious reservation, "But all things are in the power of the Most High" (i, 92).

See also E. Bretschneider, *Mediaeval Researches from Eastern Asiatic Sources*, vol. 1, London, 1888. p.154:

> The *lung chung yang* (literally, "sheep planted on hillocks") are also produced in the western countries. The people take the navel of a sheep, plant it in the ground and water it. When it hears thunder it grows, the navel retaining a connection with the ground. After the beast has become full grown they take a stick and frighten it. Then the navel breaks off and the sheep begins to walk and eats grass. In autumn it can be eaten. The flesh of the navel (of the butchered sheep) can be planted again.

To which he adds the following lengthy note (416):

> It is not difficult to divine that this miraculous story of a lamb which grows like a plant is nothing other than the reproduction of the mediæval legend of the lamb-plant, Tartarian lamb, *Agnus scythicus*. Friar Odoric, in the fourteenth century, was the first European traveller who referred to this story (Yule's "Cathay," 144), but it must have been current much earlier in Western countries, for the Chinese authors mention it in the ninth century. In the *T'ang shu*, chap. cclviii. *b*, article *Fu-lin* (Byzantine empire), I find the following account: "There are in the country of Fu-lin sheep which grow from the ground. The people wait till they shoot out, and then surround (the plant or beast) with a wall, to protect it against wild beasts. If the umbilical cord connecting the lamb with the ground is cut off, it will die. (There is another method to keep it living.) A man, duly caparisoned mounts a horse and rushes upon the lamb. At the same time a great

noise is made to frighten it. Then the lamb cries, the umbilical cord breaks off, and it goes to graze." According to Odoric's report, these lambs are found in large melons. *Hieron. Cardanus*, and after him *J. C. Scaliger* (both in the first half of the sixteenth century), in their account of this miraculous lamb, state that the *Agnus scythicus* is found in the lands of the noble Tartar horde called *Zavolha* (meaning beyond the Wolga, for *za* in Russian = beyond). The seed is like that of a melon, but the plant, which is called *barometz*, or "the lamb" (*barun* = sheep in Russian), grows to the height of about three feet in the form of that animal, with feet, hoofs, ears, &c., complete, only having in lieu of horns two curly locks of hair. If wounded, it bleeds; wolves are greedily fond of it. In 1725 Dr. Breyn of Dantzig first declared that the pretended Agnus scythicus was nothing more that the root of a large fern covered with its natural yellow down, and accompanied by some of the stems, &c., in order, when placed in an inverted position, the better to represent the appearance of the legs and horns of a quadruped. Linnæus in 1752 received a fern from Southern China, gathered by Osbeck, and did not hesitate in declaring it to be the Agnus scythicus, and to name it *Polypodium Barometz*. Loureiro ("Fl. Cochin.," 675) found the same plant in Cochin-China and China. He gives *keu tsie* as the Chinese name (i.e., *kou ts'i*, dog's back, from the resemblance of the rhizoma of the plant to a dog, as the Chinese botanical works state). Modern botanists called the plant *Cibotium Barometz*. It is a tropical plant, found in South China, Assam, and on the Sandwich Islands. Nowhere in the books at my disposal can I find mention of it near the Wolga. The English Cyclopædia (quoted by Yule), in assigning to this plant an elevated salt plain to the west of the Wolga, derived its information, it seems, only from Scaliger's conjecture. How then can Th. Moore state in the "Treasury of Botany" that the Agnus scythicus is without doubt the Cibotium Barometz? Mediæval travellers as well as the Chinese annals agree in assigning to this marvellous plant-animal the countries of Western Asia or Eastern Europe.

Furthermore, in Jewish sources, such as *M. Hullin* 9:6, *B*. ibid., 126b, we read of a rat half of which is flesh and half of which is soil, apparently substantiated by the Rambam in his commentary to the Mishnah ad loc., and the Mordechai, in his discussion to this particular phenomenon (sect. 735), also refers to the lamb that grows on a tree, (see also *Darchei Teshuvah* to *Shulhan Aruch Yoreh Deah* 84, note 170). Of course, Biblical Adam was created out of the dust of the earth (taken from all four quarters of the world) (*Genesis* 2:7), but this, again, is too broad a subject to be dealt with here. See, however, L. Ginzberg, *The Legends of the Jews*, vol. 1, Philadelphia 1909, p. 55; idem., vol. 5, Philadelphia, 1925, notes 14, 15, pp. 71–73; to which may be added: E. A. Wallis Budge, *The Book of the Cave of Treasures*, London, 1927, pp. 51–52, that Adam was created out of the four elements, dust, water, air and fire.

Additional material may be found in Pinhas Zvihi, *Sefer Ateret Paz*, Jerusalem, 2008, pp. 17–21, note 7, who also claims to have heard from reliable sources (*mi-pi magidei*

This extreme sensitivity to nature may also be found in Muslim sources. Martin Palmer and Victoria Finlay, ibid., p. 52, write as follows:

> One day, according to the Hadith (a book of traditional and authenticated accounts of the words and actions of the Prophet Muhammad), the Prophet was traveling from one town to the next with his followers. They were just crossing a river when it became time for prayers. Naturally they used the river to perform the ritual ablutions required before prayer. However, the followers of the Prophet were astonished to see him enter the river with a little bowl. This he filled with water and it was this water with which he performed the ablutions. When asked why, surrounded by a whole river, he took so little water to use, he said that just because there is plenty this does not give us the right to waste or to take more than we really need.[70]

They conclude:

> This is one of the most powerful stories that Muslims use to teach about our need to respect the environment. And even today, in the modern world, when Islamic teachers and leaders need to remind people not to waste resources this is one of the main examples they will use. Sometimes when faith-based environmentalists work on projects, all they need to do is remind local people of the stories they know already.[71]

---

emet) "that in India there is a tree out of which emerge small birds...."

All the above – and doubtless more than I have found – is in the realm of folklore. But perhaps these traditions reflect an understanding of the interrelationship between all aspects of nature.

70. *Ibn Maja, Sunan Ibn Maja*, ed. F. 'Abd al-Baqi (Turkey, 1972), 1, 146. This Muslim story is echoed in the Hindu saying: "Everything animate or inanimate that is within the universe is controlled and owned by the Lord. One should therefore accept only those things necessary for himself, which are set aside as his quota, and one should not accept other things."

71. See also what I wrote in my *On the Relationship of Mitzvot Between Man and His Neighbor and Man and His Maker*, Jerusalem and New York, 2014, p. 30, citing *M. Negaim* 12:5, and my *Darkah shel Torah*, Jerusalem, 2007, pp. 93–99, 140.

And R. Eliezer of Metz, writing in twelfth-century Germany, in his *Sefer Yeraim* (ed. A. A. Schiff, Vilna, 1892–1902, p. 402, sect. 382 ad fin.) goes so far as to say,

> And a person should take heed of this prohibition. For we have found that a great man was punished for this transgression, as it is written, "[Now King David was old and stricken in years;] and they covered him with clothes, but he got no heat" (*1 Kings* 1:1), and [concerning this] the rabbis said: For he shamed garments, when he tore Saul's cloak, therefore he had no benefit from them (*B. Berachot* 62b). And he who destroys, transgresses two prohibitions, "thou shalt not destroy" – *lo tash'hit*, and

---

A similar theme, but this time with a more socio-ethical emphasis, may be found in a tale told of R. Yisrael Lipkin Salanter (1810–1883), related in R. Yehudah Leib Maimon's *Sarei ha-Meah*, vol. 2, pp. 272–273, and cited and discussed by me in my *On the Relationship*, chapter 23, pp. 151–153:

> It once happened that Reb Yisrael Salanter, during his stay in Kovno, lived for a while in the house of a wealthy pious man, Reb Yaakov Karpas, and would dine at his table. Members of the household noted that when he washed his hands before the meal, he would do so with a minimal amount of water, even though a bucket full of water was prepared for him. They wondered in amazement: Should not a *tzaddik* like Reb Yisrael rule more stringently (*mehadrin*) to wash his hands with a plentiful amount of water! They went and spoke to Reb Karpas, who examined the matter and found that indeed Reb Yisrael would wash his hands with no more than a *reviit ha-log*. He too was most surprised, and when they sat together for a meal, he asked Reb Yisrael: "Forgive me, our Master, but this is a matter of Torah and I must learn about it. Why then does it suffice you to wash your hands with a *reviit*? Surely, it is a clear ruling in the *Shulhan Aruch* (*Orah Hayyim* 155:10), 'even though the amount (for handwashing) is a *reviit*, one should wash more plentifully.' Why then do you, sir, not do so?"
>
> Reb Yisrael answered as follows:
>
> "I have seen that the maid brings the water from afar, from a well in the valley. Your house is situated high on the hill, and the maid almost collapses under the weight of her burden, when she brings up the pail of water on her shoulders. *And it is forbidden for a person to be overly religious* (le-hader) *at the expense of others*" [My emphasis – D. S.].

On the halachic background of this tale, see what I wrote ibid.. pp. 152–153. note 2.

| "thou shalt not cut down – *lo tichrot* (*Deut., ibid.*).[72]

There is indeed ample talmudic evidence that the principle of *lo tash'hit* was applied to all manner of destruction. Thus, in *B. Kiddushin* 21a, we read that Rav Huna tore his clothing in front of his son, and the Gemara asks: Surely he transgressed *bal tash'hit*! And in *Shabbat* 129a, Rava is said to have broken a bench himself, and Abbaye reacted in surprise that surely this constitutes a transgression of *bal tash'hit*.[73]

Thus wanton destruction, or, to use a different formulation, the wasteful use of natural resources, is clearly eschewed by biblical law, expounded and expanded by rabbinic law.

This, however, should be understood within a broader ideological context. For the reason given for not destroying the fruit trees, even for the purpose of optimizing military objectives, is because "thou mayest eat of them," meaning they constitute a vital resource for the continuity of life. Even during periods of war, one must take into account the basic injunction to preserve the world's resources and its environment for future generations. Indeed, Adam, the prototype human being, on entering the Garden of Eden, was enjoined *"le-ovdah u-le-shomrah"* (*Genesis* 2:15), "to tend it and to preserve it."[74] The Hebrew word

---

72. See the editor's note 4 ad loc., referring to *Ba'al Halachot Gedolot,* negative commandments, nos. 218, 219. See further Ramban's additions to Maimonides's *Sefer ha-Mitzvot,* positive commandment no. 6, who also regards *lo tichrot* as a separate injunction, and "for thou mayest eat of them" – *ki mimenu tochel* – as a positive commandment, differing on this point from Maimonides' (ibid.) negative commandment no. 57.

73. See R. Moshe of Coucy's *Semag* (= *Sefer Mitzvot Gadol*), negative commandment 229, who brings these and additional sources to this effect. See also *B. Shabbat* 67b, and *Bava Kama* 91b for examples of *bal tash'hit.* See also Roberta Kalechofsky, *Vegetarian Judaism,* Micah Publications 1998, chapter 6, pp. 149–165.

74. Kalechofsky, ibid., p. 153, quotes David Shapiro, in his article "God, Man and Creation" (without a detailed reference), as follows:

> But even though man was converted into a conqueror he was never to forget his original relationship to the earth, which was to work it and watch over it. The second chapter of *Genesis* emphasizes that man's origin was derived from the earth. "The Lord God formed man from the dust of the earth." (2:6) The earth is not only the seat of man's activities and that of other creatures; it is not only the

"*le-shomrah*" bears two meanings: to look after it and to preserve it. These two meanings, which might seem to be almost identical, in actual fact reflect two different though related notions, both of which are alluded to by the use of this biblical term. *Le-shomrah*, looking after something, indicates that the thing does not belong to you, that you are its *shomer*, its steward. Adam is being told, as it were, that "the world and all that is in it belongs to God" (*Psalms* 24:21), but that "*ha-Aretz natan li-vnei adam*" (*Psalms* 115:16), that the earth has been given over to human beings to be tended and guarded over. Martin Buber, in his *Tales of the Hasidim*, New York, 1991, Book Two: The Later Master, p. 317, relates that:

> When Rabbi Hanokh [of Alexander, died 1870] had said the verse in the *Psalms*: "The heavens are the heavens of the Lord, but the earth hath He given to the children of men," he paused and then went on to say: "'The heavens are the heavens of the Lord' – you see they are already of a heavenly character. 'But the earth hath He given to the children of men' – so that they might make of it something heavenly."

Le-shomrah also has the semantic meaning "to preserve" something for its continued use in the future. So we are mandated to preserve the world's natural resources, which are not really ours to waste, for the continuing benefit of future generations.[75]

And there is the spiritual dimension of this issue. For we live in two different interrelated dimensions. We live in the dimension of space,

---

medium of their substance, it is the very source of man's existence as well as that of the other land-animals, just as the water is the origin of life. The earth is the mother of man, from which he emerged and to which he will ultimately return.... God did not create the world to be wasteland. He made it to be inhabited.... It is man who makes possible the extension of blessings to the earth, just as he is answerable for the curses that the earth suffers when he departs from God and the righteous way of life. Because of man's sinfulness, the earth can no longer perform its functions properly.

75. See my discussion on "Jewish Environmental Ethics" in *The Edah Journal* 2:1, 2002, pp. 1–5.

and we live in the dimension of time.[76]

In terms of the dimension of time, we can do well by quoting at length what Rabbi Yonatan Neril wrote in his *Eco Bible*, vol. 1: *An Ecological Commentary on Genesis and Exodus* (Jerusalem) 2020, pp. 166–168, on the implications of the Sabbath from an ecological viewpoint:

> *Exodus* 35:2 – *On six days work may be done, but on the seventh day you shall have a Sabbath of complete rest, holy to the Lord, whoever does any work on it shall be put to death.*
>
> So impactful is this commandment, today most of the world's population enjoys a "weekend" that can be traced back to this command.
>
> Rabbi Norman Lamm writes:
>
> Perhaps the most powerful expression of the Bible's concern for man's respect for the integrity of nature as the possession of its Creator, rather than his own preserve, is the Sabbath... The six workdays were given to man in which to carry out the commission to "subdue" the world, to impose on nature his creative talents. But the seventh day is a Sabbath; man must cease his creative interference in the natural order (Jewish law's definition of *melakha* or work), and by this act of renunciation demonstrate his awareness that the earth is the Lord's and that man therefore bears a moral responsibility to give an accounting to its Owner for how he has disposed of it during the days he "subdued it"... A new insight into Jewish eschatology: not a progressively growing technology and rising GNP, but a peaceful and mutually respectful coexistence between man and his environment, (N. Lamm, "Ecology in Jewish Law and Theology," apud *Faith and Doubt: Studies in Traditional Jewish Thought*, 3 ed., ed. Bernard Scharfstein, New Jersey 2006, p. 163–164).

---

76. See my article in *Emor* 1, January 2010, pp. 23–35, entitled "The Sanctity of Space, Time and Person: A Jewish Perspective," especially pp. 25–28, on the various levels of sanctity and their halachic implications, and the discussion of *M. Kelim* 1:6–9. I have also discussed this issue in greater detail in my article entitled "Jerusalem: Axis Mundi," in the *Joshua Schwartz Volume ...* which is vol. 12–13 of *A Journal for Land of Israel Studies and Archeology* 2020, pp. 179[x]–184[x].

On Shabbat, traditionally observant Jews stop working, stop traveling, stop creating. The Ten Commandments teach us that on Shabbat, "You shall not perform any kind of creative work," (*Exodus* 20:10). Rabbi Hirsch, in his commentary on this verse, explains that physical exertion is not one of the basic criteria of the term "creative work." According to the Torah, if one lifts a heavy piece of furniture on Shabbat, one is not guilty of violating the prohibition against work, even though such an activity is not necessarily in keeping with the spirit of Shabbat. If, however, one plucks a leaf off a tree or plants a seed in the earth, then one has violated the mandate not to perform work on Shabbat. A study of Torah law reveals that the definition of work on Shabbat is an activity in which a person transforms anything in the environment for his or her own use, such as for food, clothing, or shelter.

Rabbi Abraham Joshua Heschel taught, "To set apart one day a week for freedom, a day on which we would not use the instruments which have been so easily turned into weapons of destruction, a day for being with ourselves, a day of detachment from the vulgar, of independence of external obligations, a day on which we stop worshipping the idols of technical civilization, a day on which we use no money, a day of armistice in the economic struggle with our fellow men and the forces of nature – is there any institution that holds out greater hope for man's progress than the Sabbath?" (Abraham Joshua Heschel, *Between Man and God*, New York, 1959, pp. 221–222).

Observance of Shabbat – taking a day each week to refrain from the transformation of nature – has the potential to alter a person's feeling of creative and technological control over nature. In early nineteenth-century Germany, Rabbi Samson Raphael Hirsch senses the profound relevance of Shabbat for industrial society, exclaiming, "Sabbath in our time! To cease for a whole day from all business, from all work, in the frenzied hurry-scurry of our time!... The pulse of life would stop beating and the world perish! The world perish? On the contrary, it would be saved," (S. R. Hirsch, "The Jewish Sabbath," in *Judaism Eternal: Selected Essays from the Writings of Rabbi Samson Raphael Hirsch*, ed. Dayan Isidore Grunfeld, London 1956, p. 30). This message of Shabbat is sorely needed in today's Western society.

The mentality and lifestyle of "doing" without regard to "being," of transforming the natural world without taking time to reflect on the value of that transformation, is taking an environmental toll on the planet. A society that never rests nor reflects is the same society that over-extracts and over-consumes. This mastery of the earth without sufficient contemplation of its consequences has produced ecological destruction on the local, regional, and global level.

Air and water pollution. Species loss. Climate change. These are problems not of the environment, but of a society bent on doing and producing seven days a week. A *New York Times Magazine* article commented on American lifestyles, saying, "A nation of remarkably productive, often well-paid workers... are becoming increasingly reluctant to pause from their labors and refresh their souls." Meanwhile, the countries with the largest percentage of people working 60 hours a week or more in their main job are Turkey (23.3 percent) and South Korea (22.6 percent). On Shabbat, we are to walk on the earth without asserting our mastery over it, in order to acknowledge the sovereignty of the Creator. In this way, we will remember that we are only the custodians of the earth with the responsibility "to work it and to guard it," (*Genesis* 2:15).

And, of course, the sabbatical year, discussed below is also an example of the dimension of time and its ecological aspect.

We live in the dimension of space, and we must know that we cannot waste and overexploit the space in which we live, i.e., our physical resources. We live in a dimension of time and we must know how to utilize time and optimize our use thereof. Our lifetime is limited and we must put it to its best use. And though we live in the present, we must constantly be sensitive to the results of our actions in the future.

Now space, the universe in which we live, though physical, also has a degree of sanctity, an intrinsic sanctity in that all creation comes from God and is therefore imbued with an element of innate sanctity.[77] For

---

77. I find Abraham Joshua Heschel's remarks on the Jewish concept of the holiness of space being subordinate to that of time questionable. See his *The Earth is the Lord's* and *The Sabbath*, New York and Philadelphia, 1963, p. 79. See above note 130.

since everything in the universe, in nature, everything physical and in a sense spiritual, is the result of the divine will, it has an element of divinity or of sanctity. Ultimate dominion over all things with which we can have any contact, is only that of God; as is stated in *Deuteronomy* 10:14, "Behold, the heaven and the heaven of heavens is the Lord Thy God's, the earth also, with all that is therein." And in the language of the liturgy (*Amidah*), "who possesses all" (*Koneh ha-kol*). Mankind has been given that well-known mandate, which is also a privilege, to tend the Garden of Eden, the world – a metaphor – and to guard over it (*Genesis* 2:15). To guard over it for future generations, that is our mandate and that actually presents us with an awesome responsibility.

And as part of this responsibility the rabbis went even further, warning against overindulgent wastage. Thus, R. Hisda (Babylonia, third century CE.) says: Whosoever can eat bread made from barley, and eats bread made from wheat[78] transgresses the prohibition of *bal tash'hit*. And Rav Pappa (two generations later) added: Whosoever can drink beer and drinks wine, transgresses the prohibition of *bal tash'hit* (*B. Shabbat* 140b).[79] It is true that the Talmud indicates that these opinions were not accepted, for one should not eat inferior food, but rather take care more for one's health than one's purse. However,[80] from above we

---

78. See my note in *Tarbiz* 33, 1967, pp. 99–101, on the different classes of bread in talmudic times.

79. See *Shevut Yaakov* of R. Yaakov Reisha, vol. 3, no. 71, that even for personal monetary or medical benefits the principle of *bal tash'hit* applies. On the trade and consumption of wine and beer in Amoraic Babylonia, see the extensive discussion of M. Beer, in his *The Babylonian Amoraim: Aspects of Economic Life,* Ramat Gan, 1974 [Hebrew] index s.v. *yayin, shechar*, especially pp. 159–180, 318–324.

80. The debate, then, is what are the limits, and as Jeremy Bernstein in his *The Way to Judaism and the Environment*, p. 100, has rightly written:

> ... but this is exactly the debate we need to have: what are the limits, what "uses" are actually abuses, and what demands do holiness and sustainability make on our lives and lifestyles.

He then quotes the thirteenth-century *Sefer ha-Hinuch* (sect. 530) who "saw in this *mitzvah*" – a very general principle, a *middah*, a virtue to be cultivated:

> ... This is the way of the righteous and those who improve society ... that

can nonetheless deduce that when the foods are equally healthy, we should prefer the cheaper brand. Indeed the rabbis regarded waste of monetary resources as something that the Bible strongly advises to be avoided,[81] and they waged a constant battle against the overindulgent use of luxuries, for "the Torah expressed concern for the financial resources of the individual – *Ha-Torah hasah al memonam shel Yisrael*" (*B. Yoma* 39a, based on *Leviticus* 14:36).[82] Hence, Jewish law enjoins

---

nothing, not even a grain of mustard, should be lost ... [and] if possible they will prevent any destruction that they can. Not so are the wicked, who rejoice in the destruction of the world, and they are destroying themselves.

81.   See Rabbenu Bahya's commentary to *Exodus* 12:4, ed. Chavel, Jerusalem, 1967, pp. 89–90; *Torat Kohanim, Metzorah* 5; *Rosh ha-Shanah* 3.4 and *Bavli* ad loc.; *B. Menhahot* 76b; *B. Yoma* 39a, *M. Negaim* 12.5. For a full survey of this concept, see *Encyclopedia Talmudit* II, Jerusalem, 1965, pp. 240–245.

82.   Most recently in my book entitled *The Importance of the Community Rabbi: Leading with Compassionate Halachah*, Jerusalem and New York, 2020, pp. 42–45, note 2, I discussed this principle in considerable detail. Here I quote what I wrote there:

The principle is "*Ha-Torah Hassah al Memonam shel Yisrael*." Cf. R. Akiva's statement, in *B. Bechorot* 40a, where he ruled leniently in a certain case, in opposition to the ruling of R. Yochanan ben Nuri. And R. Akiva said to him, "Till when are you going to waste the assets of [the people of] Israel?" To which R. Yochanan ben Nuri replied, "Till when are you going to feed *neveilot* to [the people of] Israel?" See further Y. Y. Bronstein, *Avnei Gazit*, Jerusalem, 2002, p. 183, quoting the view of Maharatz Chajes, to *B. Hulin* 49b, that this principle does not apply to *issurei Torah*, things forbidden by biblical law. Here is the place to comment on that which is found in the book *Minhah Belulah* (cited by M. M. Kasher. *Torah Shleimah*, vol. 9, p. 90, note 56) on the verse from *Exodus* 9:19: "'Now therefore send, hasten in your cattle and all that you have in the field; for every man and beast that shall be found in the field, and shall not be brought home, the hail shall come down upon them, and they shall die.' The rabbis were wont to say that the Torah takes pity on the finances of the Jewish people, and here it is proven that it also takes pity on the finances of the nations of the world." (Rabbi Avraham Menachem ha-Cohen Rappaport, *Minchah Belulah*, Verona, 1594.) See *Hulin* 49b where Rava declared it proper to use impure fat to stop up a hole because the Torah takes pity on the finances of the Jewish people. And Rav Papa asked him: "This is a Torah prohibition, and you say that the Torah takes pity on the finances of the Jewish people?" Tosafot writes there: "The law is in accordance with Rav Papa that in a Torah prohibition, it is not relevant to say that the Torah takes pity on the finances of the Jewish people, that in a Torah prohibition we do not permit for that reason, and even Rava revoked his opinion."

Also see the comment of Maharatz Chajes (in his gloss on *Hulin* 49), where he makes a distinction between positive and negative commandments in this regard: "That it is not relevant to say that the Torah takes pity on the finances of the Jewish people with regard to a negative commandment, because we have established in accordance with the Rema *(Orah Hayyim* 656) that for a negative commandment a person must use up all of his money rather than transgress, which is not the case for a positive commandment, in which he does not have to use up his money." See also Rabbi Shimon Leib Eckstein, *Toldot ha-Habif* (Rabbi Hayyim Palache), Jerusalem, 1999, p. 201, note 91.

In this connection we may relate a very moving story told of R. Yisrael Salanter when he went to visit the Rebbe of Ger, R. Yitzhak Meir Alter. The Rebbe exhibited great respect for the founder of the *Musar* movement, and at the end of his visit he accompanied him on the way. In short, the Gerer Hasidim heard that a great visitor had arrived, and so when R. Yisrael came to the nearby synagogue to pray *Minhah,* the place was immediately filled with people who came to pay him their respect. The Hasidim noted carefully how R. Yisrael prayed, and were most surprised to see that he prayed briefly, like a simple person, and did not pray lengthily as they would have expected. At the end of the service, R. Yisrael became aware of the feeling of surprise that permeated the synagogue, and so he explained to the Hasidim as follows:

> I saw that on my account people had interrupted their work: the tailor his sewing, the cobbler his last, the blacksmith his anvil. They all left their work to see me. Had I prayed lengthily I would have been causing them a loss of income. Hence, I prayed briefly.

We learn here of the need for extreme sensitivity on the part of the rabbi for the fortunes of his constituents.

This principle finds expression in many different halachic contexts. (See my *Netivot Pesikah,* 2nd edition, Jerusalem, 2008, pp. 136–139, for a number of examples.) See, for example, *Mishnah Keritot* 1:7 (Herbert Danby's translation, Oxford, 1933, p. 564):

> Once in Jerusalem a pair of doves cost a golden *denar.* Rabban Simeon b. Gamliel said: By this Temple! I will not suffer the night to pass by before they cost but a [silver] *denar.* He went into the court and taught: If a woman suffered five miscarriages that were not in doubt, or five issues that were not in doubt, she need bring but one offering, and she may then eat of the animal-offerings; and she is not bound to offer the other offerings. And the same day the price of a pair of doves stood at a quarter-*denar* each.

Similarly, though It is thought to be mandatory to eat fish on Shabbat, the *Mishnah Berurah (Orah Hayyim* 222:2) ruled that if the price of fish is raised by the vendors to an unreasonable level, he would forbid the purchase of fish for Shabbat, in order to cover the price.

See also responsa *Tirosh ve-Yitzhar,* by R. Tzvi Yehezkel Michelsohn, Bilgurai, 1937, sect. 88, who urged all the rabbis of Poland, after the Second World War to forbid the eating of fish, the price of which had risen beyond what he thought to be reasonable, in order to bring down the prices. (His suggestion was not accepted.) In R. Yaakov Hayyim Sofer's *Kaf ha-Hayyim, Orah Hayyim* ibid. sect.12, he relates this issue to the *Mishnah* in *Keritot* cited above.

And yet another example is the case that was brought before R. Aaron Levine, the Rabbi of Sombar in Galitzia (responsa *Avnei Hefetz,* Bilgurai, 1934, sect. 95). In 1921 there was a dearth of *schach* to cover the *Sukkot,* and the merchants raised the price very considerably, so that the local inhabitants, who were generally poor, could not afford to buy it. The locals approached the Rabbi asking, whether they could cut down branches growing in the cemetery. According to the plain understanding of the law, one may gain no benefit from all that grows in a cemetery *(Shulhan Aruch, Yoreh Deah* 368:1, based on *Semag* [*Sefer Mitzvot Gadol*], *Hilchot Evel* 245c; *Mordechai Megilah* 830; *Rosh Megilah* sect. 9; and cf. *Shach* in the name of the *Bah, Shulhan Aruch* ibid. sect.6; *Gesher ha-Hayyim* vol.I, chapter 27 sect. 5). But the Rabbi allowed it, for the benefit of the poor, arguing, inter alia, that this prohibition is in order to accord respect to the dead (Rema ibid.); but in this case the dead would surely agree that people cover their *sukkot* in order to perform the mitzvah as required.

Of course, he could also base his permission on additional sources, such as what we read in B. *Sanhedrin* 47b:

> It was the practice of people to take earth from Rav's grave and apply it on the first day of an attack of fever. When Samuel was told of it [that people were using an object belonging to the dead, which is forbidden] he said, "They do well; it is natural soil, and natural soil does not become forbidden, for it is written, '*And he cast the dust thereof upon the graves of the common people*' (2 *Kings* 23:6), thus he compares the graves of the common people to idols. Just as idols [are] not forbidden, when they are 'attached' [to the earth], for it is written, '*Ye shall destroy all the places … upon the high mountains*' (*Deut.* 12 : 2), i.e., their gods, which are *upon* the high mountains, but not the *mountains* which themselves are their gods'; so here too, what is 'attached' is not forbidden."

But his clearly expressed avowed purpose was to break the monopoly for the good of his poor constituents.

See also *Igrot Moshe Yoreh Deah,* vol. 3, sect. 134, where R. Moshe was told of a *Hevrah Kaddisha* who had raised the prices of their services inordinately, against the rulings of the local rabbis. They asked R. Moshe if they were permitted

us not to make demands that go beyond the means of the individual. And this, too, as we have seen above, comes under the category of *bal tash'hit,* as does excessive and wasteful use of any resources. And on the basis of such a principle Jewish communities throughout the ages instituted bylaws limiting overspending, such as wearing extravagant clothing and jewelry. We find detailed rules of this nature enacted by the heads of Italian Jewish communities at Forli in 1408, and followed by rulings in Spanish Castile in 1432, etc. And already in the period of the Tosafists in the thirteenth century, we learn how the rabbis of the Rhineland limited the extent of feasts and banquets. Likewise, limits were placed on the number of invitees to wedding and other celebrations, as well as the fare offered them at such banquets, and such local communal enactments are to be found throughout Europe right up until the Second World War.[83] Such measures were taken to protect the poorer classes from societal pressures as well as to preserve the precious resources of the communities. We see, then, the extent to which this concept has been expanded in its practical applications. And indeed, the great nineteenth-century scholar, Rabbi Samson Rafael Hirsch, saw

to direct their constituents to other *Hevrat Kaddisha,* who had more reasonable prices, or whether this would constitute *hasagat gevul* (encroachment on the rights of the *Hevrah Kaddisha).* He replied that actually they were duty-bound to do so, to save the poor families from extortion. On the other hand, the *Aruch ha-Shulhan, Hoshen Mishpat* 231:20, is at pains to point out that one may not permit a shopkeeper to lower his prices so much as to prevent other merchants from making any sort of profit, and thus severely damaging their businesses....

As to the apparent contradiction between the principle of *Ha-Torah Hasah al Memonam shel Yisrael,* on the one hand, and *Ain Aniyut bi-Mekom Ashirut,* on the other, see the analysis of R. Hayyim Uri Lifshitz, in his *Pri Hayyim,* vol. 1, Jerusalem, 1980, pp. 105–113. For bibliographic references to articles on *hasag gevul,* see N. Rakover, *Otzar ha-Mishpat,* vol. 1, Jerusalem, 1975, pp. 434–435; vol. 2, Jerusalem, 1990, pp. 451–452; idem, *The Multi-Language Bibliography of Jewish Law,* Jerusalem, 1990, p. 707.

83. This subject has been extensively discussed by Bezalel Landau in *Niv ha-Midreshiah,* 1971, pp. 213–226. See further S. W. Baron, *The Jewish Community: Its History and Structure to the American Revolution,* Philadelphia, 1942, vol. 1, p. 320, vol. 2, pp. 301–307, 326, vol. 3, pp. 200–202; L. Finkelstein, *Jewish Self-Government in the Middle Ages,* New York, 1964, pp. 87, 262, 373 (clothing), 103, 143, 244, 374 (festivities). And see what I wrote in my *Minhagei Yisrael,* vol. 8, Jerusalem, 2007, pp. 34–35, note 13.

bal tash'hit as "the most wide-ranging warning to man not to abuse the position he has been given in the world for moody, passionate, or mindless destruction of things on Earth" (commentary on *Deuteronomy* 20:20).

The preservation of our natural resources is a concept that permeates biblical and rabbinic thought. Let us consider one simple example, *shemitah*, the sabbatical year, as it has much to teach us. On a strictly agricultural level, one may not exploit the earth without pause. The soil cannot generate crops year after year without losing its nutrients. You have to let the earth, the soil, rest – "*az tirtzeh ha-Aretz et shabtotehah*," "then shall the land be paid her Sabbaths" (*Leviticus*, 26:34). We know that in the medieval era, the feudal system divided parcels of land into three fields, one of which was left fallow at any given time. This made for a double *shemitah*, as it were. Similarly, it appears that in the Land of Israel in talmudic times the fields were left fallow once every two or three years, and not merely in the seventh.[84] The earth has to gather its strength, as it were, to recharge its batteries, in order to be able to continue to produce crops and remain fertile.[85]

At times we may argue that immediate short-term benefits – metaphorically the use of fruit trees for siege-engines –may justify the long-term diminution of resources. The immediate and urgent necessity to deal with vast amounts of waste products – nuclear or less volatile – and distance them from population centers by dumping them in the sea, or burying them in unpopulated areas, may indeed offer attractive, utilitarian, short-term solutions – and usually politically satisfactory ones! However, the long-term effect of pollution, both of seawater and of freshwater sources, constitute a threat to future life, and the momentary benefits of our generation – i.e., the immediate "siege benefits" – must in no way jeopardize our future progeny's ability to eat "the fruit of the trees."

---

84. See J. Feliks, *Agriculture in Palestine in the Period of* the *Mishna and Talmud*, Tel-Aviv, 1963, pp. 30–37 [Hebrew]. For the effects of irresponsible overexploitation of the soil in talmudic times, see my *Roman Palestine 200–400: The Land*, Ramat-Gan, 1978, pp. 45–69.

85. For a further discussion of this issue see my article in *The Edah Journal*, ibid.

Thus, the principle of *bal tash'hit* touches upon the most basic mandate of the conservationist – the absolute prohibition of wasting our natural resources.

One might argue: surely there are other fruit trees, not in the immediate vicinity of the besieged city. Let us use those trees for our immediate needs, and there will be enough elsewhere to satisfy our future requirements. The Bible clearly remonstrates against any such thinking. Ultimately, the planet on which we live has limited resources. We can optimize them to a certain extent, but in the final analysis we live in a "closed system." Any wanton destruction and irreversible damage reduces these resources and diminishes capabilities of the survival of future generations. Furthermore, in view of the present world population explosion, this has become a far more acute problem. Uncontrolled deforestation for short-term monetary gains,[86] dumping

---

86. On the catastrophic effects of deforestation, see David Wallace-Wells, ibid., pp. 76–77. See also what I wrote in my *Roman Palestine 200–499 The Land*, Ramat-Gan, 1978, pp. 46–51, section entitled "Denudation."

It is, perhaps, of interest to read what Edgar Thurston (and K. Rangachari) wrote in *Castes and Tribes of Southern India*, vol. 7, Madras, 1909, p. 139:

> With the view of protecting the Toda lands, [in the Nilgiris] Government took up the management of these lands in 1893, and framed rules, under the Forest Act, for their management, the rights of the Todas over them being in no way affected by the rules of which the following is an abstract:
>
> No person shall fell, girdle, mark, lop, uproot, or burn, of strip off the bark or leaves from, or otherwise damage any tree growing on the said lands, or remove the timber, or collect the natural produce of such trees or lands, or quarry or collect stone, lime, gravel, earth of manure upon such lands, or break up such lands for cultivation, or erect buildings of any description, or cattle kraals; and no person or persons, other than the Todas named in the patta concerned, shall graze cattle, sheep, or goats upon such lands, unless he is authorised so to do by the Collector of the Nilgiris, or some person empowered by him.

The Todas are a simple, somewhat primitive pastoral tribe living on the Nilgiri Plateau, and maintaining a large-horned race of semi-domesticated buffaloes which migrate from place to place, on whose milk and its products (butter and whey) they still largely depend (see Thurston, ibid., p. 117). I met some Todas on one of my trips to India in the early '60s, and though they generally keep shy of strangers – even Indian ones – they were friendly and invited me into their *mand* (hamlet), probably out of curiosity for the peculiar white man.

Out of wholly incidental interest, and perhaps largely through stream of consciousness, I'd like to describe the Toda *mand* (see Edgar Thurston, *Caste and Tribes of Southern India*, vol. 7, Madras, 1909, pp. 116–117, based on D. M. Rivers, *The Todas*, 1906):

> The abode of the Todas is called a mad or mand (village or hamlet), which is composed of huts, dairy temple, and cattle-pen, and has been so well described by Dr. Short that I cannot do better than quote his account. "Each mand [= mund]," he says, "usually comprises about five buildings or huts, three of which are used as dwellings, one as a dairy, and the other for sheltering the calves at night. These huts form a peculiar kind of oval pent-shaped [half-barrel-shaped] construction, usually 10 feet high, 18 feet long, and 9 feet broad. The entrance or doorway measures 32 inches in height and 18 inches in width, and is not provided with any door or gate; but the entrance is closed by means of a solid slab or plank of wood from 4 to 6 inches thick, and of sufficient dimensions to entirely block up the entrance. This sliding door is inside the hut, and so arranged and fixed on two stout stakes buried in the earth, and standing to the height of 2½ to 3 feet, as to be easily moved to and fro. There are no other openings of outlets of any kind, either for the escape of smoke, or for the free ingress and egress of atmospheric air. The doorway itself is of such small dimensions that, to effect an entrance, one has to go down on all fours, and even then much wriggling is necessary before an entrance is effected. The houses are neat in appearance, and are built of bamboos closely laid together, fastened with rattan, and covered with thatch, which renders them water-tight. Each building has an end walling before and behind, composed of solid blocks of wood, and the sides are covered in by the pent-roofing, which slopes down to the ground. The front wall or planking contains the entrance or doorway. The inside of a hut is from 8 to 15 feet square, and is sufficiently high in the middle to admit a tall man moving about with comfort. On one side there is a raised platform or pial formed of clay, about two feet high, and covered with sāmbar (deer) or buffalo skins, or sometimes with a mat. This platform is used as a sleeping place. On the opposite side is a fire place, and a slight elevation, on which the cooking utensils are placed. In this part of the building, faggots of firewood are seen piled up from floor to roof, and secured in their place by loops of rattan. Here also the rice-pounder or pestle is fixed. The mortar is formed by a hole dug in the ground, 7 to 9 inches deep, and hardened by constant use. The other household goods consist of three or four brass dishes or plates, several bamboo measures, and sometimes a hatchet. Each hut or dwelling is surrounded by an enclosure or wall formed of loose stones piled up two or three feet high [with openings too narrow to permit of a buffalo entering through it]...."

toxic waste into fresh water lakes as a cheap and easy solution for major industrial concerns, irresponsible disposal of nuclear waste, etc., have already done disastrous and irreversible environmental harm, bringing drought, famine, and widespread sickness to millions of earth's inhabitants. It is against just such practice that the Bible enjoins us, prohibiting and warning us in its characteristically laconic fashion.

One does not have to be a Bible-believer to understand the incontrovertible logic of this argument. One just has to be willing to look slightly farther afield, beyond one's immediate needs and environment, and to think in a broader geographical and temporal context.

However, for the believing Jew, on the other hand, saving electricity and fuel,[87] the reduction in the use of non-biodegradable materials, and a hundred other little things of which one is hardly consciously aware, but which can reduce wastage – these may all be perceived as coming under the category of a positive mitzvah. Indeed, the Talmud in *B. Shabbat* 67b states in the name of Rav Zutra:

---

87. Again I shall quote one of the Buddhist monasteries notices I saw in Sikkim:

SAVE ENERGY AND BECOME CARBON NEUTRAL

1. Personally, plant a tree.
2. Plant bamboo trees.
3. Carpool!!
4. Use energy-efficient lighting.
5. Use lighting efficiently in main shrine rooms.
6. Place floor and ceiling lighting in the corners of the room.
7. If available, use power strips (with several electrical outlets) instead of plugging in electronic appliances to many outlets.
8. Use rechargeable batteries.
9. Shut down your computer at night.
10. Unplug chargers and others electronic devices when not in use.
11. Give your old phone to someone else or recycle it.
12. When buying a computer for the monastery, consider a laptop.
13. For dark rooms on the top floor or in shrine rooms, set up sun pipes.
14. Use solar energy in areas where sunlight is plentiful and consistent.
15. Explore the possibility of wind energy.

Whoever covers an oil lamp, or uncovers a naphtha lamp, transgresses two prohibitions of *bal tash'hit* (since these acts cause the lamp to burn with unnecessary speed).[88]

Thus, the use of both sides of writing paper, changing to energy-saving devices, lighting systems, air conditioners, washing machines, etc., may all be viewed as the carrying out of a divine commandment. For there are halachic authorities who regard the words "for thou mayest eat of them" as a separate positive commandment, i.e., eating in such a way as to enable the fruits to be eaten also in the future.[89] Indeed, one who does not take account of such matters, and even thoughtlessly indulges in wanton wastefulness, according to some rabbinic opinions transgresses three biblical prohibitions![90]

How much do we waste in our bar/bat-mitzvah and wedding celebrations, or in our weekly communal *kiddush*? Whether it be the sumptuous food,[91]

---

88.   See, for instance, the responsum of R. Yosef Hayyim, in his *Responsa Torah li-Shmah,* Jerusalem, 1973, no. 76, who writes: "And I ruled for those whose custom it is to leave a candle with two wicks every weekday night to have some light in the house, and they leave the candlelight also while they sleep until the morning … that they should take out the wick while they sleep, and leave only one wick burning, since they do not need so much light while they are asleep, and if they have two wicks [burning] together it uses up [more] oil wastefully, and this constitutes bal tash'hit...."

See also *Sefer Kedosh Yisrael,* on Reb Yisrael of Vishnitz, by Natan Eli' Roth, Bnei Brak, 1976, pp. 228–229, who describes the extent to which the Vishnitze Rebbe was sensitive to *bal tash'hit.* He relates (ibid., p.228) that he would light his cigarette from a lit candle, rather than use a match, because specially lighting a match would be wasteful and constitute a transgression of the command, *bal tash'hit.* For further discussion on *bal tash'hit* see most recently Daniel Farbstein, *"Be-gidrei Issur de-bal tash'hit," Moriah* 28 (325–326), 2006, pp.126–131.

89.   Rabbenu Hillel to *Sifre Deuteronomy* ibid.; *Minhat Hinuch* no. 629; *Entziklopediah Talmudit* 3, Jerusalem, 1951, 335, note 8.

90.   R. Hillel's reading in the *Sifre,* ibid.

91.   Tzvi Bisk notes in his article in the *Jerusalem Post* of December 8, 2019, p. 10, that:

Our food supply system is catastrophically inefficient. From field to fork, 40% of food is wasted in both America and Europe, producing landfill methane. American families throw away $1,500 worth of food yearly. Improved logistics (and smart refrigerators) could conceivably reduce agriculture's greenhouse emissions (20% of total anthropogenic emissions) by half – more than maritime and aviation combined.

the disposable dishes,[92] the extravagant invitations, and the overabundance of flowers – all of these could well be seen as coming under the possible category of *bal tash'hit*, and they should be weighed against communal norms and societal conventions.

The world in which we live can no longer be perceived as a place in which communities are disparate and unrelated because of their separate locations. Everything is inextricably interconnected, and what happens in one location can and does affect people who live in other parts of the globe. *Sadna de-arah had hu*, said the rabbis (*B. Kiddushin* 27b), "The land is one single block,"[93] and never is this more evident and relevant

---

And cf. above note 122 and the long note preceding it.

92. See Wallace-Wells (ibid. p. 151) who sees the "plastic panic" as merely "another exemplary climate parable," but also that it is "a climate red herring," because though plastics "have a carbon imprint, plastic pollution is simply not a global warming problem." He adds that "it has slid into the center of our vision... occluding... the much bigger and much broader climate threat."

However, the Ellen MacArthur Foundation warns us that there would be more plastic than fish (by weight) in the ocean by 2050. In fact, it claims, only 14% of the world's masses of plastic packaging materials is collected for recycling. Furthermore in Y. Neril and L. Dee's *Eco Bible*, vol. 1: *An Ecological Commentary on Genesis and Exodus*, (Jerusalem, 2020), pp. 23–24, we read:

> Contemporary researchers investigating nonbiodegradable plastics in our planet's ocean find that they "are ubiquitous even at depths of more than 6,000 meters and 92 percent are single-use products and that these plastics are harmful to sea life and ultimately to us as they are accumulated in our food chain," (Matthew Savoca, "The Bad News Is That Fish Are Eating Lots of Plastic. Even Worse, They May Like It," *The Washington Post*, September 4, 2017). Single-use plastic has even reached the world's deepest ocean trench at 10,898 meters," (Sanae Chiba et al. "Human Footprints in the Abyss, 30 Year Records of Deep Sea Plastic Debris," *Marine Policy* 96, Oct. 2018, pp. 204–212). By 2050, some analysts believe there will be more plastic (by weight) in the oceans than fish ("The New Plastic Economy: Rethinking the Future of Plastics," *World Economic Forum*, 2016). Much of this plastic breaks down into tinier pieces, which are then eaten by fish and make their way into both the wild and human food chain. So in a sense, we are experiencing a flood of plastics that threatens to blot out sea life, and we must transform our planet into an Ark to preserve God's creation.

93. On the halachic implications of this principle in the context of land conveyances (*kinyanim*), see what I wrote in my *Roman Palestine 200:400: The Land*, Ramat-Gan, 1978, pp. 195–198.

than in our own "globalized" world. It is, therefore, our religious, as well as our humanistic duty to develop a greater sensitivity to conserving and preserving resources, and to see this as a central mitzvah that regulates all manner of our activities.

We all are acquainted with the famous story of Honi ha-Ma'agel (or Ma'agal), who saw an old man planting a carob tree, and asked him, "How long does it take until this tree will bear fruit?" "Seventy years," the old man replied. "But," he continued," as I came to the world and found carob trees that were planted by my grandparents, so too I am planting trees for my grandchildren" (*B. Taanit* 23a).

This parable advises us to think not only of our immediate material benefit, but to think ahead to coming generations. And this because there is a mandate of *horashah* bequeathing of that which is not yours, and one has no right to decline to pass it on to the next generations. And wasteful destruction of resources is tantamount to denying their continuing benefits to future generations.[94]

A somewhat similar motif may be found in *Midrash Tanhuma*, ed. Buber, Lvov 1885, vol. 2, *Kedoshim*, sect. 8, p. 76, on the verse in *Leviticus* 19:23, "And when ye shall come unto the land [of Israel], and ye shall have planted all manner of trees for food…":

It happened that the emperor Hadrian went to war, and he passed through a country with his armies to fight against those who had revolted against him, [and] he came upon an old man who was planting fig trees. Hadrian said to him, "You are an old man and you toil for other?" He replied, "My Lord, the Emperor, I am planting so that if I merit it I will eat the fruits of my labors. And if not, my children will do so." The Emperor went to battle, and three years later returned [to the same spot]. What did the old man do? He took a basket and filled it with first-fruit of ripe figs and presented them to Hadrian. He said to him, "My Lord, the Emperor, please receive from me these figs, for I am the same old man who you met on your onward journey, and you were puzzled that an old man should toil for others. Behold, this is the result of that labor, with which

---

94. See what I wrote in *Forward*, June 17, 2003, p. 13.

the Lord has blessed me..." Said Hadrian to his servants, "Take the basket from him, and fill it with gold coins." And this they did, and the old man took it and went off full of praises [for the Lord], and told the story to his family.[95]

It is, therefore, incumbent upon our religious leaders most forcefully to convey this message to their constituent communities, so that all can participate in the primordial mitzvah of le-shomrah, and avoid the dire transgression(s) of bal tash'hit.[96]

---

95. See the comments of Z. W. Zichermann, in his Otzar Plaot ha-Torah, Brooklyn, 2016, pp. 783–784, Moshav Zekenim from the tosafists, who derive from the word u-netatem – "and you shall have planted" (Leviticus, ibid.) that it is a positive injunction to plant fruit trees.

96. For further bibliographic references to the issue of bal tash'hit, see N. Rackover, A Multi-Language Bibliography of Jewish Law, vol. 1, Jerusalem, 1975, pp. 285–286 (nos. 7034–7044), vol. 2, Jerusalem, 1990, pp. 278 (nos. 4660–4669) [Hebrew]. Additional discussions may be found in passing in Be'er Moshe, by R. Moshe Stern, Jerusalem, 1984, vol. 3, no. 22, p. 26. On the extravagant spending in festive halls for banquets he relates: "I was asked by a very learned scholar, [concerning the fact] that many times people make weddings... here in New York in large hotels.... (But, much to our distress, what will they answer when they are called to order on the waste of money without any earthly benefit?).... And see further vol. 4, no.147, section 31, pp. 236–237:

> Furthermore, I wish to alert people to a bitter phenomenon, that takes place here, namely, the waste of Jewish money in organizing weddings and other festivities. Lunacy has seized hold of almost every woman whose husband has an extra dollar in his purse, that for every such event she needs a new dress, and that it is shameful[ly] unbecoming to appear twice in the same garment. And in this way they impoverish their husbands with additional stupidities... which is a criminal act.... Just the other day I was at a wedding that was full of flowers, and the experts said that the flowers cost thousands of dollars, may heavens be shocked! – On the next day all these flowers are thrown into the garbage.... It is the duty of the rabbis to gather together and to decide to announce a prohibition against the excessive use of flowers, and costly garments for a wedding.... And without doubt it is within the power of the rabbis to protest, and all will hearken [unto them], for many are awaiting this, and they will all listen to their decisions and prohibitions. Would that it were so.

Here it is worth quoting in full what we read in Y. Neril and L. Dee's *Eco Bible*, vol. 1: *An Ecological Commentary on Genesis and Exodus* (Jerusalem) 2020, pp. 158–159:

SUSTAINABLE CLOTHING

Exodus 29:29 – *The sacral vestments of Aaron shall pass on to his sons after him, for them to be anointed and ordained in.*

The Torah describes in great length and detail the eight special garments of the High Priest, which were to be made by hand by embroiderers, weavers, and artisans. Indeed, the clothing of the High Priest is the focus of more Torah verses than any other item aside from the Sanctuary. It is therefore fitting that these garments would not be thrown out upon his death but rather would be used and reused from generation to generation.

The Torah states that Aaron's holy garments were to be passed on to and worn by his sons, (*B. Yoma* 72b, where the Talmud explains that the High Priest's clothing could be used by the temporary priest appointed during a war, *meshuah milhamah*). When Aaron dies, later on in the Torah, God says to Moses and Aaron, "Strip Aaron of his vestments and put them on his son, Eleazar. There Aaron shall be gathered unto the dead," (*Numbers* 20:26). Despite the fact that Aaron wore these garments for about 40 years in the desert, including while conducting animal sacrifices and sprinkling blood and ash, they were not discarded upon his passing, but worn by his son, Eleazar. These garments were likely worn thousands of times, over multiple generations, and repaired when torn.

We would do well to learn from the long-term use of clothing by the high priests of Israel. In Britain today, the average piece of clothing is worn seven times before being thrown out, (Dana Thomas, "The High Price of Fast Fashion," *The Wall Street Journal*, August 29, 2019). Some $3.4 billion in clothing is purchased each summer in Britain alone for one-time use at weddings, barbecues, and festivals, ("Bernado's Call for People to Think 'Pre-Loved' before Buying New Clothes," *Bernado's* July 19, 2019). Only 1 percent of the materials from discarded clothing are recycled, ("Apparel and Footware in 2016: Trend, Developments and Prospects," *London Euromonitor International* 2010).

Our use and reuse of clothing has global impacts. Today, clothing accounts for around 10 percent of global greenhouse gas emissions ("U.N. Helps Fashion Industry Shift to Low Carbon," *United Nation Climate Change News*, September 6, 2018). Many garments could be worn hundreds of times, repaired, and then worn some more. Donating our used clothes to charity shops, or sharing them with friends and relatives, can reduce lifecycle emissions by over 50 percent of global total emissions, (Laura Farrant, Stig Irving Olsen and Arne Wangel, "Environmental Benefits from Reusing Clothes," *The International Journal of Life Cycle Assessment* 15/7, August 2010, pp. 726–736).

So *bal tash'hit* is not only a socio-economical commandment to protect us from the harm we do to ourselves, but also a deeply religious mandate, underscoring our status of stewardship[97] on a planet which we do not possess and resources which ultimately we do not control.

On the other hand, it is clear that not all acts that might appear to be destructive come under the category of *bal tash'hit*. Obviously, we are allowed to pull out weeds or to prune trees because such forms of "destruction" are for useful positive purposes. Thus, for example, when one is unable to access earth for the purposes of fulfilling the mitzvah of *kisui ha-dam* – covering the blood of an undomesticated animal or bird after slaughter,[98] a garment may be burned to provide ashes for this purpose, even though burning a garment would ordinarily be forbidden, coming under the rubric of *bal tash'hit*.[99] And on this basis, namely that *bal tash'hit*, by its very definition, does not include "constructive destruction," Shimon Greenfeld (1881–1930), in his *Teshuvot Maharshag*, vol. 2, 1944, no. 243, s.v. *ve-Hinei lo*, argues that the injunction against *hashhatat zera* (masturbation),[100] a sin of biblical severity,[101] if it be performed as a preventive measure in order to *avoid transgression*, as, for example, on the part of a homosexual to avoid homosexual activity, then his "spilling of seed" is not "in vain," and "he has not really committed a sin."[102]

Already the great Kabbalist, R. Mosheh Cordovero (1522–1570) in his *Tomer ha-Devorah* (1589), chapter 3, wrote:

> And wisdom will give life to all, as it is written, "And the wisdom will give life to its owners" (Eccles. 7:12), so will it teach life to all

---

97. See Seidenberg, ibid., index s.v. stewardship, p. 385a.

98. *Leviticus* 17:13; Rambam, *Hilchot Shemitah*, chapter 14; *Shulhan Aruch, Yoreh Deah* 28.

99. *B. Hulin* 88b; R. Shneuer Zalman of Liady; *Shulhan Aruch ha-Rav, Hilchot Shemirat ha-Guf ve-ha-Nefesh*, no. 14.

100. As the waste of seed.

101. See *Exodus* 20:13; *B. Niddah* 13b, etc. See *Entziklopediah Talmudit*, vol. 11, Jerusalem, 1965, 129–141, for a full analysis of all aspects of this issue.

102. See R. Chaim Rapaport, *Judaism and Homosexuality: An Authentic Orthodox View*, London, Portland, ORE, 2004, pp. 141–142 note 11.

the world and cause them to have life in this world and the next and give them life....

And His mercies are spread over all creatures, so that they be not dishonored nor destroyed, since the supreme wisdom is spread over all creatures, inanimate, growing, live and articulate, and it is for this reason we have been warned against spoiling food, for on this [too], just as the supreme wisdom does not dishonor (or spoil) any existing object, and all is created from there, as it is written "and all You created is wisdom" (*Psalm* 104:24), so too should man's mercy be upon all His creatures, may He be blessed.... And accordingly, one should not dishonor anything at all, for all [have their roots] in wisdom, and one should not uproot any plant other than when needed, and not kill any living thing except when required ..., [and one may do so] only to elevate them from the status of living creatures to articulate ones [i.e., to humankind]. For under such circumstances one may pluck the vegetable and slaughter living [animals] to harm them in order to give them merit.[103]

This, of course, is formulated in mystical terms. But the gist of the statement in halachic terms is that "constructive destruction" is permissible and does not come under the category of *bal tash'hit*.

Some might then argue that industrial pollution, to take a random example, is by no means wanton destruction, since it is normally part of the process of positive industrialization, one which certainly yields immediate and short-term beneficial results to society. Nonetheless, I would argue, on the basis of our earlier analysis, that it most surely comes under the category of *bal tash'hit*, since its harmful effect to the atmosphere is patently evident, and this negativity certainly outweighs any short-term merit it may profess to have.

---

103. See also Seidenberg, p. 164, citing additional passage from *Tomer ha-Devorah* (chapter 2, and 3:18, 20), and see also ibid., p. 186:

> [A person's] mercies need to be distributed to all creatures, not despising them and not destroying them, for so is the upper/highest wisdom distributed to all creatures, silent and growing and moving and speaking (i.e. rocks, plants, animals and humans).

In point of fact, the rabbis were quite explicit on the issue of the potential danger of waste and the need for its proper disposal. Thus, in *B. Baba Kama* 30a we read that:

> The Rabbis taught: *Hassidim Rishonim* – the early Pious Ones – would hide their thorns and broken glass three handbreadths deep in the fields, so as not to hold up the plowing. Rav Sheshet would throw his into the fire, while Rava would throw his into the Diglat (the Tigris River). Rav Yehudah said, "Whoever wants to be a *hassida* – a pious person – should observe the laws of damages (*nezikin*).

These examples obviously reflect the situation in Amoraic times when disposal solutions consisted either of incineration or discharge into a local river. Note that *B. Taanit* 24b tells us that "the gutters of Mehoza emptied themselves into the Tigris," i.e. this was their sewage system. However, nowadays we are not dealing with glass shards or nettles and thorns, but with dioxins, petrochemicals, and non-biodiversic materials.[104] But the basic principle of protecting life and health by keeping dangerous materials out of the public sphere is still extremely relevant.[105] And, of course, we can no longer just dump our wastage in the local river but must find new ways of sewage treatment.

I became keenly aware of the issue of pollution of rivers, when I recently visited Varanasi, India, a sacred town on the banks of the "sacred Ganga" (Ganges).

For the Ganges is now a toxic river. Its levels of pollution are severely health- threatening. Dead bodies, ashes of burnt bodies, industrial effluent and untreated sewage pollute its waters. Hundreds of major industries all along its banks release their untreated waste directly into it. In addition, bathing, washing clothes, bathing of animals, dumping of harmful untreated sewage all add to its sorry plight. And though it begins as a crystal-clear river high in the Himalayan Mountains, where it meets the Indian subcontinent with its high-density population, it is transformed into toxic sludge. It is considered the sixth most

---

104. Not to mention plastics, see above note 143.
105. Cf. Bernstein, ibid., pp. 127–128.

polluted river in the world.[106] I have read that 200 tons of half cremated decomposing bodies enter the Ganges just at Varanasi every year. However, on February 20, 2009, the Central Government of India declared the Ganges the "National River" of India, and in 2011 the World Bank approved $11 billion in funding to the National Ganges River Basin Authority (NGRBA) to begin the "clean-up." But in 2010 the Indian government had embarked on a $4 billion campaign to ensure that by 2020 "no untreated municipal sewage or industrial runoff enters the 1,560-mile river."

The task is enormous for already in 2012:

> Every day, it is polluted by some three billion litres of sewage and chemical waste, threatening the health and lives of millions. Its ecology, containing some of the world's rarest plants and wildlife, is under similar threat.
>
> (Pamphlet *Journey of Peace*, published by Parmate Wiketin, Uttarakhand India, under the direction of Swami Chidanand Saraswati.)

And this is only one of the many rivers bordering on great industrial complexes all over the world.[107] The problems are vast

---

106. See above note 74.

107. Here I should like to cite an illuminating passage in Martin Palmer and Victoria Finlay's *Faith in Conservation*, pp. 52–53:

> The ancient legend tells that once upon a time, an evil serpent lived in the sacred Yamuna River that flows across the center of India and into the Ganges. The serpent's foul breath blasted the crops growing along the river and its polluting body fouled the water, injuring all life. The people started to weep and the creatures of the river started to cry out, and eventually their distress reached the ears of the Lord Krishna. He sped to the river and – after a dramatic three-day battle – killed the serpent and freed the waters and the people from its evil influence.
>
> In the 1990s it became evident that the Yamuna was reaching dangerous levels of pollution. Hindu communities were able to draw upon this legend and use it to awaken local awareness of the problem. They stated that the pollution was the return of the evil serpent in a new and more ugly form. Today, they said, Krishna needs human beings to be his hands in the battle against the serpent – and it is

and overawing but must be faced before it is too late.

We should also be aware of these negative aspects of huge urban sprawls with their dense populations and vast areas of heavy industry. Indeed, one of the great challenges of the present world is population growth and the problems it brings, both with regards to adequate food production, as well as environmental degradation.[108] Add to that mass migrations and the intermingling of human populations (especially with air-transportation) which help diseases trespass the earlier limits of stable ecosystems, as is preeminently evident in the present global Corona pandemic, and then in addition to climate-change and global

---

humans who must work together to eliminate pollution in the sacred river. Once again, it is the specific Krishna nature of the story and the insight into tackling this very real environmental issue that has made this possible.

To the above we may add that Yamuna, also called Katindī, which joins the Ganga of Prayāga, the confluence of which is called Sangama, is black, from when Siva plunged into the river (*Vāmana Purana*, chapter 6). She is Krishna's wife. See Vettam Mani, *Purānic Encyclopedia*, Delhi, 1975, pp. 375 s.v. Katindī, 894 s.v. Yamunā.

And when mentioning the problematic plight of many of India's great rivers – and, of course, the same is true throughout the world – I should like to quote what I wrote in a recent essay entitled *"Our Journey through Tamil Nadu and Kerala,"* 2020, note 7, on the effects of dams over such great rivers:

The dams, while being essential elements in the expansion production and provisioning of electricity to villages etc., also frequently cause serious ecological damage. They may have a negative effect upon the fish population, as they fragment and isolate them from their downstream or upstream sweeps, thus effecting their migrational patterns. In addition, while the upstream reaches may be marginally affected, downstream the water volume is considerably reduced during the dry season, resulting in the frequent appearance of the river changing into pools alternating with dry stretches for as many as nine months in the year. And due to the decreased water discharge, these shallow pools have their temperature rise in the daytime and decline sharply at night, resulting in rooted plants growing wild in the riverbed. Reduction in riverine fish production, of course, effects the livelihood of local fisherfolk, who must seek employment in other areas, alien to their personal tradition. On the other hand, clearly the hydro-electric power produced is a great boon to the local inhabitants. This is the sort of conundrum that the local authorities have to deal with.

108. See my remarks in *Forward*, January, 17, 2003, p. 13.

warming, thus spreading plagues in ever expanding areas.[109]

So let us consider that the forty-eight Levitical cities had clear biblical guidelines for their layout. They had to have an empty open space – *migrash* – surrounding them, that functioned both as grazing land and a "green lung" for the city's inhabitants (see *Numbers* 35:1–8), and it was forbidden to build in these open spaces and to expand the city at their expense (*Sefer ha-Hinuch* sect. 342; Rambam, *Hilchot Shemitah ve-Yovel* 13:4–5, based on *B. Arachin* 33b and *B. Baba Batra* 24b). R. Shimshon Refael Hirsch (1808–1888), in his commentary to *Leviticus* 25:34, comments:

> It appears that these laws are designed to maintain an urban population with a connection to agriculture. [They] served to prevent cities from growing into metropolises and severing connections with rural life. This, then, is yet another great challenge facing our generation.

As we mentioned in our Introductory Note, the problems discussed above are global, and global society is slowly becoming more aware of them and seeking ways of relating and combatting these enormous challenges.

> [Most recently], more than 11,000 scientists from 153 countries have declared a state of emergency, warning of "untold suffering" unless urgent action is taken.
>
> Despite 40 years of debate about the issue, humans have largely failed to address climate change, leaving the planet in a "profoundly troubling" state, the experts warned.
>
> Dr. Thomas Newsome, at the University of Sydney, said: "Scientists [and I would add: religious leaders and, of course, politicians] have

---

109. See, e.g. David Wallace-Wells, *The Uninhabitable Earth: A Story of the Future*, Penguin Books, 2019, pp. 110–111. We might add that in theological terms global warming and other eco-disasters are seen as punishments for human iniquitous behavior. This is clearly evident in numerous biblical passages such as *Leviticus* 26:31–33; *Deuteronomy* 29:21–28. It is also expressed in the form of a parable at the end of the *Book of Jonah* (4:10–11), see below.

a moral obligation to warn humanity of any great threat. From the data we have, it is clear we are facing a climate emergency."

The study was released a day after the US officially began pulling out of the landmark 2015 Paris climate agreement, with secretary of state Mike Pompeo labelling it an "unfair economic burden." The controversial US exit will [probably] become official the day after the 2020 presidential elections.

The researchers from Australia, the US and South Africa used indicators such as sustained increases in human populations, the amount of meat consumed, the number of air passengers and global tree-cover loss, as well as carbon emissions and fossil fuel consumption.

However, the paper, published in the journal *Bioscience*, has suggested a six-point plan including: replacing fossil fuels with low-carbon renewables; restoring natural forests; eating mostly plant-based foods, and stabilizing, and gradually reducing, the world population.

(Metro, Wednesday, November 6, 2019, p. 12.)

Let us recall the last chapter of the book of *Jonah* (chapter 4) according to which when God wanted to teach Jonah a moral lesson he used the vehicle of "[global] warming":

(1) But it displeased Jonah exceedingly, and he was angry. (2) And he prayed unto the LORD, and said, "I pray Thee, O LORD, was not this what my saying, when I was yet in mine own country? Therefore I fled beforehand unto Tarshish; for I knew that Thou art a gracious God, and compassionate, long-suffering and abundant in mercy, and repentest Thee of the evil. (3) Therefore now, O LORD, take, I beseech Thee, my life from me; for it is better for me to die than to live." (4) And the LORD said, "Art thou greatly angry?"

(5) Then Jonah went out of the city, and sat on the east side of the city, and there made him a booth, and sat under it in the shadow, till he might see what would become of the city. (6) And the LORD God prepared a gourd, and made it come up over Jonah, that it might be a shadow over his head, to deliver him from his evil. So Jonah was

exceedingly glad because of the gourd. (7) But God prepared a worm when the morning rose the next day, and it smote the gourd, that it withered. (8) And it came to pass, when the sun arose, that God prepared a vehement east wind; and the sun beat down upon the head of Jonah, that he fainted, and requested for himself that he might die, and said: "It is better for me to die than to live." (9) And God said to Jonah: "Art thou greatly angry for the gourd?" And he said: "I am greatly angry, even unto death." (10) And the Lord said: "Thou hast had pity on the gourd, for which thou hast not labored, neither madest it grow, which came up in a night, and perished in a night. (11) And should not I have pity on Nineveh, that great city, wherein are more than six score thousand persons that cannot discern between their right hand and their left hand, and also much cattle?"

Indeed, we read in the current press so many articles warning us of the great danger of global warming. (See, e.g., *Jerusalem Post*, Wednesday, December 4, 2019.)

And in the same newspaper, from the same date:

Hot and dry: Climate report spells disaster
By Idan Zonshine

It's going to get a lot hotter.

An Israeli delegation was sent to the global UN Climate Change Conference, COP25 in Madrid, led by Minister of Energy Yuval Steinitz, and including representatives from the Ministry of Environmental Protection (MEP), the Ministry of Energy and other government officials. The aim of the conference is reducing greenhouse gas emissions, mitigating global warming and encouraging global cooperation.

As part of the conference, the MEP released their report on the effects that climate change is expected to have on Israel and the region.

The report focuses on four climate trends expected to negatively impact Israel: higher temperatures, higher humidity, rising sea levels and more extreme weather fluctuations.

The report details the projected effects of the climate change trends on a number of factors in everyday Israeli life, describing an expected rise in the risk of natural disasters, famine, floods, water contamination, forced migration, pandemics and increased border tensions.

"The goal of the report is to ensure a high level of preparation from the State of Israel for dealing with the impacts of a changing climate, implementation of plans and policy measures intended to reduce health, environmental and economic risk, which will exploit potential climate change opportunities and benefits," an MEP spokesperson said, summarizing the report.

"The Middle East is a known hot spot in terms of global warming, meaning it will be more heavily affected by climate change," the MEP spokesperson added. "This week's conference in Madrid is a reminder that it is imperative that not just Israel, but all the world's countries be prepared for the effects."

Also, an increase in the frequency of the number of hot days and nights is expected per year, along with a decrease in the frequency of cold days and nights – a current trend that is expected to continue.

According to the report, there will also be a reduction in precipitation by more than 15–25% by the end of the century. The downward trend in precipitation has existed over the past 30 years and is expected to continue.

According to Tuesday's Meteorological Service Report, the average temperature in Israel has already risen by about 1.4 degrees Celsius since 1950 and is expected to rise by another 0.9–1.2 degrees by the end of 2050; so a rise of more than 2 degrees Celsius is expected within 100 years.

An increase in the frequency and intensity of heat waves is expected and stronger storms are expected.

A change in rainfall distribution is expected in the broader geographical layout, changes in frequency, duration and intensity of precipitation – with larger amounts of rainfall falling in shorter times.

Earth's climate likely marks hottest decade on record:

MADRID/LISBON (Reuters) – The past decade [2009–2019] is almost certain to be the hottest on record, weather experts warned on Tuesday, painting a bleak picture of vanishing sea ice, devastating heat waves and encroaching seas in a report launched at a climate summit in Spain.

An annual assessment of the Earth's climate by the Geneva-based World Meteorological Organization (WMO) underscored the stakes at two weeks of talks aimed at shoring up the 2015 Paris Agreement to avert catastrophic global warming.

"Heat waves and floods which used to be 'once-in-a-century' events are becoming more regular occurrences," WMO Secretary-General Petteri Taalas said in a statement.

"Countries ranging from the Bahamas to Japan to Mozambique suffered the effect of devastating tropical cyclones. Wildfires swept through the Arctic and Australia," he said.

Among the report's findings:
• Average temperatures for the five-year (2015–2019) and 10-year (2010–2019) periods are almost certain to be the highest on record.

• 2019 is on course to be the second- or third-warmest year on record.

• Sea water is 26 percent more acidic than at the start of the industrial era, degrading marine ecosystems.

• Arctic sea-ice neared record lows in September and October, and Antarctica also saw record-low ice several times this year.

• Climate change is a key driver of a recent rise in global hunger after a decade of steady declines, with more than 820 million people suffering from hunger in 2018.

• Weather disasters displaced millions of people this year and affected rainfall patterns from India to northern Russia and the central US, and many other regions.

The report also noted surges in sea temperatures known as "marine heat waves," which devastate underwater life, had become more common.

The report said the concentration of CO2 in the atmosphere hit a record level of 407.8 parts per million in 2018 and continued to rise in 2019. Opening the climate summit on Monday, [former] United Nations Secretary-General António Guterres had warned that 400 parts per million had once been considered an "unthinkable" tipping point.

A drumbeat of dire reports from climate science in the past year [2019] has fueled environmental activism, prompted some companies to commit to slashing emissions and raised concerns among investors about the stability of asset prices.

Nevertheless, delegates in Madrid are facing an uphill battle to persuade major emitters to embrace the kind of radical change needed to shift the Earth's climate system onto a more habitable trajectory.

Climate activist Greta Thunberg, who stands at the forefront of that battle, arrived in Lisbon on Tuesday after crossing the Atlantic from New York aboard a catamaran ahead of her appearance at a summit in Madrid to demand urgent action on global warming.

The boat, *La Vagabonde*, carried the Swedish campaigner, who refuses to travel by plane, across the ocean so she could attend the COP25 climate summit in Madrid. She will spend the day holding meetings with Portuguese [climate activists and resting before her departure for Madrid.]

President Marcelo Rebelo de Sousa said it was a "great pleasure" to have her in Lisbon but did not feel it was his place to personally greet the activist.

Surely these are wake-up calls, not to a solitary prophet, but to the governments of the global society for a new attitude and policy on what we might call "ecological morality.

ESSAY THREE
Business Ethics and Ethical Investment

This leads us on to yet another area in which I believe contemporary rabbis must develop a degree of competence, in order to be able to advise their constituents and influence them actively to involve themselves in right and proper business ethics[1]

---

1. First published in *For the Sake of Humanity: Essays in Honour of Clemen N. Nathan,* eds. Alan Stephen, Ralph Walders, Leiden, Boston, 2006, pp. 303–307. I have made some modifications and additions at the end.

There is a considerable body of literature on Jewish business ethics. Here we shall list a few significant items:

- S. Albeck, *Dinei Mamonot ba-Talmud,* Tel Aviv, 1976.
- Idem, *Yediot be-Dinei Mamonot ba-Talmud,* Jerusalem, 1994.
- A. Kirchenbaum, *Equity in Jewish Law: Halakhic Perplexities in Law: Formulation and Flexibility in Jewish Civil Law,* New Jersey and New York, 1991.
- Idem, *Equity in Jewish Law: Beyond Equity: Halakhic Aspiration in Jewish Civil Law,* New Jersey and New York, 1991.
- Nahum Rakover, *Commerce in Jewish Law* (Hebrew: *Ha-Mishmar ba-Mishpa ha-Ivri*), Jerusalem, 1987.
- Idem, *Unjust Enrichment in Jewish Law* (Hebrew: *Osher ve-Lo be-Mishpat*), Jerusalem, 1987.
- *Keter: Mehkarim be-Kalkalah u-Mishpat al-Pi ha-Halachah,* eds. S. Ishon, Y. Bazak, vol. 1, 1996, vol. 2, 1999, 4, 2004.

And for further bibliographic references to articles on this subject, see Rakover's *Otzar ha-Mishpat,* vol. 1, Jerusalem, 1975, pp. 433–436, nos. 10941–11023; vol. 2, Jerusalem, 1990, pp. 449–454, nos. 8176–8273, and also ibid., p. 448, nos. 8161–8165. Likewise in his English bibliography, entitled *The Multi-Language Bibliography of Jewish Law,* Jerusalem, 1990, pp. 202–708, nos. 13975–14116.

There is, of course, much more, but these references to classic volumes should suffice.

Here we may call attention to two more significant books dealing with some of these issues:

- N. Rakover, *Ethics in the Marketplace: A Jewish Perspective,* Jerusalem, 2000.

and in social ethical investment.[2] And our stress on the latter is because irresponsible investment, such as investing in harmful products, for example those that contaminate our planet (see above

---

• Idem, *Unjust Enrichment in Jewish Law*, Jerusalem, 2000.

(These are translations of his Hebrew originals on these themes.)

To which I would also add: Asher Meir, *The Jewish Ethicist: Everyday Ethics for Business and Life*, Northdale, NJ, 2005, and the review of this book by Aaron Levine in *Tradition* 41/1 2008, pp. 78–97.

2. The United Kingdom's first ever ethical investment fund, "Friends Providence Stewardship" was launched in 1984, but this sector remains a tiny population of the investment world. Many new initiations have sprung up since then. Thus, for example, the "Charles Stanley Direct" investment platform has launched an "Investment with Conscience" knowledge hub to raise awareness:

> Patrick Connolly, chartered financial planner at Chase de Vere, said the belief that ethical investors have to sacrifice performance is changing: "Many ethical and ESG funds are now performing well and there is an argument that sustainable businesses doing the right things should deliver better long-term returns."
>
> Ethical companies are more likely to be smaller, by nature, and tend to outperform markets when large energy stocks such as oil companies struggle, as they are today, although this may not always be the case.
>
> If interested, Connolly tips investment fund BMO Responsible UK Income, which targets quality growth companies with a clear commitment to sustainability.
>
> He also flags up Janus Henderson Global Sustainable Equity, which invests in companies rising to the challenge of climate change, population growth, resource constraints, and ageing populations. "It is one of the best performers in its sector," he said.
>
> Connolly highlights Rathbone Ethical Bond fund: "It shuns armaments, animal testing, tobacco, nuclear power and predatory lending, instead targeting, say, disabled charities, companies employing ex-offenders, and sports centres in deprived areas."
>
> Chelsea Financial Services managing director Darius McDermott said 2019 was the year the world woke up to climate change and this is fuelling interest in ESG and SRI: "Having morals does not mean sacrificing investment returns, as many ethical funds have outperformed global markets for some years."
>
> McDermott tips Pictet Global Environmental Opportunities and the recently launched Investec Global Environment, which invests in companies that can work to keep global warming in check.
>
> "I would also recommend EdenTree Amity UK, as the group is one of the pioneers of responsible investing, and research capabilities are second to none."
>
> (Henry Jones, *Sunday Express*, February 16, 2020. p. 46.)

Essay Two) or impoverish sectors of the population, and even impair their health, is to be firmly and vociferously opposed.

Now there are those who say, "Money doesn't smell," or as the English proverb has it, "Money is welcome though it come in a dirty clout."[3] What they mean by this is that the source of one's wealth, and the means by which one acquired it, is largely irrelevant. One does with one's possessions whatever one wishes, good deeds or otherwise, without regard to their source.

But this certainly is not the view expressed in the Bible. In *Deuteronomy* 23:19 we read,

---

3. See W. G. Smith, *The Oxford Dictionary of English Proverbs*, Oxford, 1952, p. 429b:

> 1629 HOWELL *Lett.* 3 Aug. (1903) I. 309 Nor would I receive money in a dirty clout, if possibly I could be without it. 1659 Id. *Eng. Prov.* 13/2 Money is welcome, though it come in a shitten clout. 1721 KELLY 249 Money is welcome in a dirten clout. L. *Ducis odor lucre ex re qualibet.* 1723 DEFOE *Col. Jack* ii. Wks. (1912) I. 280 People say, when they have been talking of money that they could not get in, I wish I had it in a foul clout.

And of ibid., p. 429a:

> Money is a good servant, but a bad master.
> 1633 MASSINGER *New Way* IV (Merm.) 173 *L. All.* I must grant, Riches, well got, to be a useful servant, But a bad master. 1855 BOHN 453.

We might add R. Nachman Bratzlav's pungent statement:

> A small coin before the eye will hide the biggest mountain (*Likkutei Moharan*, 1806, p. 235).

And compare Lipkin's formulation in D. Katz, *Tenuat ha-Musar*, Tel Aviv, 1946, vol. 1, p. 272:

> A small coin before the eyes will hide all from sight.

See *A Treasury of Jewish Quotations*, ed. Joseph L. Baron, New York, London, 1956, pp. 314–315, nos. 554.23, 554.28.

Thou shalt not bring the hire of a whore, or the price of a dog, into the house of the Lord thy God for any vow: for even both these are an abomination unto the Lord thy God.

In other words, money gained by prostitution or other unsavory practices may not be brought to the Temple to fulfill the obligation of a vow. Or to formulate this in more modern terms: "tainted money" has no place in the house of God – and all the world is the house of God (Psalms 24:1; 47:8; 57:6, 12, etc.) – even if the intent is to use it for an honorable cause.[4]

Indeed, any kind of fraudulent activity in business dealings, extortion, buying or selling above or below the "true price" (*ramaut*) is strictly forbidden, so much so that the Rambam devoted several chapters in his *Hilchot Mechirah* (the Laws of Sale), with highly detailed rulings on all aspects of business activities, and definitions of honest business (*noseh ve-noten be-emunah*).[5] Money earned through such practice would, of course, also be "tainted money."

However, returning to our earlier types of "tainted money" it is not only inappropriate for it to be presented to the house of God (cf. *Malachi* 1:7–8), but indeed, any God-fearing person should distance himself from such "spoiled goods." It is for this reason that usury is

---

4. Cf. *Treasury* ibid. p. 39 no. 93.2:

> In the field of modern business, so rich in opportunity for the exercise of man's finest and most varied mental faculties and moral qualities, mere money-making cannot be regarded as the legitimate end ... since with the conduct of business human happiness or misery is inextricably interwoven.

Brandeis, address, Brown University, 1912.

5. See chapters 12–18, *Entziklopediah Talmudit*, vol. 1, pp. 153–161, s.v. *ona'ah*. And this includes, according to many opinions, the prohibitions of such practice towards Gentiles too (ibid., pp. 158–159, note 202). I discussed the subject of Ona'ah in my *Roman Palestine 200–400: The Land, Ramat Gan*, 1978, chapter VII, pp. 136–159, where (in note 2 on p. 137) I also referred, inter alia, to P. Dickstein's article in *Ha-Mishpat ha-Ivri*, vol. 1, Tel Aviv, 1926, pp. 15–155, entitled *"Mechir Tzedek ve-Ona'ah"*; E. Z. Melamed's article in *Yavne* 3, Jerusalem, 1942, pp. 35–56, on "The Development of the Laws of Ona'ah in Mishnaic and Talmudic Sources"; S. Shilo, in *Encyclopedia Judaica*, Jerusalem, 1971, vol. 12, 1391–1395, etc.

forbidden by biblical and rabbinic law,[6] as it is also in Islamic law, although legal fictions were later developed to accommodate these laws to modern society and its economic infrastructure.[7] Actually, the Hebrew word for usury is *neshech,* from the root *nashach,* "to bite," for usury bites into one's possessions as a beast bites into the flesh (cf. *M. Baba Metzia* 5:1), and ibid., 60b: for he bites (*nahit*) [the debtor] by receiving what he had not given.

And, indeed, the Talmud has many references to the immorality of usury, with its legal implications. Thus in *Y. Baba Metzia* 5:1, ad init. we read:

> Said R. Yannai (early III cent. C.E.): This is interest (*ribit*) which may be confiscated (from the creditor who has already illegally claimed it) by the court (literally: judges).

Thus the *halachah* permitted the confiscation of illegally and unethically acquired *ribit.*[8]

---

6. *Exodus* 22:24; *Leviticus* 25:35–37; *Deuteronomy* 23:20; *Ezekiel* 18:8, 17; *Psalms* 15:5; *Proverbs* 28:8; *Sifra Leviticus* 25:37, ed. Weiss 109b; *B. Makkot* 24a; *M. Sanhedrin* 3:3; *M. Baba Metzia* 5:1; *Shulhan Aruch, Yoreh Deah* 159–177, etc.

7. See, e.g., Ezra Batzri, *Dinei Memonot,* Jerusalem, 1942, vol. 4, subject index: s.v. *iska,* p. 441, s.v. *ribit,* pp. 478–479; D. Mishan, "*Hebeitim Hilchatiim u-Mishpatiim shel Heter Iska,*" *Keter* 2, 1999, pp. 405–464; A. Meir, "*Heter Isuk – Heter Iska Hadash,*" ibid., pp. 422–465; Y. Ben Shahar and Y. Hess, "Ribit be-Taagidim," *Keter* 1, 1996, pp. 231–337, etc.

See, e.g., on the *heter iska,* Israel Schepansky, *Ha-Takkanot be-Yisrael,* vol. 2, Jerusalem, New York, 1992, pp. 439–441, and vol. 4, pp. 210–211. In the Rambam this subject is to be found in *Hilchot Shluhin ve-Shutafin* 6:2–3. This is a vast and complex subject, which is beyond the scope of this study. As to the Islamic approach to *riba* – usury, see Niel B. E. Baillie, *A Digest of Moohummudan Law,* Lahore, 1957, pp. 791–798.

8. However, the passage continues:

> They (the students of the academy) asked R. Yohanan (died Palestine, 279 C.E.): The interest – may it indeed, be confiscated by the judges? He replied: If from this (i.e. if we were actually to confiscate interest claimed), we would leave nothing to the great ones of the Land of Israel.

And just as one may not extract usury,[9] so, too, we read in *Exodus* 22:26–27,

> If thou at all take thy neighbor's raiment to pledge, thou shalt deliver it unto him by the time that the sun goes down. For it is his raiment for his skin: Wherein shall he sleep? And it shall come to pass when he crieth unto Me, that I will hear, for I am gracious.

For just as He is gracious, so, too, are we enjoined to be gracious (see *B. Shabbat* 133b).

In fact, any kind of fraudulence, both in sale and in purchase, is strictly forbidden, as the Mishnah in *Baba Metzia* 4:11 makes very clear with detailed rules emphasizing the necessity for extreme honesty in sale and purchase. Thus:

> Produce may not be mixed together with other produce, even fresh produce with fresh, and, needless to say, fresh with old; howbeit they have permitted strong wine to be mixed with weak, since this improves it. Wine lees may not be mixed with wine, but the buyer may be given lees that come from the same wine that he has bought. A man whose wine is mixed with water may not sell it in a shop unless he has told the buyer [that it is mixed]; and he may not sell it to a merchant even if he has told him, since he [would buy it] only to deceive therewith. In any place where they are

---

Apparently in R. Yohanan's time, around the third quarter of the third century C.E., wealthy individuals with large estates called mockingly "the great ones of the Land of Israel," had acquired multiple properties largely through money-lending at interest.

See the discussion in my *Roman Palestine 200–400: The Land*, Ramat-Gan, 1978, pp. 192–193; A. Gulak, *Le-Heker Toldot ha-Mishpat ha-Ivri bi-Tekufat ha-Talmud*, 1, *Dinei Karkaot*, Jerusalem, 1929, pp. 192–193; G. Alon, *Toldot ha-Yehudim be-Eretz-Yisrael Bi-Tekufat ha-Mishnah ve-ha-Talmud*, Tel-Aviv, 1955, vol. 2, p. 1556; and cf. *B. Baba Kama* 94b; M. Gil, "Land Ownership in Palestine under Roman Rule," *RIDA* 3/17, 1970, pp. 32–33 (where some corrections are required); F. Oertel, "The Economic Life of the Empire," *Cambridge Ancient History*, vol. 12, p. 254.

9. See also the "In-Depth Study" on usury, in Aaron Kirschenbaum, *Equity in Jewish Law, Beyond Equity: Halakhic Aspirationism in Jewish Law*, Hoboken, NJ, New York, 1991, pp. 25–44.

accustomed to put water into wine, they may do so.

And the next Mishnah, ibid., tells us that:

> He may not sift crushed beans. So Abba Saul. But Sages permit
> it. But they agree that he should not sift them [only] at the entry of
> the store-chamber, *since so he would be a deceiver of the eye.* He should
> not bedizen that which he sells, whether human-kind, or cattle, or
> utensils.[10]
> (Transl. Danly Oxford, 1933, p. 355)

And thus, the Rambam in his *Hilchot Mechirah* 18:1 (and cf. *Shulhan
Aruch Hoshen Mishpat* 228:6) clearly summarizes that:

> It is forbidden to deceive people in buying and selling or to
> deceive them[11] by creating a false impression.... If one knows that an

---

10. But see *Yerushalmi*, ad loc. (chapter 4 ad fin). That one may improve the nature
and appearance of food according to the opinion of R. Avdima of Malha, though food
is not mentioned in the Mishnah. However, R. Aha bar Yaakov disagreed with him,
forbidding this too. (See the commentary on R. Eliyahu of Fulda ad loc.) See also the
comments of Yisachar Tamar, in his *Alei Tamar* to *Baba Metziah*, Givatayim, 1983, p.
43, on the importance of aesthetic appearance.

11. Furthermore, this ruling applies to a Jew's deceiving a non-Jew in sales too. See
Rambam, *Hilchot Geneivah* 7:8:

> He who does business with a Jew or with a non-Jew, if he measured or
> weighted less [than the true measure or weight], transgresses a negative biblical
> commandment [i.e. *Leviticus* 19:35–36, "Ye shall do no unrighteousness in
> judgment, in meteyard, in weight, or in measure. Just balances, just weights, a
> just *ephah*, and a just *hin*, shall ye have...."], and he is dutybound to return [to
> him any loss]. And so too it is forbidden to deceive the non-Jew in calculations,
> but rather one must be precise with him (citing the verse in *Leviticus* 25:50)....

Cf. *Shulhan Aruch, Hoshen Mishpat* 231:1. And there are views that theft from a
non-Jew is even more serious than that from a Jew (*Tosefta Baba Kama* 10:15; see S.
Lieberman's comments in *Tosefta ki-fshutah* 9, New York, 1988, p. 121 to line 49,
referring us to *Sefer Hasidim* sect. 1014, ed. *Mekitzei Nirdamim* p. 343; *Semag Laavin*
152, 58b; *Semak* sect. 275 ad fin.; *Hagahot Maimoniyot, Hilchot Gezeila* 1:2, etc.). See
in detail the various opinions on the issue of theft from a non-Jew in *Entziklopediah*

article he is selling has a defect, he must inform the buyer about it. It is forbidden to deceive people even by words.

... and this even if the purchaser suffers no economic loss as a result of the misrepresentation.[12] And in the next *halachah* he exemplifies this by saying that:

One should not dress up... an animal or old vessels so that they appear new ...

And the *Shulhan Aruch*, ibid. (228:9), adds:

It is forbidden to soak meat in water so that it will look whiter and then fatter ...

And the Talmud in *B. Hullin* 94a rules that:

A man should not sell his neighbor shoes made of the hide of an animal that died, [representing them] as made of the hide of a living animal which was slaughtered; there are two reasons: first, because he is deceiving him, and secondly, because of the danger.[13]

Talmudit, vol. 5, Jerusalem, 1958, s.v. *Gezel ha-Goi*, 487–495, where the dominant view is that this is a serious infraction of biblical law. See also *Seder Eliyahu Rabba*, ed. M. Ish Shalom, Vienna, 1901, pp. 74–75, where we read as follows:

He said to me, "Rabbi, the following happened with me. I sold a non-Jew four *kurim* (a measure) of dates, and I measured (i.e. weighed) them in a dark house, half and half. He said to me, 'You and God in Heaven know the measures that you are measuring for me.' And while I was measuring, I did so short of three *seahs* of dates. Afterwards I took the money and bought with it a jug of oil, and placed it in the same place where I sold the dates. The jug broke and the oil was lost." I said to him, "My son, the verse says, "Thou shalt not oppress thy neighbour, [nor rob him]..." (*Leviticus* 19:13) – "Your neighbour is like your brother, and your brother is like your neighbour. From this you learn that theft from a non-Jew is theft ....."

12. See Rakover, *Ethics in the Marketplace*, pp. 33–37, for copious additional references.

13. See Rashi ad loc.

Likewise, ibid., we are told that:

> One should not send one's colleague a barrel of wine with oil floating on top. [Since oil is more expensive than wine, and the recipient thinks he has received a barrel of oil].[14]

In like fashion, the *Aruch ha-Shulhan, Hoshen Mishpat* 227:1 writes that if merchandise:

> ... is slightly damaged and this is not apparent to the purchaser, or if one sells an item as new when in fact it is old.... This type of fraud is forbidden even when there is no overreaching in the price, and this applies with even greater force when there is overreaching in the price.

And see *Seder Eliyahu Rabba*, ed. M. Ish Shalom, Vienna, 1901, p. 140, who writes as follows:

> "And thou shalt love the Lord thy God" (*Deuteronomy* 6:5) – that you cause people to love the name of heaven; that you know your business practices and your activities in the market-place and with people [to be honest]... so that people may say: Blessed be so and so who has learned Torah...; how pleasant is his behavior, his ways and his works: ... and thus is the name of heaven sanctified. But when a person... [doesn't act in this manner]... people say, 'Woe is this man.... See how evil and crooked are his ways....' And from here they said: A person must distance himself from theft both from Jews and non-Jews, and indeed from anyone in the market-place....

This, then, is a classic plea for business morality to all people, Jew and non-Jew. Indeed, the *Beer ha-Golah* to *Hoshen Mishpat* 348 subsection 5, writes:

---

14. See Rashi ad loc., and the continuation of the Talmud with the sad tale of one who did this and its tragic consequences.

And I write this for [all future] generations; for I saw many who grew rich from deceiving non-Jews, and ultimately they were not successful, and fell into penury.... While those who sanctified the [name of] God, and returned to non-Jews any loss through default, grew rich and successful, and left behind a heritage to their children.[15]

And it was to this end that the rabbis established a price-control system, thus legally diminishing the possibilities of extortion in sole, "price-fixing" and fraudulent pricing,[16] which of course, aims specially at protecting the poor.

For sensitivity to the plight of the "have-nots" is a common theme throughout rabbinic literature. We are well-acquainted with the famous *Mishnah* in *Keritot* 1:7, which we cited above on page 177, in which the price of doves was brought down radically.

And based on this text the *Beer Haiteiv* to *Shulhan Aruch, Orah Hayyim* 242:1 cites a number of authorities (such as *Pri Hadash, Minhagei Issur*, sect. 15, etc.) who rule that even though there is an obligation (according to *Tikkunei Shabbat*) to eat fish at each Shabbat meal, if the price of fish went up steeply, one should desist from doing so until the price drops again. And we have seen elsewhere, in *B. Moed Katan* 27ab, that there were a number of rabbinic enactments instituted to take account of the plight of the poor. Indeed, the Torah was keenly aware of the economic stratification of society, as is evident from the gradated sacrifices (*korban oleh ve-yored*) listed in Leviticus 5:6, 7, and 11:

---

15. See further Eliyahu Schlesinger, *Otzar Hemdah*, vol. 1, Kiryat Sefer, 2018, pp. 122–123, who cites additional later sources on the issue of absolute business honesty to all people.

16. See *B. Baba Metzia* 40b; Rambam, *Hilchot Mechirah* 14:1; *Shulhan Aruch Hoshen Mishpat* 227–239, on the laws of the "unfair price."

And cf. Rambam, ibid., 14:6, based on *B. Baba Batra* 90b, that anyone who creates extortionate prices is like one who extorts usury, and transgresses the biblical directive, "and thy brother shall live with thee" (*Leviticus* 25:36).

As to price-fraud, *ona'ah* (or *hona'ah*), cf. *Leviticus* 25:14, see Rakover, *Ha-Mishar ba-Mishpat ha-Ivri (Commerce in Jewish Law)*, Jerusalem, 1987, chapter 1, pp. 19–46; (ibid., pp. 28–32, on price hiking, and 32–43, on price control) (= *Ethics in the Marketplace*, pp. 47–70).

6. And he shall bring his trespass offering unto the Lord for his sin which he hath sinned, a female from the flock, a lamb or a kid of the goats, for a sin offering; and the priest shall make an atonement for him concerning his sin.

7. *And if he be not able to bring a lamb*, then he shall bring for his trespass, which he hath committed, two turtledoves, or two young pigeons, unto the Lord; one for a sin offering, and the other for a burnt offering.

11. *But if he be not able to bring two turtledoves*, or two young pigeons, then he that sinned shall bring for his offering the tenth part of an ephah of fine flour for a sin offering; he shall put no oil upon it, neither shall he put *any* frankincense thereon: for it *is* a sin offering.

There are numerous additional examples of such special consideration for the impoverished.[17]

And here I cannot resist retelling the story that I heard from my father:

Once, my father saw his father, the Gaon Rabbi David Sperber, without the large silver watch that was always hanging from his vest by a silver chain (my grandfather, who was very poor and sufficed with very little, had received the watch as a gift from a member

---

17. See, e.g., what I wrote in my *Darkah shel Halachah*, Jerusalem, 2007, pp. 98–99, etc., and in my book, *The Importance of the Community Rabbi: Leading with Compassionate Halachah*, Jerusalem and New York, 2020, pp. 109–112, section entitled "Beyond the Letter of the Law," and pp. 203–211, "Sensitivity to the Have Nots."

We could, for instance, point to the *Mishnah* in *Eruvin* 4:9, where special consideration was afforded to poor people with regard to the complex laws of *Eruvin*, according to R. Meir who said: We are concerned with the poor man only. (However, there are a variety of interpretations of the term *ani*, a poor person, in the *Rishonim*, such as that of Rabbenu Hananel [to *B. Eruvin* 51b] who remarks that "all travelers may be regarded as poor people, since normally they do not have a loaf [for the *eruv*] available to them." Nonetheless the simple understanding of the Talmud's explanation in *B. Eruvin* 51b, is that "it was for the poor person the Sages ruled with this leniency." See also the well-known Talmudic dictum, "He who has a loaf in his basket is in no way similar to him who has no loaf in his basket" [*B. Yoma* 18a, 67a, 74b, *B. Yevamot* 37b, *B. Ketubot* 62b]. This is a broad topic that requires its own treatment.)

of the community). But he did not say anything to him. Some time later, my father saw the same watch in the possession of one of the wealthy residents of the village. My father asked his father to explain why he had given his watch to the rich man? My grandfather answered that this rich man had lost his wealth, and his situation was so bad that he had to sell his own watch in another city. Since it was beneath this man's dignity to be seen without the watch, and it would reveal his condition, he gave him his watch. In my father's bewilderment, he asked – "We need to help him to that extent?" My grandfather explained that this is an explicit halacha: "If the personal habit of this poor person was to ride on a horse and to have a servant run before him ... we should buy a horse for him to ride and a servant to run before him."[18]

Indeed, the halachah took great cognizance of the poor and the starving. So we find that a tailor who is poverty-stricken and hungry, is permitted to ply his trade after the first of Av, and even during *Tish'a B'Av*, if this be the only was he can support himself. So ruled R. Yosef Hayyim, the *Ben Ish Hai*, despite the fact that the Rema, in *Shulhan Aruch, Orach Hayyim* 551:7, as explained in the *Mishnah Berurah*, ibid., note 51, and the *Kaf ha-Hayyim*, ibid., notes 109, 110, forbade this. This was already the opinion of R. Yisrael Bruna (c. 1400–1480) in his responsa no. 10, where he wrote that:

A Jewish tailor is permitted to sew new clothing if he has not what to eat, just as a mourner [may] after the [initial] three days [of mourning].[19]

R. Ovadyah Yosef, in his *Halichot Olam*, vol. 2, Jerusalem, 1998, pp. 140–143, goes so far as to permit this even on *Tish'a b'Av* itself, and

---

18. See *The Importance of the Community Rabbi*, p. 206, and see the remarkable story told of R. Yehoshua Yehuda Leib Diskin, in Yosef Scheinberger, *Amud Aish: Toldot Hayyav ve-Poalav Shel Maran Moshe Yehoshua Leib Diskin*, Jerusalem, 1955, pp. 145–146, which bears many similarities to the above.
19. This is also cited by the *Kaf ha-Hayyim*, ibid., note 104.

even when there is pleasure involved (*ve-afilu be-binyan shel simhah*), comparing this situation with that of a poor worker who needs to earn a living on *Hol ha-Moed*.

Indeed, the Torah is replete with mitzvot relating to charity (*tzedakah*) to the poor (e.g., *leket, shikhah* and *peah*, etc.), and clearly takes into account different social classes (e.g., *korban oleh ve-yoreid*, *Leviticus* 5:7–22), etc.[20]

See, for example the very moving passage in *Deuteronomy* 15:7–14:

> 7. If there be among you a poor man of one of thy brethren within any of thy gates in thy land which the Lord thy God giveth thee, thou shalt not harden thine heart, nor shut thine hand from thy poor brother:
>
> 8. But thou shalt open thine hand wide unto him, and shalt surely lend him sufficient for his need, in that which he wanteth.
>
> 9. Beware that there be not a thought in thy wicked heart, saying, The seventh year, the year of release, is at hand; and thine eye be evil against thy poor brother, and thou givest him naught; and he cry unto the Lord against thee, and it be sin unto thee.
>
> 10. Thou shalt surely give him, and thine heart shall not be grieved when thou givest unto him: because that for this thing the Lord thy God shall bless thee in all thy works, and in all that thou puttest thine hand unto.
>
> 11. For the poor shall never cease out of the land: therefore I command thee, saying, Thou shalt open thine hand wide unto thy brother, to thy poor, and to thy needy, in thy land.
>
> 12. And if thy brother, a Hebrew man, or a Hebrew woman, be sold unto thee, and serve thee six years; then in the seventh year thou shalt let him go free from thee.
>
> 13. And when thou sendest him out free from thee, thou shalt not let him go away empty.

---

20. But this is a field beyond the scope of this study on which there is, in any case, considerable literature. See, e.g., Yehudah Berg, *Ha-Tzedakah be-Yisrael: Toldotav u-Mosdotav*, Jerusalem, 1943; Betzalel Landau, "*Ha-Tzedakah be-Hayyei ha-Tzibbur*," *Mahanayim*, 1961, etc.

14. Thou shalt furnish him liberally out of thy flock, and out of thy floor, and out of thy winepress: of that wherewith the Lord thy God hath blessed thee thou shalt give unto him.[21]

And conversely, the *mitzvah* of *tzedakah* – charity[22] – is a sort of investment,

---

21. See what I wrote in my *The Importance of the Community Rabbi: Leading with Compassionate Halachah*, pp. 203–211, section entitled "Sensitivity to the Have Nots."

22. See what I wrote in my *On the Relationship of Mitzvot – between Man and his Neighbor and Man and his Maker*, Jerusalem, New York, 2014, in chapter 16 (pp. 115–123), entitled "The Overriding Importance of Charity."

The biblical verse in *Deuteronomy* 14:22, "Thou shalt surely tithe …," – *aser te'aser* – was interpreted by R. Yohanan (died c. 270 C.E.) in *B. Taanit 9a: Aser bi-shvil she-tit'asher*, tithe in order to become wealthy. (And see comment on this in *Torah Temimah* ad loc., note 36.) And I found an amusing parallel in a folktale from Orissa in India, cited in A. K. Ramanujan, *Folktales from India*, New York, 1991, pp. 82–85:

The old sage returned from his pilgrimage, and the young disciple spent two more years with him. At the end of these years, when the boy was five and the girl two, the disciple himself decided to go on a pilgrimage to the Himalayas. The thought of the growing children [of the sage] and the miserable life that was waiting for them filled him with pain and even anger, though he consoled himself again and again with thoughts of fate. [For Brahma had said to him]:

"Son, I'll tell you what it wrote [invisibly on his forehead at birth]. But if you tell anyone about it, your head will split into a thousand pieces. The child is a boy. He has a hard life before him. A buffalo and a sack of rice will be his share in life; he'll have to live on it. What can be done?"

"What! O Father of the Gods, this child is the son of a great sage. Is this his fate?" cried the disciple.

"What do I have to do with it? Such are the fruits of a former life. What's sown in the past must be reaped in the present. But remember what I said: if you reveal this secret to anyone, your head will explode in a thousand pieces." …..

With his guru's permission, he left the forest hut and his guru's family, and journeyed towards the Himalayas. He visited many towns and learned men, lived with and learned from many sages. He wandered for twenty years, examining the world, understanding human nature, pondering the ways of providence. Then he decided to return to his guru's place on the banks of the river where he had begun his studies.

But when he got there, he found that his guru had died and so had his wife. His heart heavy with sorrow over their passing, he went to the nearest town in search of his guru's children. After a while, he found a coolie with a single buffalo. He at once recognized his guru's son in this poor man. What Brahma's iron pen had written on his forehead had come to pass. The disciple's heart grew heavier. He could hardly bear to see his great guru's son a poor man living off a single buffalo. He followed the poor man to his hut, where he had a family, a wife and two ill-fed children. There was a sack of rice in his house and no more. Each day the family anxiously took out a little of it, husked it, and cooked it. When the sack was empty, with his coolie's savings he was able to get one more sack, that's all. That's how they lived, just as the stylus of Brahma had written.

The disciple started a conversation with the sage's son, calling him by name, and asked, "Do you know me?"

The coolie was astonished to hear his name from the lips of an utter stranger. The disciple introduced himself and explained who he was and begged him to follow his advice. As soon as you wake up tomorrow, take your buffalo and sack of rice and sell them in the market for whatever price they'll fetch. Don't think twice about it. Buy whatever you need for a great dinner for you and your family, and finish it all by tomorrow evening. Leave not even a mouthful for the next day. Reserve nothing. With the rest of the money, feed the poor and give gifts to the best Brahmans in town. You'll never regret it. I'm your father's disciple and I'm telling you this for your own welfare. Trust me."

But the coolie couldn't believe him. "What will I do to feed four months in this house if I sell it all tomorrow?" he cried. "You Brahmans are always advising poor people like me to give it all to Brahmans. It's all very well for you. You are at the receiving end."

But his wife, who had overhead this conversation, intervened. She said, "This gentleman looks like a wise man, just like your father who was his guru. He must know something we don't. Let's follow his advice for one day and see."

The coolie's doubts broke down when she also supported the holy man. The next day, somewhat anxiously, he sold his buffalo and his sack of rice. What he bought with the money was enough to feed fifty Brahmans morning and evening as well as his own family. So that day he fed people other than his own family for the first time in his life. When he went to bed that night after this unusual day, he couldn't sleep. He got up in the middle of the night and found his father's disciple sleeping on the flat ground outside his hut. The disciple was wakened by the coolie's arrival and asked him what the matter was. The coolie said," "Sir, I've done as you've told me. In a few hours it'll be dawn. What will I do when my wife and children wake up? What will I feed them? I've nothing left, not a piece, not a handful of rice, and no buffalo to give us milk."

The disciple showed him some money he had, enough to buy another buffalo and a sack of rice, asked him to go back to bed, sleep well till morning, and see what happened.

The coolie had bad dreams that night and woke up early. When he went out to wash his face at the well, he looked at the makeshift shed where he used to feed his buffalo some straw the first thing every morning. The thought occurred to

albeit primarily a spiritual one. And this surely is the meaning of the

---

him that he didn't have a buffalo to feed this morning. But, to his astonishment, he found another buffalo standing there. He thought, "Fie on poverty! It makes you dream of buffaloes when you have none." It was still dark. So he went in and brought out a lamp to see if the buffalo was real. It was a real beast! And beside it was a sack of rice! His heart leapt with joy and he ran out to tell the holy man, his father's disciple. But when he heard the news, the disciple said with a disguised air, "My dear man, why do you care so much? Why do you feel so overjoyed? Take the beast and the sack of rice at once, and sell them as you did yesterday. Give your family and the Brahmans another terrific meal."

The coolie obeyed this time without any misgivings. He sold the buffalo and the sack of rice, bought provisions, and again fed his family and fifty Brahmans, keeping nothing back. Thus it went in the house of the sage's son. Every morning he found a buffalo and a sack of rice, which he sold and fed his family and the Brahmans, keeping nothing back. Thus it went in the house of the sage's son. Every morning he found a buffalo and a sack of rice, which he sold and fed his family and the Brahmans with the money. A month passed. The holy man was now sure that this kind of good life had become an established fact in the life of his guru's son. So one day he said, "When I heard that my great guru's son was living a retched life, I had to do something about it. I've done what I could. You're now living comfortably. Continue to do what you've been doing. Reserve nothing for yourself. If you do, your happiness will end. If you hoard the money, this good fortune will desert you." .....

On the day of his departure, he woke up too early. The moon was up. He had heard the crows cawing and mistaken it for the signs of dawn. He got up and began his journey. He had not gone too far when he met a beautiful person walking towards him leading a buffalo; he carried a sack of rice on his head, and a bundle of pearls was slung over his shoulder.

"Who are you, sir, walking like this in the forest?" asked the holy man.

The man with the buffalo threw down the sack at this question and almost wept as he relied, "Look, my head has become almost bald from carrying this sack of rice every night to that coolie's house. I lead this buffalo to that man's shed. My iron pen wrote [his] fate on [his] forehead, and thanks to you, you wretched clever man, I have to supply [him] whatever was promised at [his] birth. When will you relieve me of [this] burden?"

Brahma wept, for it was none other than Brahma himself.

"Not till you grant [him] a good ordinary life and happiness!" said the holy man. Brahma did exactly that and was relieved of his troubles.

Thus were fate and Brahma outwitted.

This moral tale seeks to teach us how charity can even overcome fate. However, see ibid., pp. 189–191, on the inevitability of fate.

verse in *Ecclesiastes* 11:1, that states "Cast your bread [*lahmecha*] upon the waters, for you shall find it after many days," usually interpreted as "benevolent giving" (*BDB Lexicon*, p. 537b), *lehem*, here meaning "livelihood" as in *Proverbs* 31:14, etc. Thus, give benevolently, for in the fullness of time it will return to you and reward you. (See Ibn Ezra ad loc.).[23] Indeed, though the rabbis state that a person will never fall

---

23. The verse was taken literally in this amusing footnote recorded by Ellen Frankel, in her *The Classic Tales: 4,000 Years of Jewish Lore*, Northvale, NJ, London, 1993, no. 191, pp. 385–387 (based on *Alpha-Beta de-Ben Sira*, sect. 7, *Otzar Midrashim*, ed. J. D. Eisenstein, New York, 1915, p. 37). And because of its charm I shall cite it in full:

> Once there lived a man who performed many deeds of charity. Before he died, he made his son swear that he would follow his father's example and always stretch out his hand to the poor.
> "The Bible tells us," said the dying man, "'Cast your bread upon the waters, for you shall find it after many days.' Heed this teaching, my son, and you shall never suffer want."
> The son promised to do what his father asked.
> After his father died, the son went down to the shore each day and cast a loaf of bread into the sea. And each day a certain fish ate it. In time the fish grew so large that the other fish went to complain to King Leviathan.
> "So large has this greedy creature grown that he swallows twenty of us in one bite!" they cried. "We can no longer live together with him!"
> Leviathan summoned the fish and asked him, "Your brothers and sisters who live in the teeming depths of the sea are not half as large as you who live by the ocean's edge. How do you account for this?"
> "There is a man who feeds me every day, "explained the fish. "Each morning he casts a loaf into the sea, and I gobble it up."
> "Bring me that man!" commanded Leviathan.
> The next day the fish dug a tunnel in the sand where the man always stood to cast his loaf and placed his gaping mouth at the bottom of the tunnel. When the man stepped there, he fell down into the hole and was swallowed up by the fish, who brought him before Leviathan.
> "Spit him out!" ordered the King of the Fishes.
> So he spat him out, and Leviathan swallowed him.
> "Why have you cast bread into the waters each day?" asked Leviathan.
> "Because my father taught me to do so," replied the man.
> Then Leviathan spit him out and kissed him and offered him a gift: either half the treasures of the deep or the knowledge of all the languages of human beings and beasts. He chose the latter, so Leviathan instructed him until he understood all the tongues on earth.

into penury by giving charity,[24] and no harm will come to him from such activity (*Maimonides, Hilchot Matnot Aniyim* 10:2). Maimonides continues that:

Then Leviathan brought him to a far shore and flung him up on the sands. Lying there, he looked up and saw two ravens flying overhead.

One raven said, "Father, I see a man lying there. Is he alive or dead?"

"I don't know, my son," replied the other.

"I shall go down and pluck out his eyes, which are my favorite dainties," said the younger bird.

"Do not go!" warned the father, "for if he is alive, he will capture you and kill you!"

But the son did not heed his father's words and flew down to the man lying motionless on the shore.

The man had understood everything the ravens said, and when the bird landed on his head, he grabbed it by its feet.

"Father, Father!" cawed the captive bird. "I am lost!"

"Alas, my son!" the father cried, "if you had only listened to me!" Then he flew lower and said to the man, "May God grant you the wisdom to understand my words! Let my son go, and I will show you a treasure beyond your wildest imaginings!"

Immediately the man released the bird. The grateful father said, "Dig under your feet and you will find the treasures of King Solomon."

He dug in the sand and found chests filled with jewels and pearls and much fine gold. From that day on, he and his family never suffered want. And he continued to stretch out his hand generously to the poor, just as he had promised his father.

24. See also *M. Pe'ah* 8:9, which teaches us that:

...He that needs to take them [i.e. charitable donations] yet does not take them, shall not die of old age before he has come to support others out of his own (possessions), [i.e., he will be rewarded with riches]. Of such a one is written, "Blessed is the man that trusteth in the Lord, and whose hope the Lord is" (*Jeremiah* 17:7).

Presumably, this is because in not taking charity for himself, he is enabling others to receive that aid, and it is as if he is, in effect, given others charity, for which he will be rewarded by God.

See *Tosfot Yom Tov* and *Melechet Shlomoh* ad loc. as to whether the words "shall not die of an old age" are indeed a correct reading, and Yisachar Tamar's comment in *Alei Tamar*, vol. 1, Givataim, 1979, p. 400a.

And cf. *Sheiltot Exodus* 39; *Semag Asin* 162; *Semak* 248; *Sefer Yere'im* 162; *Or Zarua* 1, *Tzedakah* 15; *Kaftor va-Ferah*, chapter 44.

All who have compassion over others [the Lord] has compassion over him, as it is written, "And I will show mercies unto you, and He may have mercy upon you" (*Jeremiah* 42:12).

Furthermore, in *Proverbs* 10:2 and again ibid., 11:4, we are told that "Charity saves from death" – *Tzedakah tatzil mi-Mavet*. And this belief is reflected in Jewish folklore, as for example, in the following tale found in *Folktales of the Jews*, eds. Dan Ben-Amos and Dov Noy, vol. 3, Philadelphia, 2011, pp. 281–282:

The Resurrected Dead Man
(Righteousness Saves from Death)

Told by Moshe Twiti to Moshe Rabbi

A very well-known rich man in the city of Aleppo was well on the road to poverty. Each day he sold objects from his home to support the members of his household, until he had nothing left. Out of sorrow and shame he breathed his last, and his soul went up on high.

It was during the month of Nisan. Everyone was making ready for the holiday. Misery and chilly despair filled the widow's home. There was nothing in the house and no one to take an interest in their fate, and the woman was ashamed to set foot outside her home to ask for charity.

Ezra Hamambo was the *shammash* of the Great Synagogue. He was well acquainted with all the families in town, and so, too, he knew the wealthy widow and knew that she would not want to accept anything from the community.

What did he do?

He stood one day at the door of the synagogue, holding a large handkerchief in his hand, collecting from those coming in and going out, to give charity secretly. When no worshipers remained in the synagogue, he counted the money that he had collected, and behold, it had reached the sum of forty Israeli pounds. He tied up the bundle, put in his pocket, and started walking to the house of the wealthy. He entered her house and said to her: "Please hear me, widowed madam, a certain woman deposited this bundle of money with me several months ago when she left for the Holy Land, and to this day she has not returned. The money is on this bundle, and I am not doing anything with it. Perhaps you will take it out of my hands and do some good deeds with it, distribute it to those in need, for the holiday of Passover is near, and the sum in the bundle can be put to good use."

The widow took the bundle from Ezra Hamambo's hands and said to herself, "Well, I need it." She thanked the man, and with the money bought what she needed for the holiday and celebrated the Passover holiday together with her children with joy and gladness and knew not from want.

The days passed slowly, and soon the holiday of Shavuot arrived. On the day after the Shavuot holiday, the woman heard that Ezra Hamambo, the *shammash* of the synagogue, had passed away, and that the men of the burial society had come and washed him and purified him and were ready to take him to be buried.

Without delay, the widow hurried to Hamambo's house and asked the men of the burial society to leave the room, for she wished to speak to the deceased. The men of the burial society exited the room, and the widow entered. Upon seeing the corpse on the floor, she disheveled her hair, tore her dress, and fell upon the corpse, saying, "Master of the Universe! Our sages said: 'If any man saves a single soul from Israel, Scripture imputes it to him as though he had saved the whole world,'" and this man lying here kept eight souls alive, how is it possible that he die?"

She wept.

A few moments later, the dead man began to move. She got up right away and fixed her dress and her hair. Meanwhile, the dead man rose to life, sat down, and called to the men of the burial society to enter his room. They marveled at the sight and said: "How is it possible? Hamambo has arisen to life." They sat and marveled.

He recounted that while indeed his soul had risen before the heavenly court and there it was decided that his time to die had come: "The woman standing here in this room brought the bundle of money and in it forty Israeli pounds, and she shouted and said: 'This soul had saved eight people,' and how was it possible that I die? Then it was decided in the court on high to add forty years to my life. They returned my soul to my body and here I am, alive and speaking to you."

The men of the burial society sat and feasted with him. They blessed him and went to their homes, marveling at the resurrection that they had seen with their own eyes.

May God grant that we perform many good deeds and mitzvot and merit a long life. Amen, may it be His will.

Here, the biblical phrase has been taken literally. But, of course, there are examples of people who were thought to be dead, but actually were not.[25]

And similarly, to much the same end, the Sabbatical year is a year of charity in that it annuls all debts, as we read in *Deuteronomy* 15:1–2:

At the end of every seven years thou shalt make a release [of debts]. And this is the manner of the release: Every creditor that lendeth unto his neighbor shalt release it; he shalt not extract it of his neighbor, or of his brother, because it is called the Lord's release.

And coming back to the subject of the "Sabbatical year" (already mentioned in the previous chapter) the rabbis devoted a whole chapter of the talmudic tractate *Shevi'it* to this issue.

For we have no absolute ownership over that which we possess (or think we possess). This is expressed in a story cited in *Tosefta Baba Kama* 2:13, ed. Lieberman, p. 9,[26] which may be seen as an allegory describing man's place in creation:

It happened that a certain person was removing stones from his ground onto public ground when a pious man found him and said,

25. See my *Jewish Life Cycle*, vol. 1, Oxford and Ramat-Gan, 2008, chapter 7, pp. 465–481, and vol. 2, chapter 35. And see further comments on the above tale, pp. 283–289, and especially p. 289, note 25.
26. Parallel in *B. Baba Kama* 50b, *Ecclesiastes Rabba*, chapter 6 ad fin.

"Fool, why do you remove stones from ground which is not yours to ground which is yours?" The man laughed at him. Some time later he was compelled to sell his field, and when he was walking on that public ground, he stumbled over the very stones he had thrown there. He then said, "How well did that pious man say to me: Why do you remove stones from ground which is not yours to ground which is yours?"[27]

In other words, the notion of a distinction between "private domain" and "public domain" may at times be blurred. "Yours" is really "not yours," but ultimately is "public domain," and in this allegory "God's domain." Of course, this also expresses a similar message to that of the parable of the man sailing in a ship cited in the preceding chapter.[28]

---

27. See S. Lieberman, *Tosefta ki-Fshutah*, vol. 9 (*Nezikin*), New York, 1988, p. 28, lines 70–74, who suggests that the "pious man" (*hasid*) was R. Yehudah ben Baba, in accordance with the reading in *Halachot Gedolot*, Bologna, p. 349, and cf. ibid., p. 87 to lines 51–53.

28. And that is why (theologically) there are so many constraints in the Jewish law of sale, not only the limitations of the "just price," referred to above, but also, for instance, the rules of *bar-metzra* enumerated in the last three chapters of Rambam's *Hilchot Shechenim* (12, 13, 14) devoted to the sale of adjacent plots of land, where the neighboring owner has "first right refusal." This is a law that is not mentioned in the Bible, but the rabbis induced under the blanket category of "And thou shalt do that which is right and good" (*Deuteronomy* 6:18). See Rambam, ibid., who writes that:

> It was impossible to write in the Torah all the required practices between a man and his neighbours and his colleagues, and all aspects of his business practices and the rules for the good of the community and the countries. So after many of them were mentioned, the Torah then formulates in a general fashion the principle that one should "do what is right and good" in all one's activities, and into the category fall the rules of compromise .... and the law of the neighbouring field.

Similarly writes the *Magid Mishneh* to Rambam, *Hilchot Shechenim* ad fin.

See further Schepansky, ibid. vol. 2, pp. 436–438. Here again, we cannot here further expand on this subject, for which there is a very considerable literature.

The reverse aspect of this notion, as it were, in what Rambam in his commentary to *Parashat Kedoshim* (*Leviticus* 19:2), famously calls, "*naval bi-reshut ha-Torah*," is a rascal [who acts] within the parameters of biblical law. (See ed. H. D. Chavel, Jerusalem, 1960, p. 115.) He does not transgress any explicit prohibition, but his behavior is

A prime example of this is to be found in *Y. Baba Metzia* 4:2, and *Genesis Rabba* 31:3–5, ed. Theodor Albeck, p. 279 and parallels, concerning the generations of the Deluge, as recounted in Louis Ginzburg's magisterial *The Legends of the Jews*, vol. 2, Philadelphia, 1909, p. 153:

> The other sin hastened the end of the iniquitous generation was their rapacity.[29] So cunningly were their depredations planned that the law could not touch them. If a country man brought a basket of vegetables to market, they would edge up to it, one after the other, and abstract a bit, each in itself of petty value [less than the value of a *perutah*, the minimal value of a coin], but in a little while the dealer would have none left to sell.[30]

This, indeed, is the key theme in Rakover's book on "Unjust Enrichments" referred to above, which embraces all those situations in which one person derives material benefit from another without being legally entitled thereto.

Our land, our property our wealth is God's gift to us,[31] and we are no more than guardians over it, enjoined to watch over it and preserve it

---

ethically quite unacceptable. See above preceding chapter.

29. Compare the difficult verse in *Ecclesiastes* 5:7, "If thou seest oppression of the poor (*oshek rash*), and the violent perverting of justice and righteousness in the state, marvel not at that matter; For one higher than high watcheth, and there are higher than they." In other words, high forces will deal with this evilness. (On the meaning of "the high" and "the higher than they," see R. Yosef Tuv Elem's exposition of Ibn Ezra's interpretation of these words, in Ibn Ezra's commentary to *Ecclesiastes*, ed. M. S. Goodman, Jerusalem, 2012, p. 70, note 133.) But see *The Commentary of R. Samuel Ben Meir, Rashbam, on Qoheleth*, eds. Sara Japhet and Robert B. Salters, Jerusalem, Leiden, 1985, pp. 134–135, for a different understanding of this verse, and also R. Yosef Taitachek's *Porat Yosef* to *Ecclesiastes*, Jerusalem, 1999, p. 59, for yet another interpretation.

30. Cf. ibid., vol. 5, Philadelphia, 1925, p. 174, note 18. And see the discussion of Yisachar Tamar, in his *Alei Tamar* to *Y. Baba Metziah*, ibid. (vol. *Nezikin*), Givataim, 1983, pp. 38–39.

31. See, e.g., *Zohar* 1:121b: The Holy One blessed be He gives wealth to a person so that he be able to feed the poor and carry out his commandments. If he does not do so, and has pride in his wealth, he will be punished.

for future generations. He bids us give tithes and other forms of charity from our earnings (e.g., *Leviticus* 19:9–10, ibid., 23:22, *Numbers* 18:21–24, 14:22–27, 28–29, 23:19–22), and we are obligated to preserve the sanctity – i.e., moral integrity – of our possessions. The sanctity of our possessions, and indeed the sanctity of the land we live on, is preserved by our judicious and ethical use thereof, and that which is "tainted" carries with it a stigma that bids us distance ourselves from it. As the rabbis have said *(Derech Eretz Zuta* 2:8),[32] "Distance yourself from that which leads to sin, and all that is like it;" or again (ibid. 1:12): "Distance yourself from the unsightly and all that is like it."[33] We

---

32. See my edition, Jerusalem, 1994, pp. 81, 98, for parallels and the literature analyzing this statement in its various versions.

33. Compare ibid., 8:2. And when the text talks of "unsightly and all that is like it," the intention is that a person should distance himself even from those things which are not truly unsightly, but close to being so. And in *Kala Rabbati*, ed. M. Higger, New York, 1936, 3:17, p. 242, we read:

> From where do you know this? From that which is written, "Therefore shall ye keep My charge [*u-shemartem et mishmarti*], (that ye do not any of these abominable customs, which were done before you, and that ye defile not yourselves therein; I am the Lord your God)" (*Leviticus* 18:30). *Hukotai* (my laws) is not mentioned, but rather *mismarti*. Take heed [*shemor*] of the guard [*mishmeret*], lest you enter into [the realm of] law (i.e. contravening the law).

Cf. *Tosefta Yevamot* 4.7, ed. Zuckermandel p. 245, ed. Lieberman, p. 12, *B. Hulin* 44a: But keep away from the unsightly and what is similar to it; and cf. *Derech Eretz Zuta* 1:12, 8.2. See further *Mechilta* to *Deuteronomy* (*Midrash Tannaim*, ed. Hoffmann) p. 134; *Avot de-R. Natan*, version 1, chapter 1, ed. Schechter, p.9; *Tosefta Hulin* 2:24, ed. Zuckermandel, p. 503, all of which cite this statement. And a similar formulation is found in *Seder Eliyahu Rabba*, chapter 14, ed. Ish Shalom, p. 69: They distance themselves … from the unsightly thing, etc. See further *Tzavaat R. Eliezer ha-Gadol.* sect. 44; Rambam, *Hilchot Ishut* 15:18, and cf. Higger's reference in his *Masechtot Zeirot*, New York, 1929, p. 129. Rav Saadiah Gaon in his *piyyut, Essa Meshali*, ed. B. M. Lewin, Jerusalem, 1943, p. 34 line 13, wrote much the same thing. See the historical analysis of G. Alon, in *Tarbiz* 11, 1940, pp. 135–136 (= *Mehkarim be-Toldot Yisrael*, vol. 1, 1957, pp. 282–284), and further comments by S. Lieberman, in his *Tosefta ki-Fshutah*, vol. 6, New York, 1967, p. 34; J. J. Rabinowitz, *Jewish Law*, New York, 1956, pp. 180–181. In my edition of *Derech Eretz Zuta*, Jerusalem, 1984, p. 81, I brought further citations of this maxim, all of which demonstrates clearly how central a notion this is in Jewish ethical and halachic thought.

have a further obligation to do all within our power to discourage the
continuation of such unseemly activities.

Similarly, rabbinic literature has a number of (aggadic) sources that
are intended to teach us that wealth is accumulated as a result of positive
ethical behavior, in other words, as God's gift. Thus, the Talmud, in *B.
Kiddushin* 31a[34] tells the following story:

> The students asked Rav Ulla (Eretz Yisrael, flor. second half of the
> third century C.E.), how far the obligation to honor one's parents
> extend. He answered them as follows: Go and see what a certain non-
> Jew, called Dama ben Natinah, did in Ashkelon. The Sages wished
> to do a deal [with him] for sixty-thousand [dinars] which he would
> earn, but the key was under his father's pillow, and he was unwilling
> to disturb him. And Rav Yehudah said in the name of Shemuel (early
> third century C.E.) ... that the Sages sought [to purchase] precious
> stones for the *Efod* [the High Priest's tunic], and his payment would
> be sixty-thousand [dinars], but the key was under his father's pillow,
> and he was unwilling to disturb him. The following year the Holy
> One blessed be He rewarded him with a red heifer that was born in
> his herd. The Sages of Israel came to him [to purchase it from him].
> He said to them: I know full well that if I request from you any
> earthly sum, you will give it to me. But all I ask of you is that you
> give me the sum I lost through honoring my father.

A similar tale is told of Rav Safra (Babylonia and Eretz Yisrael, flor.
late III and early IV cent.) in Rashi to *B. Makkot* 24a citing the *Sheiltot*,[35]

---

34. Parallel in *B. Avodah Zara* 23b–24a; *Y. Pe'ah* 1:1, *Deuteronomy Rabba* 1:14.
However, it would appear that he lost his fortune when he began to perform charitable
acts for the sake of his own honor and prestige, or when he did not give in accordance
with his means. See *B. Ketubot* 66b–67a, and see Judah Nadich, *Jewish Legends of the
Second Commonwealth*, Philadelphia, 1983, p. 385 note 80.

35. The source is in the *Sheitot de-Rav Ahai Gaon* (died 752 C.E.), ed. S. K. Mirsky,
Genesis, vol. 2, Jerusalem, 1961, p. 252 (*Sheilta* 38); ed. and commentary by the Netziv
(R. Naftali Tzvi Yehudah Berlin), vol. 1, Jerusalem, 1969, p. 235 (*Sheilta* 36), who
points out that this tradition is brought anonymously in the Rashba to *Baba Batra* 88.

namely that he had something he wished to sell, and a man came to him while he was reciting the *Shema*, and said to him, "Give me this object for such and such a sum of money," and Rav Safra did not answer him as he was involved in prayer. The [potential] purchaser thought that he had not offered him enough, and it was for this reason that he had not responded; so he offered him a higher price. After Rav Safra concluded his prayers, he said, "Take this object at the rate of your original offer, for at that time it was my intention to agree to the sale."

Rabbi Leo Jung, in his article "The Ethics of Business," apud *Contemporary Jewish Ethics*, ed. Menachem Marc Kellner, New York, 1978, p. 341, writes as follows:

> The world firm of Beer, Sondheimer and Company is reported to owe its tremendous expansion to the following fact: On a Friday in 1870, just before the Franco-German War broke out, Mr. Beer left his office for the Sabbath rest. He had large holdings in copper and other metals necessary for the waging of war. The porter received a number of telegrams which he presented on Sunday morning to his employer. They came from the War Ministry and offered to buy all metals in the possession of Mr. Beer; each successive wire increased the price. When Mr. Beer, on Sunday, went through these messages, he informed the War Department that he would have accepted the first offer and only failed to answer it because it was the Sabbath. He was, therefore, prepared to let the government have all his merchandise at the rate originally suggested to him. The War Ministry was so impressed by this example of living Judaism that they made the firm its main supplier and thus established its global significance. But Mr. Beer, consciously or unconsciously, acted on a precedent reported in the *Talmud* about Rav Safra!

Further, the Talmud in *B. Taanit* 19b–20a relates the tale of Nakdimon ben Gurion's righteousness, that when there was a drought in the land and the wells were empty, and the pilgrims coming for the foot-festivals had no water to replenish their thirst; he made a deal with

---

See Netziv's comments ad loc.

a certain wealthy individual that he would lend him twelve full wells and he would return them full at a given date, and if we could not fulfill this deal he would give you twelve thousand talents of silver. The story continues that when the day came to return the twelve wells full of water, they were empty, because the drought had continued, and the owner of the wells came to claim his money. But Nakdimon prayed to God, and miraculously the rains came even before the deadline of nightfall and filled up all the wells. So through his piety and generosity he retained his wealth.[36]

And here we add the following tale found in *Folktales of the Jews*, eds. Dan Ben-Amos and Dov Noy, vol. 1, Philadelphia, 2006, pp. 213–214:

The Honest Merchant
Moshe Rabbi

Hakham Judah Levi (died 1932), one of the earliest sages of Haifa, more than sixty years ago, lived on the Street of the Jews. He was a true scholar, well-versed in the Talmud and decisors. He had a sweet voice and frequently led the congregation in prayer. The Jewish community appointed him their rabbi, but he did not want to derive any benefit from the community treasury and went into trade. The man was honest and his business flourished. Everyone knew there was no point in haggling with him. The price he set was not to be changed. Non-Jews, too, used to go into his shop to buy from him.

Once an emir from Transjordan was sitting in the store and resting. He removed his broad belt (in which people used to keep their money, watch, and other paraphernalia) from his *kumbaz*·and laid it on the counter. After a long conversation with Hakham Judah, he purchased a large quantity of goods and paid for them. Hakham Judah wrapped up the merchandise and gave it to the emir. The emir took his purchases and left the store. But he forgot his belt in the shop.

Hakham Judah saw the belt, which was full of gold dinars. He wrapped up the belt and put it into a cupboard, because he didn't see

---

36. Parallel in *Avot de-Rabbi Natan* 6:3, ed. Schechter, version 1, p. 32.

the emir, who had already gone back to Transjordan and forgotten his belt.

Three years later, the emir returned to Hakham Judah's shop on the Street of the Jews. When Hakham Judah saw the emir, he recognized him and said, "Listen, my friend the emir! You have something on deposit with me!"

"What?" asked the emir. "I don't remember giving you anything for safekeeping."

Hakham Judah replied. "You'll see straightaway!" He went over to the cupboard, opened it, and took out the belt with the money inside, The emir looked at the belt and recognized it.

Please, count the money," said Hakham Judah. "Check that it's exactly the amount you left there.

"I don't have to count it," said the emir.

If you've saved the belt for three years, do you think I won't trust you?"

"Nevertheless, I want you to count the money," said Hakham Judah.

The emir counted his money. It was all there. He thanked Hakham Judah Levi for his honesty. When he went back out to the street, he spread the story among his Muslim friends. From that time on, Hakham Judah was well known among the gentiles, too. Everyone respected him for his honesty, saying, "There is none so honest and trustworthy as Hakham Judah Levi the Jew.[37]

These and other such rabbinic tales reflect the notion that one's wealth is a divine reward for charity and piety,[38] just as the fall into poverty is a punishment for the lack thereof. And already the author of *Ecclesiastes* (5:9) assured us that "He that coveteth silver [i.e. money]

---

37. For an analysis of different aspects of this tale – cultural, historical and literary – see ibid., pp. 215–216.

38. See e.g. *Y. Pe'ah* 1:1, the statement of R. Aba (flor. c. 290–320 in Eretz-Yisrael) that if one gives charity, one will be saved from the Roman taxes. On taxation in Roman Palestine, see my *The City in Roman Palestine*, New York, Oxford, 1998, pp. 28, 30, 110–111, 116, 122. There is, of course, a considerable bibliography on this subject, but the above should suffice in this context.

shall not be satisfied with silver," i.e., greed does not necessarily lead to wealth, and certainly not to a feeling of satisfaction. Indeed, the Palestinian rabbis advised with a punning adage: *Aser bi-shvil she-titasher* – give tithes [which is a form of charity] in order to become rich (*B. Shabbat* 119a, *B. Taanit* 9a), and it is by that merit R. Yishmael ben R. Yossi claimed (ibid.) that the rich men of Israel gain wealth. As to Babylonia, where there is no obligation of tithing, they merit it by the honoring of the Torah... and furthermore, the rabbis counselled, in the name of R. Yossi: Let the money of your neighbors be as precious to you as your own (*Avot* 2:17). So all these sources stress that it is ethical behavior that brings the reward of material wealth, or, in other words, the accumulation of wealth should be grounded in ethical practice, both for the individual and the general public.

Perhaps, this is already indicated in Abram (Abraham)'s reply to the King of Sodom, in *Genesis* 14:21–24:

> And the King of Sodom said unto Abram: Give me the persons and take the goods to thy self. And Abram said to the King of Sodom: I have lifted up my hand unto the Lord, God Most High, Maker of Heaven and Earth [i.e. I have sworn], that I will not take a thread not a shoe-lachet nor ought that is thine, lest thou shouldest say: I have made Abram rich; save only that which the young men have eaten, and the position of the men which went with me, Aner, Eshkol and Mamre, let them take their portion.

And shortly after, ibid. 15:1, we read:

> After these things the word of the Lord came to Abram in a vision, saying: Fear not, Abram, I am thy shield, thy reward shall be exceeding great ...

Walter S. Wurzberger, in his *Ethics of Responsibility: Pluralistic Approaches to Covenantal Ethics*, Philadelphia and Jerusalem, 1994, pp. 42–43, writes as follows:

> Numerous sources buttress the view that Jewish ethical principles

are based upon concern for the well-being of society. The Bible frequently concludes its appeal for compliance with the provisions of the Covenant by stating that such provisions are intended for our own good (e.g. *Leviticus* 20:3–46; *Deuteronomy* 6:1–3, 9–16, 10:12–22, 11:13–21, 28:1–69, 29:9–28, 32:1–47). Maimonides unequivocally declares that the ethical laws of the Torah are designed for the improvement of the material well-being of society:

As for the well-being of the body,[39] it comes about by the improvement of their ways of living one with another. This is achieved through two things. One of them is the abolition of their wronging each other. This is tantamount to every individual among the people not being permitted to act according to his will and up to the limits of his power, but being forced to do that which is useful to the whole. The second thing consists in the acquisition by every human individual of moral qualities that are useful for life in society so that the affairs of the city may be ordered (Maimonides, *Guide to the Perplexed* part 3, chapter 27).[40]

Since ethical conduct is conducive to the common good, obeying

---

39. We may add in parentheses, that we are not actually owners, or masters, over our own bodies, but merely wardens thereof. And it is for this reason that suicide is forbidden in Jewish law. See Sidney Goldstein, *Suicide in Rabbinic Literature*, Hoboken, NJ, 1989.

We may add to his rich bibliography the important controversy between Prof. Avraham Grossman and Prof. H. Soloveitchik on the legitimacy of suicide during the Crusader period. See, e.g., Grossman in an article "*Shorshav shel Kedushat ha-Shem be-Ashkenaz ha-Keddumah*," apud *Keddushat ha-Hayyim ve-Heruf ha-Nefesh*, eds. Y. Gafni and A. Ravitzky, Jerusalem, 1993, pp. 99–130; H. Soloveitchik, "Religious Law and Change: The Medieval Ashkenazic Example," *AJS Review* 12, 1987, pp. 205–221; idem, "Halakhah, Hermeneutics and Martyrdom in Medieval Ashkenaz," 11/1, *JQR* 94/1, 2004, pp. 77–108; 11/11, *JQR* 94/2, 2004, pp. 278–299, etc.

40. See Michael Shwartz, ed., Vol. 3, Tel-Aviv University Press, 2002, p. 516, note 4, referring to Yonah Ben-Sasson, "Law and Justice in the Thought of Maimonides," apud *Maimonides as a Codifier of Jewish Law*, ed. Nahum Rakover, Jerusalem, 1987, pp. 130–131; Y. Gellman, "Human Action in Rambam's Thought: Individual Autonomy and Love of God," *Jewish Thought* 2/1, 1992, pp. 127, 131; Howard Kreisel, *Maimonides' Political Thought: Studies in Ethics, Law and Human Ideal*, Albany, NY, 1999, pp. 103, 168.

the Torah's moral legislation confers this-worldly benefits upon society as a whole. Moreover, Maimonides takes it for granted that individuals performing moral acts are bound to benefit from the improved social conditions engendered by their behavior. This, in Maimonides' opinion, accounts for the traditional distinction that is made between the rewards that are received for the fulfillment of moral versus ritual commandments. Whereas observance of the commandments between human beings and God yields only spiritual rewards in the world-to-come, commandments governing relations between people belong to a different category. While their spiritual reward, too, is reaped only in the hereafter, there are this-worldly benefits as well:

> When man fulfills the commandments which are based upon utility for human beings... he will obtain good in this world. His having engaged in a good practice will influence others to do likewise and he will in turn benefit from this practice (Maimonides, *Mishnah Commentary* to *Peah* 1:1).

He goes on to show its important legal ramifications of this principle. But to summarize: activities which are based upon utility for human beings, that is to say which benefit society, and therefore fulfil the requirements of social-ethical practice, will bring benefit both to the individual – which for some will be wealth and comfort – thus in more modern terms, we may find in the above, a contemporary ideology for ethical investment too.

However, wealth certainly poses numerous problems and challenges, as Meir Tamari, onetime chief economist to the office of the Bank of Israel, in his seminal work *With All Your Possessions: Jewish Ethics and Economic Life*, New York/London, 1987, p. 25, wrote:

> Ever since the dawn of history, material possessions and wealth have been seen as posing basic ethical and spiritual problems. All religions, therefore, have had to offer some perspective regarding the scope and legitimacy of economic activity. Judaism is no exception in

this respect, though it differs radically from all other religions in the answers it provides to the relevant questions.

Two distinct sets of problems within the general issue of material wealth would seem to require a religious perspective: the proper allocation of time between work and spiritual activity (such as prayer, religious study, or the fulfillment of religious obligations), and the challenges to ethics and morality. Inequalities in wealth have given rise to injustice, theft, and often bloodshed, and the accumulation of wealth often looks as though it is linked to human lust.[41] All of these behaviors are inconsistent with the ethical and moral teachings of almost all religions. In Judaism's approach to these and allied issues, we will be able to discover the foundations for a specific ethical framework with respect to economic activity, on the part of both the individual and society.

And indeed, in his 340-page book he attempts to paint a portrait of the vision of Jewish ethical economics.[42]

From a broader viewpoint, at a global level, we may note that "the capitalist free market, perhaps the greatest innovation of the modern economic system, one that has triumphed over its socialist and totalitarian foes, permits the individual, to exert a good deal of control over his own private world. But capitalism is ill-equipped to redress injustice and inequity; in fact inequity is front-loaded into the system."[43]

As Rabbi Jonathan Sacks, z"l, the former Chief Rabbi of the United Kingdom, in his *The Dignity of Difference: How to Avoid the Clash of Civilizations* (New York, 2002, p. ii), so eloquently stated:

41. Cf. *Ecclesiastes* 5:9: He that coveth silver [i.e. money] shall not be satisfied with silver; nor he that loveth abundance with increase; this is also vanity.

42. Other books have confronted this subject. See, for example, most recently: Aaron Levine, *Free Enterprise and Jewish Law: Aspects of Business Ethics*, New York, 1980; Moses L. Para, *Business Ethics: A Jewish Perspective*, USA, 1997.

43. David Sasha, "Cultural Diversity without Moral Relativism: A Review Essay of *The Dignity of Difference: How to Avoid the Clash of Civilizations*, by Rabbi Jonathan Sacks," *The Edah Journal* 3:2, 2003, p. 4. The following citations for Rabbi Sacks's book are quoted in Sasha's article.

The liberal democracies of the West are ill-equipped to deal with such problems. That is not because they are heartless – they are not; they care – but because they have adopted mechanisms that marginalize moral conditions. Western politics have become more procedural and managerial. Not completely: Britain still has a National Health Service, and most Western countries have some form of welfare provision. But increasingly, governments are reluctant to enact a vision of the common good because – so libertarian thinkers argue – there is little substance we can give to the idea of the good we share. We differ too greatly. The best that can be done is to deliver the maximum possible freedom to individuals to make their own choices, and the means best suited to this is the unfettered market where we can buy whatever lifestyle suits us, this year, this month. Beyond the freedom to do what we like and can afford, contemporary politics and economics have little to say about the human condition.

And he continues (ibid., p. 32):

Not only has the dominance of the market had a corrosive effect on the social landscape [and, we may add, the physical ecological landscape, too – D.S.], it has also eroded our moral vocabulary arguably the most important resource in thinking about the future. In one of the most influential books of recent times, *After Virtue* [University of Notre Dame Press, 1981], Alasdair MacIntyre argued that "We possess indeed simulacra of morality, we continue to use many of the key expressions. But we have – very largely, if not entirely – lost our comprehension, both theoretical and practical, of morality." The very concept of ethics (Bernard Williams [in his *Ethics and the Limits of Philosophy*, 1985] called it "that peculiar institution") has become incoherent. Increasingly, we have moved to talking about efficiency (how to get what you want) and therapy (how not to feel bad about what you want). What is common to both is that they have more to do with the mentality of marketing (the stimulation and satisfaction of desire) than that of morality (what ought we desire).

And in what may seem to be an obvious statement, but I believe is a very significant formulation, he remarks (ibid. p. 42),

> Religion and politics are different enterprises. They arose in response to different needs: in the one case to bind people together in their commonality, in the other to mediate peaceably between their differences.

Economic considerations play a key role in the political process. However, the single greatest risk of the twenty-first century (to paraphrase a Sacksian statement) is that economics become "religionized." Religion should guide economics and not the reverse. Hence, ethics and morality should form the foundations of economic policy, whether at governmental or non-governmental levels.

However, as David Wallace-Wells wrote in his "epoch-defining book" *The Uninhabitable Earth: A Story of the Future*, Penguin Books, 2019, p. 237, which is primarily concerned with global warming and climate change, and paints a terrifying nightmarish picture of the future:

> … unless we take dramatic action and reshape the whole conglomerated machine of modern life away… we may comfort ourselves, perversely, by remembering that the world has always had droughts and floods and hurricanes, heat waves, famines and war. And will likely fall into spasms of panic, considering that a future of so many more of them seems so unlivable, unconscionable, even uncontemplatable today. In between, we will go about our daily business as though the crisis was not so present… lamenting our burned-over politics and our incinerated sense of the future… and now and again by making some progress, then patting ourselves on the back for it, though it was never enough progress, and never in time.

And this is a scenario we must do all in our ability to avoid.

I therefore believe that it should be our aim, and indeed the universal aim of all faith groups, actively to encourage the socially responsible deployment of our assets[44] and engage in a concerted effort to combat the use of unethical and harmful means to accumulate wealth. And this, of course, includes the use of industrial "short-cuts" with their immediate and very attractively financial returns, but also with their often devastating ecological effects.

Now though the urgency maybe clear, the ways and means are less so. For I am keenly aware that there are great complexities involved in the application of the notion of ethical investment, and ever more so of so-called "ethical divestment." For moral standards many vary according to different political aspiration. Thus, the Arab boycott of West Bank Israeli products could from their point of view be ethically justified, though for Israel's West Bank Jewish settlements it can be extremely harmful. Moreover, many huge multinational companies and corporations have, for the purpose of "sound investment," very mixed portfolios. These might well include commercial shipping lines, factories producing motor-cars, even electric ones and the like, but also tanks, fighter aircrafts and a variety of weaponry. Similarly, the large energy-producing giants not only market oil, and even at times coal and other fossil fuels, which are ecologically calamitous, but also have immense wind and solar-energy fields, producing "clean" energy. How, then, does one maneuver one's way through this labyrinthine maze of

---

44. And we should also add that people should be careful not to live beyond their means. This we may learn from an interesting halachic ruling found in *Sefer HaHinuch*, sect. 123. There, in discussing the categorization of some offerings, which may be given as costly ones or cheap ones (*Korban Oleh ve-Yored*), meaning a poor man brings a cheap one, and a rich man an expensive one, he rules that if a poor man brings a rich man's offering, i.e., a costly one, he has not fulfilled his obligation. The *Hinuch* then explains that the Lord is merciful towards the impoverished and therefore permits him to bring a cheap offering. But by bringing a costly one, he has gone beyond his means, and might even be forced to commit robbery.

This, however, might appear to contradict the *Mishnah* in *Negaim* 14:12, which states that:

If a poor leper brought the offering of a rich leper, he *has* fulfilled his obligation.

For the solution of this apparent contradiction to the *Hinuch's* ruling, see what Z. W. Zichermann cited in his *Otzar Plaot ha-Torah, Leviticus*, Brooklyn, 2016, pp. 195–197.

what are from an ethical viewpoint diametrically opposed products.

But together with that, the fact that a shareholder holds an element of ownership in a limited company, means that he also shares a degree of responsibility in its activities. The "community of shareholders" are ultimately the real owners, and not the CEO; he is subservient to their requirements. That gives the shareholder (or a group of them) a tremendous power, and, hence, a heavy burden of responsibility. And that is where the ethical element, as opposed to the short-term financial-utilitarian considerations, must be brought into play. And despite the fact that I am fully aware of the complexity involved, and the confusion andquestions arising from such thinking, and can offer no clear answer to these perplexing conundrums, I think there is great importance and, indeed merit, in recognizing them, seeking to confront them, and, perhaps in the meanwhile simply choosing clear and unequivocally positive options. Eventually, one hopes, such a path will have a cascade effect, one of such dimensions that it will truly be able to be called *tikkun olam*.

Conclusion

What does all of the above mean from a practical Jewish perspective?[1]
At the most basic level, the Rambam, in *Hilchot Deot* 3:2 (transl. M.
Hymson, Jerusalem, 1959, vol. 1, 496) writes:

> A man should direct all his thoughts and activities to the
> knowledge of God, alone. This should be his aim in sitting, rising
> and conversation. How should this be carried out? *Whether engaged*
> *in commerce* or in manual labor for profit, *one's heart should not be*
> *solely set on the accumulation of wealth,* but he should do these things
> in order to obtain therewith his bodily needs – food, drink, shelter,
> the demands of married life…. [My emphasis – D.S.]

And over and above this, Rambam (in *Hilchot Matnot Aniyim* 10:7–14)
listed eight levels of charity, the highest being to give or loan or go into
partnership or give work opportunities to the indigent in such a manner
that he will be able to support himself and no longer be in need of
charity. According to this criterion, microfinancing, as an example, in
poor emerging countries, enabling the local population to move toward
self-dependency, to improve their economic conditions as well their
physical environment, must rank high on the scale of activism. And
all such ecological projects, be they in water purification, agriculture,

---

1. The global perspective has most recently been described in frightening detail
by David Wallace-Wells in his *The Uninhabitable Earth: A Story of the Future* (referred
to above in the Introductory Note and again a few pages back), which the *Guardian*
declared to be "An epoch-defining book."

forestry, etc., which will positively benefit local populations are also a clear religious mandate. Judaism sees every individual, irrespective of race or creed, as fashioned in the image of God, and hence, deserving of dignity and respect. Thus, the qualitative status of the individual, his freedom, his physical and economic well-being, and his legally recognized rights, must be the concern of us all. The Jewish concept of *tikkun olam* must therefore address itself both to the amelioration of our environment, as well as to the bodily and socio-economic needs of the individual and, of course, to human rights. Within this broad spectrum of responsibility, we should seek to dedicate our energies and our resources,[2] and thus be ensured that we will be fulfilling the will of God.

---

2. And when I speak of resources, I am also referring to rabbis and religious leaders, not only politicians and heads of industry, who, though having the power to make meaningful change, are often those who stand to benefit most handsomely from inaction. For, as I wrote in the concluding comments of my *The Importance of the Community Rabbi*, p. 247, our spiritual leaders should always be cognizant of the statement of Rav Zutra bar Tuvia in the name of Rav, in *B. Hagigah* 12a, that,

> The world was created [on the basis of] ten principles: wisdom, intelligence, knowledge, strength, rebuke, courage, justice, law, kindness and mercy.

They must combine these characteristics in their leadership activities, having the wisdom and knowledge of what is right and what needs to be done to put things right, and the strength and courage to act, often with an independent stance, in order to achieve, or at least move in the direction, of the aforementioned goals.

About the Author

Rabbi Professor Daniel Sperber is a leading scholar of Jewish law, customs, and ethics. He taught in the Talmud Department of Bar-Ilan University, where he also served as dean of the Faculty of Jewish Studies and president of the Jesselson Institute for Advanced Torah Studies. In 1992, he was awarded the Israel Prize for Jewish Studies. For close to five decades, Rabbi Sperber served as rabbi in Jerusalem, first in Yad Tamar Synagogue in Katamon, and then in Menachem Zion Synagogue in the Old City. He now lives in Ovnat, a small religious settlement on the banks of the Dead Sea.

The descendant of a line of distinguished Orthodox rabbis, Prof. Sperber was born in 1940 in a castle in Ruthin, Wales, and studied in the Yeshivot of Kol Torah and Hevron in Jerusalem. He earned a BA in art history at the Courtauld Institute of Art and received a PhD in classics, ancient history, and Hebrew studies from University College, London.

Prof. Sperber has published more than thirty books and over four hundred articles on the subjects of Talmudic and Jewish socio-economic history, law and customs, classical philology, and Jewish art. Among his major works is a well-known, eight-volume series, *Minhagei Yisrael*, on the history of Jewish customs. More recently, he has written books on halachic methodology and rabbinic decision-making in confrontation with modernity and has established an independent *beit din* dealing with *agunah* issues. He is the author of *On Changes in Jewish Liturgy: Options and Limitations; On the Relationship of Mitzvot Between Man and His Neighbor and Man and His Maker; The Importance of the Community Rabbi: Leading with Compassionate Halachah;* and *Rabba, Maharat, Rabbanit, Rebbetzin: Women with Leadership Authority According to Halachah*, all published by Urim Publications.